Microsoft®
Surface™

FOR
DUMMIES®

A Wiley Brand

2nd Edition

Microsoft® Surface™ FOR DUMMIES®

A Wiley Brand

2nd Edition

by Andy Rathbone

FOR DUMMIES® A Wiley Brand

Microsoft® Surface™ For Dummies®, 2nd Edition

Published by: **John Wiley & Sons, Inc.,** 111 River Street, Hoboken, NJ 07030-5774, www.wiley.com

Copyright © 2014 by John Wiley & Sons, Inc., Hoboken, New Jersey

Published simultaneously in Canada

For general information on our other products and services, please contact our Customer Care Department within the U.S. at 877-762-2974, outside the U.S. at 317-572-3993, or fax 317-572-4002. For technical support, please visit www.wiley.com/techsupport.

Wiley publishes in a variety of print and electronic formats and by print-on-demand. Some material included with standard print versions of this book may not be included in e-books or in print-on-demand. If this book refers to media such as a CD or DVD that is not included in the version you purchased, you may download this material at http://booksupport.wiley.com. For more information about Wiley products, visit www.wiley.com.

Library of Congress Control Number: 2014931351

ISBN 978-1-111-89863-5 (pbk); ISBN 978-1-118-91661-2 (ebk); ISBN 978-1-118-89875-8 (ebk)

Manufactured in the United States of America

10 9 8 7 6 5 4 3 2

Contents at a Glance

Table of Contents

Introduction

• •

*W*elcome to *Surface For Dummies,* 2nd Edition! This book helps you wring the most out of Microsoft's Surface, the combination work/pleasure tablets that turn heads in coffee shops, classrooms, and lunch rooms.

This book doesn't explain *everything* you can do with the Surface. That would take at least ten volumes. No, this book explains everything you need to know to set up your Surface, introduce it to yourself and your social networks, and transform it into a natural extension of your lifestyle and work routine.

This book covers all four Surface models: the original Surface RT and Surface Pro, and the newer Surface 2 and the Surface Pro 2 models. It also covers more Official Surface Accessories than anybody could possibly afford.

About This Book

Today, most people think of desktop PCs as workhorses for creating: They create documents, spreadsheets, and whatever other boring files their boss requires. And they usually require a mouse and keyboard.

Tablets, by contrast, work best at letting you consume: videos, music, the Internet, and e-mail. And you often do it on the couch by using your fingertips.

But what if one tablet straddled both worlds, letting you both consume and create?

That's the promise of a Surface tablet. Its finger-friendly Start screen lets you watch videos, listen to music, read e-books and e-mail, and browse the web. And, come Monday morning, you can switch to the Windows desktop, click on one of the Surface's many keyboards, and put on your working cap.

How well does it hold up on that promise? That's where this book comes into play. I describe how it works in both work and play mode, as well as how to give it a few little tweaks to make it fit into your life a little more easily.

How to Use This Book

Instead of bundling a user manual with the Surface, Microsoft tossed in a single strip of paper with Ikea-like diagrams of how to fold down your Surface's kickstand. That's it.

This book takes over from that ignoble start by explaining exactly what you can and can't do with your Surface. And when it points out things you *can't* do, it offers some workarounds for going ahead and doing them anyway.

The book comes separated into basic parts, each dealing with what you need to do with your Surface at certain times: setting it up, connecting it to things, letting it entertain you, and buckling it down when work beckons.

Jump to the section you need at that particular moment in your life, absorb what you need to know, and move on. There's no need to read the entire thing from cover to cover. Everything is presented in easily digestible nuggets.

Each of this book's step-by-step instructions works with a strategically placed tap on your Surface's touchscreen. On those rare occasions when you need to type information on a keyboard, you see easy-to-follow bold text like in this sentence: Type **Sarcophagus** into the Search box.

If you're reading this book as an e-book, you'll find that all the websites are listed as active links, ready to direct you to the page with a tap of your finger.

Foolish Assumptions

Because you've purchased this book, I'm making one logical assumption about you: You've bought a Microsoft Surface tablet, or you're thinking about buying one.

So, you should know that everything in this book covers all four models of Microsoft's Surface tablet:

- ✔ **The original Surface RT and the Surface Pro:** After you've taken advantage of their free upgrade to Windows 8.1, all the instructions in this book apply to them.
- ✔ **The new Surface 2 and the Surface Pro 2:** These two new models come with Windows 8.1 installed.

This book describes how the four models differ, and I place a special icon next to material that applies only to the Surface RT and Surface 2.

If you haven't yet purchased a Surface, this book helps you understand how the models differ and which model works best in which situations.

I also cover the Surface's famous click-on Touch and Type Cover keyboards, as well as their replacements, the new Touch Cover 2 and Type Cover 2 keyboards. Because they're functionally the same, I refer to them both as simply Touch and Type Cover keyboards.

Icons Used in This Book

This book includes five basic *icons*, little symbols placed next to paragraphs of particular import. Here's what to expect when you see any of these icons:

 Keep an eye out for this icon, which alerts you to time-saving tricks that immediately leapfrog you ahead of other Surface owners.

 Avert your eyes from paragraphs marked with this icon if technical information isn't your thing — the text contains details that appeal to only a few nerdy souls.

 Remember these few key tidbits, and you'll pick up things much more quickly.

 Tread carefully with the steps in this paragraph. The information may lead to serious problems if things go wrong.

 The Surface 2 and the Surface RT (when upgraded) run *Windows 8.1 RT*. That means they differ from the Surface Pro and Surface Pro 2 in some fundamental ways. This icon calls out information that explains those differences.

Beyond This Book

The Microsoft Surface has so many cool features that I couldn't fit them all into this book. You can find additional content at the following places:

✔ **Cheat sheet:** Here you can find information on how to keep your Surface updated so that it runs smoothly, how to work with apps (what those in tablet-land call *programs*) and keep them updated, and how to use the Charm bar (if you're unfamiliar with this feature introduced in Windows 8).

`www.dummies.com/cheatsheet/surface`

> ✔ **Extras:** Visit here for step-by-step tutorials on how to play songs directly from a flash drive, as well as how to drop websites onto the Reading List app for later reading at your leisure.
>
> `www.dummies.com/extras/surface`

Where to Go from Here

New Surface owners should definitely start with a read-through of the first four chapters, with a special emphasis on Chapter 3. The walkthrough steps in there apply not only to you but to everybody with an account on your Surface.

If you don't have an attached keyboard, spend some time with Chapter 5; that chapter explains the subtleties of your Surface's built-in keyboard, which pops up when no other keyboard is attached.

Gadget hounds should jump to Part II to see exactly what will and won't work with their particular Surface models, as well as how to set up their apps and social networks.

After that, jump to your choice: the Play (Chapters 10 and 11) or Work (Chapters 12 through 14) part of the book.

If you're reading this as an e-book, use your reader's Bookmark and Search features to find what you want.

And with that, enjoy your Surface! It's a bold move by Microsoft that heralds the future of Windows, and you're at the forefront.

Part I
Introductions

getting started with

Surface

In this part . . .

- ✔ Find out why you should consider buying a Surface and which of the four models best meets your needs.

- ✔ Recognize each Surface model and identify the various buttons, ports, and sensors.

- ✔ Discover how to attach a keyboard and charge the battery.

- ✔ Turn on your Surface for the first time and set it up for your language.

- ✔ Download available updates, including security updates and updates for the bundled apps and programs.

Chapter 1

Which Microsoft Surface Do You Need?

*M*any people stay tied to a desktop PC at work. They sit in front of a deskbound workhorse that lets them create documents, spreadsheets, and whatever other humdrum files their boss requires that day.

When it's time to relax, however, many of those same people reach for a tablet. Lightweight and portable, tablets make it easy to watch videos, listen to music, browse the web, and check e-mail.

But what if you had a tablet that did it *all?* You could *create* files when work called but *consume* files during your leisure.

That's the promise of a Microsoft Surface tablet. Its finger-friendly Start screen lets you switch between videos, music, e-books, e-mail, and the web. And, come Monday morning, you can switch to the Windows desktop, fire up Outlook, Word, Excel, or PowerPoint, and get to work.

This chapter explains Microsoft's four models of Surface tablets: The two older models, Surface RT and Surface Pro, and the two new models, Surface 2 and Surface Pro 2. I describe them each in detail, highlighting their features, their strengths, and their weaknesses.

Why Buy a Microsoft Surface?

Most computer manufacturers create computers, including Windows tablets, as cheaply as possible. By coming up with the lowest price tag, they hope to undercut their competitors. Instead of taking the same road to the bottom, Microsoft created its line of Surface tablets as a showpiece, designed to show off Windows tablets at their finest.

To do that, Microsoft designed the Surface in-house with a large budget and engineering team, a luxury not available to most computer manufacturers.

Competitors cut costs by wrapping their tablets in cheap plastic. Microsoft Surface models, by contrast, come sheathed in a magnesium alloy. The rugged but lightweight casing gives the tablet a solid feel.

The Surface includes a built-in kickstand, shown in Figure 1-1. An optional attachable keyboard doubles as a cover when not in use.

Figure 1-1:
Every
Surface
model
includes a
kickstand to
prop it up at
a comfort-
able viewing
angle.

Photo image provided by Microsoft

Why not just buy an iPad? Well, they're attractive tablets that excel at what they do, but they're limited. Without a built-in USB port, iPads don't let you transfer files easily between your tablet and desktop PC. Every Surface tablet, by contrast, includes a full-sized USB port, making it easy to swap files through flash drives or even portable hard drives.

When iPad owners need to work, they usually reach for their laptop. Surface owners simply flip their keyboard into place, load the familiar Windows desktop, and head for the mainstays of Microsoft Office: Word, PowerPoint, Excel, and OneNote.

When you're ready to hit the road again, flip back the keyboard and run, taking all of your files with you.

Your Surface strips computing down to its essentials, creating a lightweight and mobile workstation that lets you add on accessories when necessary:

- ✔ **Fingers:** Your fingertips may be the only accessory you need. Touchscreens simplify many mobile computing tasks. It's easy to scroll through large documents with a flick of your finger, for example. Plus, touchscreens often seem more natural, especially when paging through digital books, maneuvering through maps, or resizing digital photos.

- ✔ **Keyboard:** A pop-up touchscreen keyboard works well for light typing. For heavier work, the optional keyboards add about a half-pound of weight and double as screen covers.

- ✔ **Monitor:** When you plug a monitor into your tablet's video port, you've created a two-monitor workstation. You can view your notes on your tablet but compose your document on the second, larger monitor. (I explain how to manage two monitors in Chapter 6.) Or, you can extend your Windows desktop across both monitors, doubling its size.

Understanding the Unique Features of a Surface

Microsoft Surface tablets introduce several features not found in other tablets:

- ✔ **Kickstand:** Place a tablet on the desk, and its screen faces the ceiling, not you. To solve the problem, each Surface includes a built-in kickstand that lets your tablet sit upright like a laptop's screen. The kickstand on the newest models, the Surface 2 and Surface Pro 2, adjusts to provide two viewing angles, handy for typing in different situations.

- ✔ **Keyboard cover:** Most tablets don't include a case or a keyboard. You can buy them as accessories, but they're two more items to carry around. The Surface, by contrast, offers a keyboard that doubles as a cover. When you're done working, flip up the keyboard, and it becomes a cover to protect the screen.

- ✓ **USB port/memory card slot:** These items come built into every Surface tablet, but you won't find them on any iPad. Ask any iPad owners how they move information to and from their iPad. Most of them get an uncomfortable expression on their faces while explaining their workarounds.

- ✓ **Windows desktop:** Nearly everybody has grown fairly used to the Windows desktop, a staple around offices for two decades. All Surfaces include the Windows desktop, but with one caveat: You can't install traditional desktop programs on the Surface RT or Surface 2.

- ✓ **Microsoft Office:** The Surface RT and Surface 2 include a copy of Office Home and Student 2013 RT. That gives you Outlook, Word, Excel, PowerPoint, and OneNote, ready to create your own documents or touch up those that arrive in e-mail. (Microsoft Office isn't included on a Surface Pro or Surface Pro 2, but you can purchase and install it yourself if you want.)

Deciding between the Microsoft Surface Tablets

Microsoft has sold four types of Surface tablets that look and behave very similarly. (A fifth Surface, available sometime in 2014, will have cellular Internet access.) All of them share many features:

- ✓ The tile-filled Start screen introduced in Windows 8
- ✓ The Windows desktop
- ✓ Downloadable apps from the Windows Store
- ✓ A USB port and memory card slot for adding storage
- ✓ The ability to create different accounts for different users

Yet the tablets differ in subtle ways that let them each serve different niches.

The following sections explain how the models differ so that you can figure out which Surface meets your needs.

Not sure which Surface you're looking at? Look for this chapter's "Identifying a Surface Model" section. It explains how to tell each model apart simply by flipping it over and reading the wording hidden on the back cover.

Note: I describe the first two Surface models, the Surface RT and Surface Pro, in the adjacent sidebar, "Upgrading first-generation Surfaces to Windows 8.1."

Upgrading first-generation Surfaces to Windows 8.1

Microsoft's first two Surface models, the Surface RT and the Surface Pro, didn't fare well in the market. The Surface RT boasted a long battery life but ran at a fairly sluggish pace. The Surface Pro was speedy and powerful but lacked a long battery life. And Windows 8 was too new to gather much enthusiasm.

Microsoft replaced the two older Surface models with the much more capable Surface 2 and Surface Pro 2.

If you own the Surface RT or Surface Pro, by all means, take advantage of Microsoft's free upgrade to Windows 8.1. To upgrade, visit the Store app with your Surface (as explained in Chapter 7), search for *Windows 8.1*, and choose to download and install the upgrade.

After you upgrade your Surface RT or Surface Pro to Windows 8.1, nearly *all* of the instructions in this book will also apply to your older Surface. (The older tablets just run more slowly or with less battery life.) If you own a Surface RT, look throughout this book for the Windows RT icon. That icon points out where the Surface RT and Surface 2 work differently than the Surface Pro and Surface Pro 2.

Microsoft no longer sells the Surface Pro, and Microsoft's website now refers to the original Surface RT as simply "Surface." You might find the "Surface" still available on Microsoft's website or at some stores for an exceptionally low price.

Surface 2

The Surface 2 works best during your leisure time, letting you watch movies, listen to music, browse the web, and connect with your friends.

Should you need to work, open the Desktop app. There, the built-in Microsoft Outlook, Word, Excel, PowerPoint, and OneNote apps should carry you through until you can get back to the office.

 The minimalist Surface 2 doesn't run Windows 8.1 but an operating system called *Windows RT 8.1*. In plain English, that means that the Surface 2 can't run traditional Windows desktop programs. Like the iPad, it's limited to *apps,* small programs downloaded from the Windows Store.

Although it can't run traditional Windows programs, the Surface 2 offers these perks:

- ✔ **Low price:** The Surface 2 comes in a 32GB version that costs $429; adding a Touch Cover keyboard adds another $79. (The newer Surface keyboards cost more, and I describe the differences between all of the Surface keyboards in Chapter 5.)

- ✔ **Long battery life:** Depending on its use, the Surface 2 averages between eight and ten hours of battery life.

✔ **Thin and light:** The Surface 2 weighs less than 1.5 pounds and is 8.9mm thin. That makes it easy to toss into a backpack or keep by the bedside table.

✔ **Better camera:** The Surface 2 sports a 3.5-megapixel camera in front and a 5-megapixel camera in back. (The Surface RT also includes that camera, but the Surface Pro and Surface Pro 2 include only 1.2-megapixel cameras for the front and back.)

✔ **USB 3.0 support:** The Surface 2 works well with natively recognized USB gadgets. That means you can plug in storage devices (flash drives, portable drives), USB hubs with more USB ports, mice, keyboards, cameras, some headsets, and some USB printers. Because it uses the new USB 3.0 standard, your information transfers much more quickly with USB 3.0 gadgets.

✔ **Bluetooth support:** Nearly anything that connects wirelessly through Bluetooth works well with the Surface RT and Surface 2. Your wireless headsets, mice, keyboards, and other Bluetooth gadgets should work without a hitch.

✔ **Memory card slot:** To add storage, slide a memory card into the built-in microSDXC slot. That slot works with microSD, microSDHC, or microSDXC cards, which let you add up to 128GB storage space.

✔ **Microsoft Office RT:** The Surface RT and Surface 2 include Microsoft Office RT, a suite of programs including Outlook, Word, PowerPoint, Excel, and OneNote. That's one less thing to buy to stay productive.

✔ **OneDrive:** Your Microsoft account gives you 7GB of free storage on OneDrive, an online cubby hole for files. (OneDrive was called *SkyDrive* until early 2014, when Microsoft changed its name.) The Surface 2 contains a certificate to increase your OneDrive storage to a whopping 200GB, free for two years.

✔ **Apps:** The Surface 2 can run only apps downloaded from the Windows Store. The Store doesn't have as many apps as Apple and Google offer, but the stock grows larger every day.

The Surface 2 differs from the Surface Pro 2 version in many subtle ways too numerous to mention here. If you own a Surface 2 or Surface RT, keep an eye open for this Windows RT icon, like the one in the margin. Paragraphs with this icon explain other ways Windows RT differs from traditional Windows.

Surface Pro 2

Whereas the Surface 2 aims to meet the consumer's needs, the Surface Pro 2 gives you the power of a desktop PC in a rugged tablet. You could say that it's two computers in one. On one hand, you have the Start screen apps for casual, on-the-go computing and staying connected while traveling.

What *can't* the Surface 2 handle?

Because the Surface 2 runs Windows 8.1 RT instead of Windows 8.1, it brings some unique compromises. Those compromises will be deal breakers for some people. Other people will say, "Who needs that, anyway?"

Here they are, in no particular order:

✔ **No desktop programs:** Surface 2 can run only apps downloaded from the Windows Store. You can't install desktop programs like you can on a desktop PC.

✔ **No Windows Media Center:** Unlike Windows 8 computers, Surface 2 won't let you install Windows Media Center for viewing DVDs and watching or recording TV shows.

✔ **No Windows Media Player:** The Surface 2 desktop doesn't include Windows Media Player. To watch movies and listen to music, you must use the built-in Music and Video apps or download replacement music and video apps from the Windows Store.

✔ **Can't start a homegroup:** When connected to a network, the Surface 2 can join homegroups and access files from other networked computers. However, those computers can't access *your* files. To share your files, you can upload them to OneDrive, copy them to a portable flash drive (or hard drive), or send them through e-mail.

✔ **No driver support:** Windows RT relies on its own set of built-in *drivers* — special software that lets it communicate with plugged-in accessories. Because you can't install drivers, the Surface 2 won't work with some USB gadgets such as TV tuners, barcode readers, GPS units, and other devices that require you to install a program.

✔ **No GPS:** Lacking a GPS chip, the Surface 2 relies on Wi-Fi to estimate your location. That narrows down your location to within a few hundred feet. (Surface 2 with a built-in 4G LTE cellular data plan also lacks a GPS.)

✔ **No NFC (Near Field Communication):** Too new of a technology to disappoint many, NFC lets two devices exchange bursts of information when they bump into each other, a feature much-welcomed by business-card swappers.

And, when work calls, you can load the full-powered Windows 8.1 Desktop app to run the same Windows programs you run on your desktop PC.

Windows 8.1 Pro also lets you pony up an extra $15 for the Windows Media Center Pack. This pack lets you play DVDs if you plug in a USB DVD drive. Plug in a TV tuner, connect a TV signal from cable or an antenna, and you've turned the Surface into a complete digital video recorder, ready to record TV shows for watching later.

The Surface Pro 2 comes with all the perks given to Surface 2 owners, including the 200GB of free OneDrive storage for a year.

I won't list all the advantages here because the Surface Pro 2 is basically a powerful desktop PC flattened into a tablet. *Any* software that runs on a Windows 8.1 desktop PC runs on a Surface Pro 2.

The same holds true for gadgets you plug into the Surface Pro 2's USB port: network ports, bar code readers, scanners, MIDI gadgets, and other specialty items.

But all that power brings a few compromises:

- ✔ **Battery life:** You can expect six or eight hours of battery life, perhaps more, depending on your use. But the battery probably won't last as long as it does on the Surface 2.

- ✔ **Higher cost:** Surface 2 pricing begins at $449 for a model with 2GB of memory and 32GB of storage. The Surface Pro 2 begins at $899 for 4GB of memory and 64GB of storage.

- ✔ **No Microsoft Office:** Unlike the Surface 2, the Surface Pro 2 doesn't include Microsoft Office. If you need that program, you must buy and install it separately.

- ✔ **No connected standby:** When the tablet's asleep, it's *really* asleep. It won't collect your e-mail in the background.

Summing Up the Differences between the Versions

Sometimes numbers mean more than words. To satisfy the other side of your brain, the specifications in Table 1-1 show exactly how the Surface 2 and Surface Pro 2 differ from each other.

Table 1-1	Differences between the Surface 2 and Surface Pro 2	
Item	*Surface 2*	*Surface Pro 2*
Operating System	Windows RT 8.1	Windows 8.1 Pro
Processor	NVIDIA Tegra 4 (T40) 1.7 GHz Quad Core	Fourth generation Intel Core i5-4200U Processor with Intel HD Graphics 4400
Memory	2GB	4GB or 8GB
Weight	1.5 pounds	2 pounds

Item	Surface 2	Surface Pro 2
Thickness	0.35 inches (8.9mm)	0.53 inches (13.5mm)
Display	10.6 inches, 16:9 ratio, 1920 x 1080 pixels, 5-point multitouch, 1080p resolution	10.6 inches, 16:9 ratio, 1920 x 1080 pixels, 10-point multitouch, 1080p resolution
Battery	31.5 watt hours	42 watt hours
Ports	USB 3.0 slot, micro-HDMI port, microSD slot, $\frac{1}{8}$-inch headphone jack, microphone, stereo speakers	USB 3.0 slot, Mini DisplayPort version 1.2, microSD slot, $\frac{1}{8}$-inch headphone jack, microphone, stereo speakers
Wireless	Wi-Fi (802.11a/b/g/n), Bluetooth 4.0	Wi-Fi (802.11a/b/g/n), Bluetooth 4.0
Storage capacity	32GB or 64GB	64GB/128GB with 4GB of memory model; 256GB/512GB with 8GB memory model
Cameras and microphones	Two 720p cameras and two microphones (one each in front and back). The front camera is 3.5 megapixels; the back is 5 megapixels.	Two 720p cameras (one in front and one in back), and one microphone on top. Both cameras are 1.2 megapixels.
Price	$449 for 32GB, $549 for 64GB. Touch and Type Covers sold separately.	$899 for 64GB, $999 for 128GB, $1,299 for 256GB, and $1,799 for the 512GB model; Touch and Type Covers sold separately
Start screen	Yes	Yes
Office RT	Includes RT versions of Word, Excel, PowerPoint, OneNote, and Outlook	No; Office must be purchased and installed separately
Stylus	Not included, but supports capacitive stylus	Digital stylus included, with built-in charger
OneDrive/Skype	Includes 200GB of free OneDrive storage for two years, one year of Skype Unlimited World calling to landlines in over 60 countries, and unlimited Skype WiFi at over 2 million hotspots	Includes 200GB of free OneDrive storage for two years, one year of Skype Unlimited World calling to landlines in over 60 countries, and unlimited Skype WiFi at over 2 million hotspots

(continued)

Table 1-1 *(continued)*

Item	Surface 2	Surface Pro 2
Sensors	Ambient light sensor, accelerometer, gyroscope, compass	Ambient light sensor, accelerometer, gyroscope, compass
Power supply	24 watts (included)	48 watts, with 5-watt USB port for charging accessories

Table 1-2 shows differences between the two original Surfaces, the Surface RT and the Surface Pro.

Table 1-2	Differences between the Surface RT and Surface Pro	
Item	Surface RT	Surface Pro
Operating System	Windows RT, with free upgrade to Windows 8.1 RT	Windows 8, with free upgrade to Windows 8.1
Processor	Quad-core NVIDIA Tegra 3	Third-generation Intel Core i5 Processor with Intel HD Graphics 4000
Memory	2GB	4GB
Weight	1.5 pounds	2 pounds
Thickness	0.37 inches (9.3mm)	0.53 inches (13.5mm)
Display	10.6 inches, 16:9 ratio, 1366 x 763 pixels, 5-point multitouch	10.6 inches, 16:9 ratio, 1920 x 1080 pixels, 10-point multitouch
Battery	31.5 watt hours	42 watt hours
Ports	USB 2.0 slot, micro-HDMI port, microSDXC slot, 1/8-inch headphone jack, stereo speakers	USB 3.0 slot, Mini DisplayPort version 1.1, microSDXC slot, 1/8-inch headphone jack, stereo speakers
Wireless	Wi-Fi (802.11a/b/g/n), Bluetooth 4.0	Wi-Fi (802.11a/b/g/n), Bluetooth 4.0

Item	Surface RT	Surface Pro
Storage capacity	32GB or 64GB	64GB or 128GB
Cameras	Two 720p cameras, front and rear	Two 720p cameras, front and rear
Price	$349 for 32GB, $449 for 64GB and Touch Cover	No longer sold
Start screen	Yes	Yes
Office (Word, Excel, PowerPoint, OneNote)	Yes, includes Home and Student version	No, Office must be purchased and installed separately
Stylus	Not included but supports capacitive stylus	Digital stylus included, with built-in charger
OneDrive/Skype	Includes 7GB of free OneDrive storage space with your Microsoft account, but no Skype credits	Includes 7GB of free OneDrive storage space with your Microsoft account, but no Skype credits
Sensors	Ambient light sensor, accelerometer, gyroscope, compass	Ambient light sensor, accelerometer, gyroscope, compass
Power supply	24 watts (included)	48 watts, with 5-wall USB port for charging accessories

Identifying a Surface Model

Not sure which Surface model you're viewing? You can find out by lifting the kickstand on the back of the tablet and peeking underneath. There, you see the word *Surface,* as well as this identifying information:

- ✔ **Surface RT:** These all-black, first-generation models list the term *Windows RT* beneath a Windows logo. You'll also see the amount of storage listed as either 32GB or 64GB. The kickstand's visible side shows a Windows logo.

- ✔ **Surface Pro:** These first-generation models list the term *Windows 8* beneath the Windows logo. You'll also see the amount of storage, 64GB or 128GB.

✔ **Surface 2:** These look much like the Surface RT tablets, down to the term *Windows RT* listed beneath the Windows logo. However, these second-generation tablets have a black front with a *silver* back. Beneath the kickstand, the amount of storage is listed as either 32GB or 64GB. Models with a 4G LTE data plan have a SIM card slot on the left edge below the volume rocker.

✔ **Surface Pro 2:** These second-generation models list the term *Windows 8.1* beneath the Windows logo. You also see the amount of storage, 64GB, 128GB, 256GB, or 512GB.

The serial number of your Surface, needed for warranty and service information, is printed directly beneath the word *Surface* under the kickstand.

The serial number of a Surface keyboard is printed on the right edge of its spine — that raised edge that clicks onto the Surface when attaching the keyboard.

Before buying a used Surface on eBay, make sure the seller posts a clear photo of the information printed beneath the kickstand. That way you know exactly what's being sold.

Understanding Your Surface's Storage Space

Microsoft sells its various Surface tablets with up to 512GB of storage space. However, Microsoft tosses some of its own software onto the tablet, which reduces storage space for your own files. Windows consumes some of that space, for example, as do the bundled apps and troubleshooting tools.

That means you can't copy 32GB of music onto a 32GB Surface. So, how much information *can* you store? Table 1-3 explains exactly how much storage space you'll have on each Surface model.

If you need more storage, you can always slip a microSDXC memory card into the microSD memory slot of any Surface.

The Surface 2 and Surface Pro 2 come with 200GB of free OneDrive storage for one year. I describe how to activate it in Chapter 3.

Table 1-3	Surface Storage Space
This Surface Model . . .	*. . . Contains This Much Storage Space*
Surface RT, 32GB	15GB
Surface RT, 64GB	45GB
Surface Pro, 64GB	30GB
Surface Pro, 128GB	89GB
Surface 2, 32GB	18GB
Surface 2, 64GB	47GB
Surface Pro 2, 64GB	37GB
Surface Pro 2, 128GB	97GB
Surface Pro 2, 256GB	212GB
Surface Pro 2, 512GB	451GB

Chapter 2

Getting Started with Your Surface

. . . .

. . . .

*W*hether your Surface arrives in the mail or in a shopping bag from your local Microsoft Store, the fun doesn't start right away. No, first you need to remove your Surface from its packaging and charge the battery — tasks I cover in this chapter.

While you're waiting for the battery to charge, take some time to identify all of your Surface's ports, slots, and attachments, all pointed out in this chapter. Some of them sit in plain sight; others hide in mysterious crevices.

But no matter where they hide, this chapter points them all out so you know what each one does. That way, you can either impress your friends or bore them to tears with your Surface port acumen.

The Grand Unboxing

The Surface comes artfully packed in a black box, shown in Figure 2-1. Look at the top-right corner, and you can see a white box protruding from inside. It's either an artful display of design creativeness or a waste of paper, depending on your mood.

Figure 2-1:
The Surface
comes
packaged in
a white box
that's been
pushed
inside a
black box.

To unpack your Surface, follow these steps:

1. **Remove the small strip of clear plastic tape holding the white box to the black sleeve.**

2. **Slide the white box out of the black sleeve.**

3. **If your Surface included a keyboard, remove the Touch Cover keyboard and its black cardboard packaging from beneath the box.**

   Microsoft bundled a Touch Cover keyboard with some early Surface RT models. Now, none of the Surface models include a keyboard; it's considered an accessory to be purchased separately.

4. **Remove the small strip of plastic tape holding the white box shut and then open the lid.**

   The lid opens, with the hinge along the right edge. As the lid opens, you see the Surface resting peacefully inside, as shown in Figure 2-2, complete with its power adapter.

5. **Remove the Surface from the box and remove its plastic wrapper.**

6. **Remove the manual and paperwork from the box beneath the Surface and remove the charger.**

And that's it. The Surface's battery comes partially charged, but before turning it on, you should plug it into the charger, as described in the next section. When you're ready to turn on your Surface, flip ahead to Chapter 3.

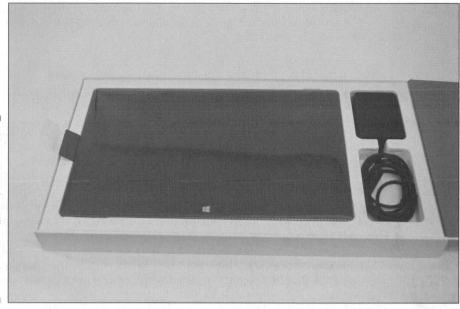

Figure 2-2:
All Surface models include a power adapter, thankfully. If they didn't, you'd be powerfully annoyed.

As you remove the Surface from its packaging, take note of these things:

✔ The Surface's manual, if you can call it that, contains illustrations with IKEA-inspired instructions: single sheets of paper with line drawings and arrows. Microsoft supplements it with a downloadable user guide available at its website: www.microsoft.com/surface/userquides.

✔ Pounce on the two blue cards, found as soon as you lift the Surface 2 or Surface Pro 2 from the box. One card has a password for 200GB of *OneDrive* (formerly known as SkyDrive) storage space, free for two years. The other card offers a year's worth of Skype WiFi and Unlimited World. I explain those services and how to redeem them, as well as their fine print, in Chapter 3.

✔ Your Surface's serial number is listed on the box's UPC code sticker. (It begins with the letters *S/N.*)

✔ Your Surface's serial number and amount of storage space also appears hidden beneath the kickstand.

If your Surface needs to be returned for service, you need to enter its serial number on Microsoft's online support site.

✔ The serial number for the optional keyboard appears on the right edge of its spine.

✔ Okay, if you can't wait, feel free to use the Surface while it's charging. But flip ahead to Chapter 3, where I walk you through the process of turning it on for the first time.

Charging the Battery

The Surface's bundled charger is lightweight, smaller, and flatter than many adapters, making it easy to carry. In the North American version, the outlet's prongs make sturdy little clicks as they fold in and out.

The charger plugs into the wall easily, politely leaving room to plug something into the adjacent outlet. The charger's other end has five little metal pins that line up with the five little metal pins recessed into a gap along your Surface's right edge.

When attached correctly, a little light begins glowing on the charger's end. If you don't see that little light, try wiggling the charger until it seats more firmly in the slot.

Follow these steps to charge your Microsoft Surface:

1. **Unfold the prongs from the charger's long end, if necessary, and plug them into an outlet.**

   On North American models, the prongs fold in for easy storage and out for plugging into a wall. Plug the charger into the wall so it doesn't cover the second wall outlet, and you'll leave room for plugging in other gadgets.

   On the Surface Pro and Surface Pro 2, you need to plug the charging cable into the charger. It's easy to see which end fits into which spot.

2. **Place the prong's small end into the charger on your tablet's lower-right side.**

   The five magnetically charged metal ports on the end of the charger cable should mesh with the five magnetically charged ports on your tablet's lower right side. The connector fits in either way, shown in Figure 2-3, with the cord pointing up or down your tablet's edge.

   If the connector doesn't snap tightly into the groove, it won't charge — even when it *feels* like it's in place. The key is to look for the little light on the connector (shown in Figure 2-4). Keep rocking the connector from side to side until the light glows. When it glows, it's charging.

   On some newer chargers, the glowing light surrounds the plug's tip; on others, it's a tiny pinpoint of light, like the one shown in Figure 2-4.

3. **Wait for the Surface to charge.**

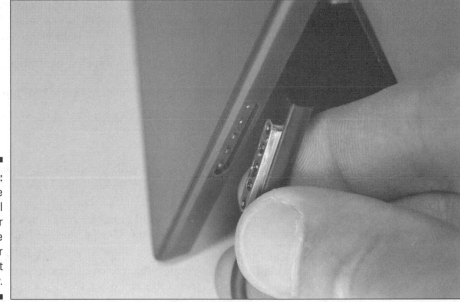

Figure 2-3:
The symmetrical connector fits into the charger socket either way.

This glowing light means the Surface is charging.

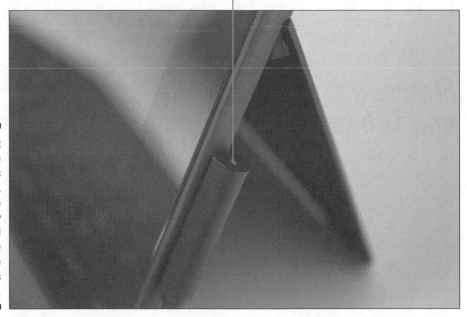

Figure 2-4:
When the connector's light glows, you've successfully fastened it, and the Surface begins charging.

Your Surface takes between two and three hours to charge completely. It may charge in less time, depending on how low its battery has drained. You can use your Surface while it's charging, but the charging time will take longer.

For such a simple device, the charger leads to a long list of stipulations:

✔ You can't charge the Surface from another computer's USB port.

✔ You *can* charge your phone or other USB gadgetry from the USB port of any Surface. If possible, though, plug your Surface into the wall first to avoid draining its battery.

✔ In a pinch, you can charge any Surface with the charger from any other Surface model. However, the Surface Pro and Surface Pro 2 charge much more quickly when using their own Pro chargers.

✔ For travelers, Microsoft offers a portable charger that plugs into a car's cigarette lighter. I cover optional Surface accessories in Chapter 17.

✔ The power connector doesn't fit very easily into the Surface RT and the Surface Pro; a gentle rocking motion usually snaps it into place. On the Surface 2 and Surface Pro 2, the connector snaps into place much more easily.

✔ Unlike the 24 watt chargers bundled with the Surface RT and Surface 2, the power adapter bundled with the Surface Pro and Surface Pro 2 puts out *48 watts*. Its adapter also includes a USB port for charging accessories, a handy feature missing from the power adapter bundled with the Surface RT and Surface 2.

Figuring Out What's Included and What's Missing

The only things included in the box are the Surface, its charger, and its miniscule paperwork.

Unless you paid extra for accessories, Microsoft left out these popular items, unfortunately:

✔ **Keyboard:** You can purchase the Surface keyboards at Microsoft's online store (www.microsoftstore.com) or at any Microsoft Store retail location. Designed specifically for the Surface, they also fold over the screen as a cover. I describe them all in more detail in Chapter 5.

If you don't want to spring for the expensive keyboard covers, you can plug any desktop PC keyboard into a Surface's USB port. Bluetooth (wireless) keyboards also work well; I explain how to connect Bluetooth devices in Chapter 6.

✓ **Cables:** You can plug your Surface into an external monitor or HDMI TV set for watching movies, gaming, or just fiddling around. Unfortunately, Microsoft didn't include the cables. For more information on the required cables, flip ahead to Chapter 6.

✓ **Memory card:** The Surface includes a memory card slot, but it's empty. Adding a memory card adds storage, as I describe in the next section.

✓ **Microsoft Office:** The Surface RT and Surface 2 include a pre-installed copy of Microsoft Office 2013 RT, the suite of programs with Outlook, Word, Excel, PowerPoint, and OneNote. The Surface Pro and Surface Pro 2 *don't* include Office, however. If you want it, you must buy and install it yourself.

✓ **Stylus:** You can draw on your Surface RT and Surface 2 with a plastic pen called a *stylus,* but only the Surface Pro and Surface Pro 2 include one. And their stylus won't work on the Surface RT or Surface 2. (Those models require a different type of stylus, which I cover in Chapter 5.)

Identifying the Parts of Your Surface Tablet

Waiting for your battery to charge can be pretty boring. So, while you're waiting for your Surface to charge fully for the first time, spend some time examining its front, back, and edges, as shown in Figure 2-5 (which shows the Surface 2 and Surface Pro 2) and Figure 2-6 (which shows the Surface RT and Surface Pro).

This section explains the holes, switches, and distinguishable doodads on each Surface model, what they do, and what they won't do.

✓ **On/Off toggle switch:** Pressing this simple on/off toggle switch in the top-right corner doesn't really turn your tablet on or off. Instead, it puts your tablet to *sleep*: a low-power state where your tablet shuts down everything but the essentials. Then, when you tap the On/Off toggle again, the Surface wakes up with all of your open apps and documents just the way you left them.

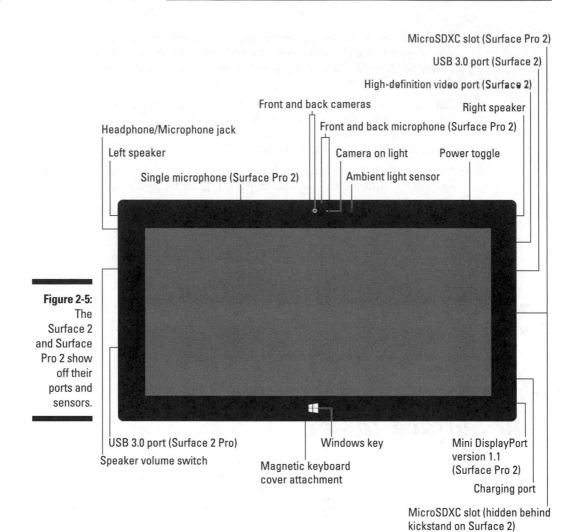

MicroSDXC slot (Surface Pro 2)

USB 3.0 port (Surface 2)

High-definition video port (Surface 2)

Front and back cameras

Right speaker

Headphone/Microphone jack

Front and back microphone (Surface Pro 2)

Left speaker

Camera on light

Power toggle

Single microphone (Surface Pro 2)

Ambient light sensor

Figure 2-5:
The
Surface 2
and Surface
Pro 2 show
off their
ports and
sensors.

USB 3.0 port (Surface 2 Pro)

Windows key

Mini DisplayPort
version 1.1
(Surface Pro 2)

Speaker volume switch

Magnetic keyboard
cover attachment

Charging port

MicroSDXC slot (hidden behind
kickstand on Surface 2)

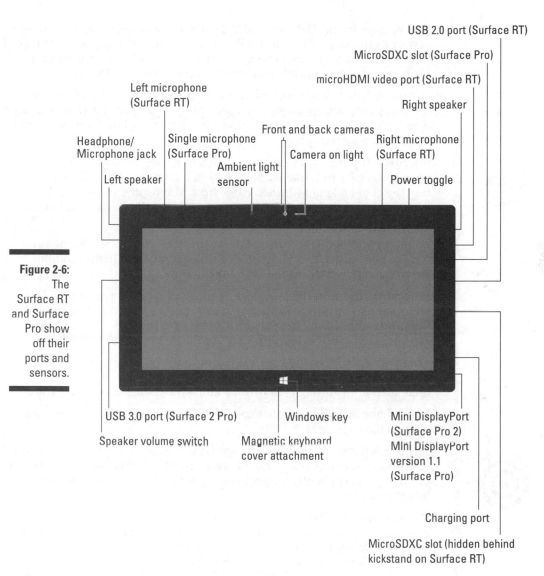

USB 2.0 port (Surface RT)

MicroSDXC slot (Surface Pro)

microHDMI video port (Surface RT)

Left microphone
(Surface RT)

Right speaker

Front and back cameras

Right microphone
(Surface RT)

Headphone/
Microphone jack

Single microphone
(Surface Pro)

Camera on light

Ambient light
sensor

Power toggle

Left speaker

Figure 2-6:
The
Surface RT
and Surface
Pro show
off their
ports and
sensors.

USB 3.0 port (Surface 2 Pro)

Windows key

Mini DisplayPort
(Surface Pro 2)
Mini DisplayPort
version 1.1
(Surface Pro)

Speaker volume switch

Magnetic keyboard
cover attachment

Charging port

MicroSDXC slot (hidden behind
kickstand on Surface RT)

- **Microphones:** Only the Surface RT boasts a pair of stereo microphones across its top edge. The Surface Pro has a single microphone on its top. The Surface 2 and Surface Pro 2 have front and back microphones for picking up the appropriate sounds when recording movies.

- **Speakers:** This pair of speakers lives near the top of your Surface's sides, providing surprisingly good stereo separation. The speakers aren't extraordinarily loud, however, which is great for neighboring hotel rooms, but not so good at your own party.

- **microHDMI port:** This port lets you send high-definition video from your Surface RT or Surface 2 to an external monitor or TV. You can buy the cool-looking $40 video cable from Microsoft's website, or you can use almost *any* microHDMI cable, which usually costs around five dollars.

- **mini DisplayPort:** The Surface Pro and Surface Pro 2 offer this newer type of port, often found on Apple laptops. It puts out high resolution video through a mini DisplayPort cable.

- **USB port:** This port, the same size as the ones found on desktop PCs and laptops, lets you plug in keyboards, mice, portable hard drives, and other USB accessories. Only the Surface RT USB port uses USB 2.0; the Surface Pro, Surface 2, and Surface Pro 2 all use the newer, faster USB 3.0 port.

- **Charging port:** Described in the previous section, this odd five-button port on the lower-right side lets you charge your Surface with your bundled adapter or through Microsoft's auto charger cable, sold separately.

- **Headphone jack:** Headphones and external speakers plug into this ⅛-inch port on the left side.

The headphone jack also accepts specially designed microphones. These microphones, compatible with iPhones and iPods, have three thin stripes on them and are slightly longer than regular microphones, which only have two thin stripes.

- **Volume control:** This rocker switch on the Surface's top-left side works as expected: Press the top portion to raise the volume; press the lower portion to lower it. As you press the control, the screen shows the current sound level. (You can also mute the volume with a Touch or Type Cover keyboard, covered in Chapter 5, or any keyboard with dedicated Windows 8 keys.)

- **Keyboard connector:** This mysterious magnetic connector on the bottom edge works only with the Surface's special click-on keyboards. To use a standard keyboard, just plug the keyboard's USB plug into the USB port on your Surface's right edge. I describe how to connect Bluetooth keyboards, mice, and other accessories in Chapter 6.

✔ **Kickstand:** Folding flush against the Surface's lower back edge, the kickstand flips out to prop up your Surface when you're working at a desk. It works on laps, as well, but doesn't feel as substantial and flat as a traditional laptop. It opens easiest from either of the two bottom corners and, in a boon for lefties, from the indent along the bottom-left side.

The Surface 2 and Surface Pro 2 add a second position to the kickstand, making the Surface easier to use on laps and airplane trays.

✔ **microSDXC slot:** This slot hides behind the kickstand on the Surface RT and Surface 2, and on the right edge of the Surface Pro and Surface Pro 2. But no matter which Surface you own, the slot accepts a microSD, microSDHC, *or* a microSDXC card, the same types found in many cell phones for the past few years. Many stores sell cards with up to 128GB of storage space.

✔ **Camera:** These two cameras, located on the top center of the Surface's front and back sides, take mediocre snapshots and shoot high-definition video. Most smartphones do a better job. One cool thing: The back camera is angled downward at 22 degrees, so it shoots straight when the tablet sits with its kickstand out on the table.

When shooting with the back camera on the Surface 2 or Surface Pro 2, keep the kickstand in its first position, or the camera won't shoot straight.

✔ **Recording light:** Barely visible next to each camera lens, this tiny white light glows whenever you're framing or shooting a photo or video. In fact, if you see it glowing, *smile:* You're being recorded.

✔ **Ambient light sensor:** Located near the front camera, this barely visible sensor constantly measures the light surrounding the screen. When you walk into a dark room, the screen dims slightly, making it easier to read (and preserving battery life). Similarly, walk outdoors in the sunlight, and the screen brightens to make it easier to read. If you find that this feature leads to constant screen flickering, I explain how to disable it in Chapter 14.

✔ **Windows key button:** Located on the bottom front of your tablet, this looks more like a logo than a button. And it doesn't physically move when pressed. But your tablet senses your finger's presence and behaves as if you've pressed your keyboard's Windows key. It returns you to the Start screen. Or, if you're already at the Start screen, it returns you to your last-used app or program.

Attaching the Keyboard

The Surface's special Touch and Type Cover keyboard covers adhere to the Surface by strong magnets, and they're not difficult to attach. (The Touch Cover 2 and Type Cover 2 keyboards come with even stronger magnets.)

Hold the keyboard's connector anywhere close to the connector on the Surface's bottom edge, shown in Figure 2-7, and they lunge for each other.

Figure 2-7: Match the Touch or Type Cover keyboard's connector with the connector on the bottom of your Surface, and they click into place.

However, like tired wrestlers, they occasionally miss. (To test the connection, press the keyboard's Windows key. If the keyboard is connected, your Surface should toggle between your Start menu and your last-used application.)

If your Surface doesn't acknowledge your keyboard's keystrokes, try holding down the keyboard and sliding the Surface to the left and right until you feel the keyboard lock into place.

Still not working? Try restarting your Surface with the keyboard attached: Swipe in from the screen's right edge to fetch the Charms bar, tap the Settings icon, tap the Power icon in the Settings pane, and tap Restart from the pop-up menu.

Still not working? Try wiping any oil or dirt from the two connectors. If it still doesn't work, it's time to drop by a Microsoft Store in your city or contact the Microsoft Surface Online Service Center (`https://myservice.surface.com`).

Positioning the Surface

Your Surface works in a variety of positions. No matter how you hold it, the screen flips to be right-side up. Although convenient, it's also disorienting: The familiar power button on the top right suddenly lives on the bottom left.

To remember which side is *really* up, take a look at the white Windows logo button on the Surface's bottom-front edge. When the logo is on the *bottom,* your tablet is right-side up, and all the buttons are where they should be. If it's on the top, either turn your Surface right-side up or remember that the buttons aren't in their normal positions.

When you're seated, fold out the Surface's kickstand from the Surface's back: Place your finger in the indentation on the back's lower-left edge and pull out; the kickstand snaps into place.

Although it looks precarious, the Surface and its kickstand actually feel pretty solid on a lap, especially with an attached clip-on keyboard. (Pull the kickstand out to its second position on the Surface 2 and Surface Pro 2 for even better lap traction.)

Finding Microsoft Website Support for the Surface

Microsoft offers several official sites dealing with the Surface, its sales, and support:

> ✔ **Microsoft Surface Tablets (`www.microsoft.com/surface`):** Microsoft's catch-all page for the Surface, this describes the latest models in detail, lets you sign up for the mailing list for product announcements, and provides links to the online store and support pages.

✔ **Microsoft Surface Support** (`www.microsoft.com/surface/support`): Visit here if your Surface doesn't seem to work correctly. You can walk through some troubleshooting steps, and if they don't work, you can contact Microsoft's technical support. They'll assess the situation and then make arrangements for a replacement if it's still under warranty.

✔ **Microsoft Community Support** (`http://answers.microsoft.com/en-us/surface/forum`): Surface owners ask questions and share tips on this Microsoft forum. Microsoft representatives also help answer questions.

✔ **Windows Compatibility Center** (`www.microsoft.com/en-us/windows/compatibility`): Here you can see what devices people report to have worked with Windows 8, Windows RT, Windows 8.1, and Windows 8.1 RT. Unfortunately, Microsoft tends to think everything is compatible until proven otherwise. Don't be surprised to see your incompatible items listed here as compatible.

Chapter 3

Setting Up Your Surface

You've taken your Surface out of the box. You've charged the battery. If you bought an optional keyboard, you've attached it to your Surface.

But your Surface *still* isn't ready for action.

This chapter walks you through everything you need to do when first turning on your Surface: Sign in with a Microsoft account (or create a new one), name your Surface, download and install updates, and then set up user accounts for each person who will be using your Surface.

Turning On Your Surface for the First Time

After prying off all the cardboard, peeling off the plastic wrappers, and charging your Surface, the fun begins. If you're near a wireless network, make sure it's turned on and that you know the network's name and password. You'll need to enter those so the Surface can connect with the Internet and download all the updates it missed while hiding in its box.

This setup is nearly identical for all four Surface models, so follow these steps to turn on your Surface for the first time:

1. **Press and release the power button on your Surface's top-right edge.**

   I describe all of your Surface's buttons in Chapter 2. Two or three seconds after you press and release the button, the word *Surface* appears in white letters on a black screen as your tablet churns its way to life. After a minute or two, it leaves you staring silently at the opening screen called *Region and Language*.

If you made a mistake while following any of the next steps, hold down the Surface's power button for about five seconds until it turns off. Release the power button, wait a second, and then press and release it again to turn on your Surface. When your Surface wakes up, it begins at the opening step, letting you start over.

2. **Tap your preferred language from the list.**

   As soon as you tap one of the listed languages, the Next button's wording changes to that language, letting you follow the menu choices in your native tongue.

3. **Verify your Country/Region, preferred App Language, Keyboard Layout, and Time Zone.**

   Your Surface asks you to verify these things:

   • **Country or Region:** Choosing your geographic location helps your Surface display information tailored to your surroundings.

   • **App Language:** Here, you can choose what language you'd like your apps to use, a boon for the bilingual.

   • **Keyboard Layout:** In another hat tip toward the bilingual, this option lets you change your Surface's onscreen keyboard to show accent marks and characters from different languages and regional dialects.

   • **Time Zone:** Choosing the correct time zone helps your Surface and its apps keep you aware of the correct time.

   The decisions you make here aren't permanent. If you want to change your Surface's keyboard layout to accommodate other languages, check out Chapter 14.

If you ponder a menu option for more than two minutes, the screen goes blank to preserve battery life. To revive it, touch the Windows key centered beneath your screen. (Or, if you have a keyboard cover attached, tap any key.)

4. **Tap Next.**

5. **When the License Terms page appears, read the License Terms agreement and tap the I Accept button.**

   Pull up a chair and relax. The Surface agreement is about 6,000 words long.

6. **When the Personalize screen appears, choose your Start screen's background color, type a name for your Surface into the PC Name box, and tap Next.**

   As you tap in different places on the colored strip shown in Figure 3-1, the background color changes to match the color beneath your finger. Spot a color you like? Lift your finger to lock that color into place. (I explain how to change the color in Chapter 14.)

Figure 3-1:
Slide your
finger along
the bar to
choose a
color and
then create
a name for
your new
Surface.

Then, tap inside the PC Name box and type a name for your Surface. If
you haven't attached a keyboard to your Surface, the tablet's built-in
keyboard pops up, letting you type your Surface's new name. (I describe
how to type on the built-in glass keyboard in Chapter 5.)

The name you choose here will identify your Surface when it connects to
networks, either at home, work, or on the Internet. Give every computer
a different name so you can tell which one is which.

After choosing a background color and name for your Surface, tap the
Next button. (I explain how to change your Surface's name in Chapter 14.)

After you leave this screen, the subsequent screens all have a backward-
pointing arrow in their top-left corner. Tapping a backward-pointing arrow
lets you return to the previous screen and change any of your answers.

**7. When the Get Online screen appears, connect to a wireless network, if
available, and tap Connect.**

If you're within range of a wireless network, the Surface lists all the wireless networks it detects, shown in Figure 3-2. If you spot your wireless
network's name, tap it; when the Connect button appears, tap it. Type
your network's password, if required, and then tap Next.

If you're connecting to your home or work network, tap Yes at the screen
asking whether you'd like to find PCs, devices, and content on the network. (That tells your Surface to find any available networked printers,
as well as anything else it can connect with.) If you're connecting to a network at a coffee shop or other public place, then tap No at that screen.

Not within range of a network? Don't know the password? Then escape
by tapping the words Skip This Step. You find out how to connect to a
wireless network in Chapter 6.

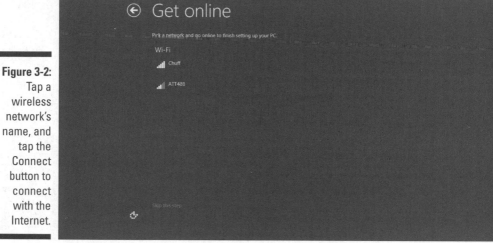

Figure 3-2:
Tap a
wireless
network's
name, and
tap the
Connect
button to
connect
with the
Internet.

8. **When the Settings screen appears, tap the Use Express Settings button.**

   The Express Settings, shown in Figure 3-3, provide a good mix of security while preserving your privacy. If you prefer to personalize your settings, however, tap the Customize button. (I explain how to change these settings later in Chapter 14.)

   The Surface Pro and Surface Pro 2 run a different version of Windows than do the Surface RT and Surface 2, so their wording differs slightly on this screen.

Figure 3-3:
Tap Use
Express
Settings to
stick with
Microsoft's
selected
settings
or tap
Customize
to approve
each setting
manually.

9. **If you successfully connected with the Internet in Step 7, type your Microsoft account e-mail address. If you didn't connect, create a Local account and type a name and password.**

   At this point, your path diverges depending on whether you were able to connect with the Internet in Step 5.

   - If you connected with the Internet and you already have a *Microsoft account* — an e-mail address you use to visit Microsoft services like Hotmail, Messenger, OneDrive (formerly called SkyDrive), Windows Phone, Xbox LIVE, or Outlook.com — type your Microsoft account's e-mail address into the white box. Type your password into the box beneath it, shown in Figure 3-4. Then move to the next steps to verify your security information.

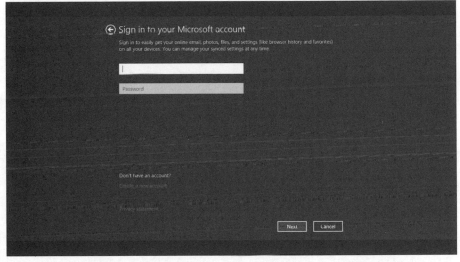

Figure 3-4:
Type your Microsoft account e-mail address, your password, and tap Next.

   - If you connected with the Internet but *don't* have a Microsoft account, tap the words Create a New Account. The setup program then walks you through the necessary steps to transform your favorite e-mail address into a Microsoft account. (You *need* a Microsoft account to get the most out of your Surface tablet.)

   - If you connected with the Internet but *don't want a Microsoft account,* tap the words Create a New Account. On the next screen, tap the words Sign In without a Microsoft Account. Then create a Local account by typing your first name, a password, and a password hint.

   - Couldn't connect with the Internet? Then create a Local account by typing your first name, a password, and a password hint.

Trusting your PC

Whenever you use a pre-existing Microsoft account on a new Windows 8 or 8.1 PC — and your Surface counts as a PC — Microsoft asks you to "Trust This PC." The words *Trust This PC* may appear on a menu on your Surface or in an e-mail.

Trust it with *what*, you may ask? Actually, Microsoft wants to know if you trust this PC with your information. This security precaution ensures that *you're* the one accessing the PC. Here's how it works:

To verify your identity, Microsoft sends a secret code to the cell phone or e-mail address that you entered when first setting up your Microsoft account. When you receive the code, visit the listed web address and enter the code into the online confirmation box.

Microsoft then confirms that *you* are the person creating an account on the Surface, and it begins syncing all your passwords and sign-in information for your apps, websites, Wi-Fi networks, social networks, and your network's homegroup if you have one.

No matter which path you take in Step 9, you tap the word Finish and then end up staring at the Windows Start screen. Welcome!

- ✔ If you signed in with a Microsoft account that you've used on other Windows 8.1 PCs, you're asked how Windows should set up your PC. Choose the option called "Set This Up as a New PC Instead" because your Surface is a new PC.

- ✔ After you enter your Microsoft account, your Surface begins stocking itself with all of the settings, online contacts, and appointments stored by your Microsoft account. It also gives you access to the OneDrive account linked with your Microsoft account.

- ✔ When the OneDrive Is Your Cloud Storage screen appears, tap the Next button. You want to take advantage of your free OneDrive storage. If you don't want free storage for some reason, tap Turn Off These Settings (Not Recommended) before tapping the Next button.

- ✔ If you couldn't connect with the Internet and instead created a Local account, I explain how to convert a Local account into a much more convenient Microsoft account in this chapter's "Setting Up User Accounts" section.

Downloading Software Updates

No doubt, your new Surface has updates waiting for it. Some of the software fixes the latest bugs; others add features. If you've been able to connect to the Internet, your Surface will probably restart as soon as you sign in for the first time. And when it wakes up, it's probably ready to download a second batch of updates.

In case your Surface still hasn't connected with your wireless network, Chapter 6 offers more details on connecting to networks. If you have only wired Internet access, head for Chapter 17: You need a USB-to-Ethernet adapter, available from the Microsoft Store.

When you've successfully connected with the Internet and you want to make sure your Surface is up-to-date with *all* of its updates, follow these steps:

1. **Summon the Charms bar and tap the Settings icon.**

   Slide your finger in slightly from the screen's right edge to fetch the icon-filled strip known as the *Charms bar.* Then tap the Settings icon at the Charms bar's bottom edge. The Settings pane appears. (I describe the Charms bar in Chapter 4.)

2. **Tap the Change PC Settings link from the bottom of the Settings pane.**

   The PC Settings screen appears.

3. **Tap Update and Recovery from the screen's bottom-left corner; when the Windows Update screen appears, tap the Check Now button. Select your waiting updates and click the Install or Install and Restart button.**

   Windows Update searches for any waiting updates, which can take a *long* time. Depending on your Surface model, a screen similar to Figure 3-5 appears. There, you see any of these updates waiting for installation:

   - **Firmware updates:** These large updates improve your Surface's most basic functions. Firmware updates can improve the sound, battery life, camera, keyboard, and other physical items. Firmware updates usually require your Surface to be plugged in, so make sure your power adapter is handy. These updates always require a restart to take effect.

   - **Important updates:** Because these updates usually fix security problems, your Surface normally downloads them automatically in the background. After they're downloaded, your Surface installs them automatically within a few days. Or, if you happen to restart your Surface, it installs them then. (Your Surface needn't be plugged in for these.)

   - **Recommended and Optional updates:** These aren't required for security, but installing them usually improves your Surface in other ways. For example, if you have an original Surface RT, the final version of Office 2013 RT will be listed here to replace your preview version. You may also see updated *drivers* — software that helps your Surface communicate with printers, networks, and other gadgets.

If your Surface says it found updates and will install them automatically, you don't need to do anything; the Surface will install them later.

If you want to force the update, perhaps before traveling, tap the words View Details. The View Details screen appears, letting you see the waiting updates and install them all with a tap of the Install button.

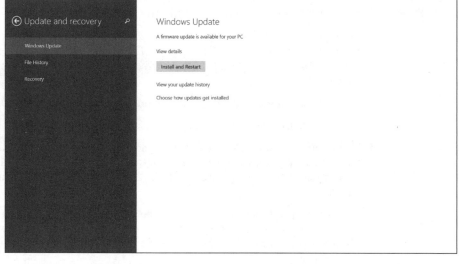

Figure 3-5:
Tap the
Install or
Install and
Restart
button to
install the
updates
waiting
for your
Surface.

4. **If asked, restart your Surface.**

    If you see a Restart Now button, tap it to restart your Surface. If you don't see that button, follow this step to restart your Surface:

    Summon the Charms bar by sliding your finger in from the screen's right edge and then tap the Settings icon. Tap the Power button on the Settings pane and, when the pop-up menu appears, tap the words Update and Restart.

When your Surface returns to life, the updates are installed.

✔ After manually downloading the first big batch of waiting updates, you probably won't need to check with Windows Update again. It will automatically download and install any waiting updates a few days after their release.

✔ Windows Apps update automatically on the Surface 2 and Surface Pro 2, as well as on the Surface RT and Surface Pro after they've been upgraded to Windows 8.1 RT or Windows 8.1.

Activating Windows

Your new Surface may toss a banner across the screen that brings everything to a halt: You need to *Activate Windows.* That means you need to link your particular copy of Windows to your Surface. Your Surface normally activates automatically when first connected to the Internet. But if you haven't yet connected to the Internet, the banner appears, asking you to activate your Surface manually.

It's a painless procedure that needs to be done only once. Tap the banner's Go to PC Settings button. At the PC Settings screen, tap Activate Windows. Then on the Activate Windows screen (see Figure 3-6) do one of the following:

- ✔ **If you're connected to the Internet, tap the Activate button.** Windows activates automatically. You're through.

- ✔ **If you're not connected to the Internet, or you're having trouble activating, tap the Activate by Phone button.** Tapping this button fetches a menu. When you choose your geographic region, your Surface lists a telephone number along with a string of 56 numbers. You need to pick up a telephone, dial that number, and, when the robot answers, enter that string of 56 numbers with your telephone's keypad.

   If you're having trouble punching the numbers into your phone, you're given the option to speak with a human. Hopefully, the human will prove more accommodating.

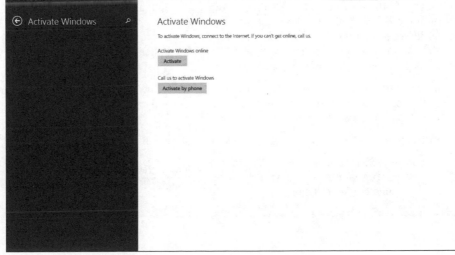

Figure 3-6:
To activate
your copy of
Windows,
tap the
Activate
button.

Downloading app updates from the Windows Store

If your Surface still runs Windows 8 or Windows RT, by all means, upgrade it to the new Windows 8.1 or Windows 8.1 RT. It's a free upgrade, and it enhances your Surface in many ways. As just one example, the new version of Windows keeps your apps updated automatically, which saves a lot of time.

If you stick with Windows 8 on your Surface RT or Surface Pro, you must update your apps manually by following these steps:

1. **From the Start screen, tap the Store tile.**

2. **When the Store app appears, tap the word Updates in the Store app's upper-right corner.**

The store lists all of your waiting updates, each selected with a check mark in its upper-right corner. (Don't want to update a particular app? Then *deselect it* before moving to the next step.)

3. **Tap the Install icon from the Store app's App bar.**

The Store app begins downloading and automatically updating your apps.

You'll have to repeat these steps every few days as new updates come out.

Creating a Recovery Drive

To be on the safe side, create a Recovery Drive for your Surface. Stored on a flash drive of 4GB (Surface RT, Surface 2) or 8GB (Surface Pro, Surface Pro 2), a Recovery Drive lets you reinstall Windows if your Surface no longer starts on its own and all resuscitation efforts fail.

Remember: You need to dedicate a flash drive to this purpose, and the process will erase everything stored on that drive.

To create a Recovery Drive, follow these steps:

1. **From the Start screen, open the Charms bar, tap Search, and type** Create a Recovery Drive **into the Search pane.**

2. **Tap the Create a Recovery Drive link that appears below the Search box; when the User Account Control pop-up appears, approve the action by tapping the Yes button.**

3. **When the Recovery Drive window appears, follow the steps to insert your flash drive and create the Recovery Drive.**

Label the flash drive as *Surface Recovery Drive* and stash it in a safe place. If your Surface ever falters, you can insert the Recovery Drive as one of the troubleshooting steps I describe in Chapter 15.

Setting Up Your Free OneDrive and Skype Accounts

Unlike the first generation Surface RT and Surface Pro, the new Surface 2 and Surface Pro 2 models come with two perks: a free 200GB OneDrive account for two years and both Unlimited World and Skype WiFi for one year.

So, what does that mean? Here's the scoop:

✔ **OneDrive:** OneDrive is a storage space that you can access from the Internet. By storing files on OneDrive, you can access them from anywhere: your Surface, your PC, your smartphone, or even any web browser. I explain how to use OneDrive, formerly called *SkyDrive,* in Chapter 6.

✔ **Skype:** Skype works like a telephone call or video conference between two PCs. Although it's free when used between two PCs, calling landlines or cell phones with Skype costs extra. The one-year Unlimited World subscription lets you use Skype to call landlines and cell phones for free in many countries. And the one-year Skype WiFi subscription lets you connect to Skype WiFi hotspots around the globe for free, as well.

To activate them, find the blue cards packaged with your Surface 2 or Surface Pro 2. Visit the websites listed on the cards and enter the code printed on the cards' backs.

Now, the fine print:

✔ You must redeem the offers within 90 days after buying your Surface. You can't redeem them after December 31, 2014. And you can redeem only one offer per Microsoft account.

✔ To read more fine print and sign up for your free OneDrive space, visit www.skydrive.com/surface.

✔ To see the countries covered by Skype's Unlimited World subscription and to sign up for your free Skype and Skype WiFi account, visit www.skype.com/surface.

Setting Up User Accounts

Unlike competing tablets, your Microsoft Surface lets you create separate accounts for different people. That lets several people use the same Surface, with all of their information stored separately on their individual accounts.

Separate accounts make it easy to share a Surface among a family, for example. You can even set up limited-access accounts for children.

Even if you're the only person who will use your Surface, you may want to set up a second account for the inevitable friends who need to check their e-mail.

Your Surface lets you set up three types of accounts:

- ✔ **Microsoft account:** This links your account with Microsoft, letting you download apps and use many of Microsoft's services. If you own a Surface, you *want* a Microsoft account.

- ✔ **Local account:** Local accounts are fine for simple work, letting you browse the web and create files using Word, Excel, PowerPoint, and One Note. But you can't download any apps from the Microsoft Store without typing a Microsoft account and password, and many of the Surface's bundled apps require a Microsoft account, too.

- ✔ **Guest account:** This handy temporary account gives you a way to let a friend borrow your tablet for a quick e-mail check *without* giving them access to any of your files. You find out how to set up a Guest account later on in this section.

To set up a new user account on your Surface (or to convert a Local account to a Microsoft account), follow these steps:

1. **From any screen, fetch the Charms bar and tap Settings.**

   Swipe your finger inward from the screen's right edge and then tap the Settings icon. The Settings pane appears.

2. **Tap the Change PC Settings link.**

   The PC Settings page appears.

3. **From the left column, tap Accounts to see the Your Accounts page.**

   The PC Settings page's Users section appears, shown in Figure 3-7.

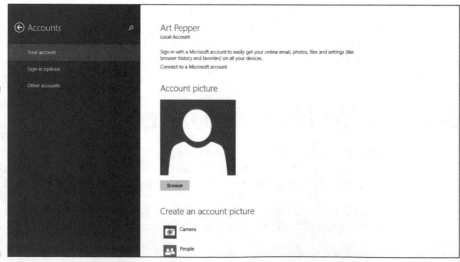

Figure 3-7:
To upgrade a Local account to a Microsoft account, tap the words Connect to a Microsoft Account.

4. **If you have a Local account and want to create a Microsoft account, tap Connect to a Microsoft Account and follow the instructions.**

5. **If you want to create a Local account, tap Other Accounts from the Accounts pane along the screen's left side. Then tap Add a User.**

   When the How Will This Person Sign In? page appears, enter the new user's Microsoft account e-mail address, if the user has one.

   The How Will This Person Sign In? screen, shown in Figure 3-8, makes it clear that your Surface prefers each account to have its own Microsoft account.

   If you know the person's Microsoft account e-mail address, type it, click Next, and move to the next step.

   If the person you're adding *doesn't* have a Microsoft account e-mail address, or you don't know it, tap Sign In Without a Microsoft Account at the bottom of the page. That takes you to a page where you can create a Local account by typing the new user's name and a simple password.

Figure 3-8: Enter the person's Microsoft account e-mail and click Next.

6. **If you're creating a Local account for a child, select the check box labeled "Is This a Child's Account? Turn On Family Safety to Get Reports of Their PC Use."**

Whether you create a Microsoft account or a Local account, that account's name then appears on the sign-in screen the next time you sign out of your account or turn on your Surface.

Signing into a new PC with a Microsoft account

When you sign into a new Windows 8 or 8.1 PC with a Microsoft account, several things happen:

✔ **Trust:** Microsoft will send a text message with a code number to your phone or an e-mail to the e-mail address you've assigned to your Microsoft account. After you enter that code number into the new PC, Microsoft will trust it with your information.

✔ **Syncing:** Because your passwords, settings, and preferences are tied to your Microsoft account, the new PC will be set up with your own wallpaper, Lock screen photo, Start screen layout, desktop themes, installed apps, Internet Explorer favorites, and other items. (These settings are stored on OneDrive; depending on the speed of your Internet connection, they may take a few minutes to appear.)

✔ **Apps:** Any apps you've purchased while on other PCs will be available to you on your new PC. (You'll still need to download them, though, by tapping their tile on the Start screen. And because the newly installed apps will arrive with their stock settings, you may need to tweak them to meet your own needs.)

You can adjust all of these settings by opening the Charms bar, tapping Settings, tapping Change PC Settings at the bottom of the Settings pane, and choosing OneDrive from the PC Settings screen. There, in the OneDrive pane's Sync Settings area, you can choose what items — if any — will travel with your Microsoft account as you move from one PC to another.

If you constantly move from one PC to another, you'll definitely want to tweak those settings to make sure you approve of what information travels with you.

✔ Family Safety offers a way of monitoring the behavior of account holders by restricting the websites they can view, the programs they can access, and the time they can spend on the computer.

✔ To turn on the Guest account, fetch the Charms bar by sliding your finger inward from the screen's right edge, tap the Search icon, and type **guest account** into the Search box. Then tap the Turn Guest Account On or Off link. When the Manage Accounts window appears, tap the Guest account icon and tap the next page's Turn On button. That places a Guest account option on the Sign In screen.

Turning Off Your Surface

This section really doesn't need to be here because you don't ever need to turn off your Surface. In fact, pushing the power button just puts it to sleep. It doesn't turn off the device at all.

The Windows RT and Surface 2 can sleep for days before the batteries give out. While the Surface sleeps, tap on the keyboard or power button to return it to life quickly with all your apps open, just the way you left it.

The Surface Pro and Surface Pro 2, however, don't offer as much battery life. When their batteries give out, the Surface copies the contents of its memory to its hard drive and then turns off. Plug it into the wall, turn it back on, and, after a few moments, all of your open apps will reappear, just the way you left them. (Leave it plugged in until it's fully charged before unplugging it.)

If you won't be using your Surface for a while, you can turn it off by following these steps:

1. **Summon the Charms bar by sliding your finger in from the screen's right edge and tapping Settings.**

2. **When the Settings pane appears, tap the Power icon.**

3. **Choose Shut Down from the Power icon's pop-up menu.**

When turned off, your Surface takes longer to start up than it does to awaken from sleep mode. And when it returns to life, you'll have to reopen your apps.

If you're already on the Start screen, you can shut down simply by tapping the Power button in the screen's upper-right corner. Then choose Shut Down from the drop-down menu.

Chapter 4

Introducing Your Surface's Start Screen and Controls

*I*f you've never experienced Windows 8 or 8.1, you're in for a surprise when you first turn on your Surface. No longer just a menu, the new Windows Start screen works like an operating system of its own, containing nearly all the tools a Surface owner needs.

Designed for tablets like the Surface, Microsoft built the new Start screen to be finger friendly and information packed. It serves up quick, informational tidbits with the least amount of effort.

If the Start screen lacks a tool you need for a particular task, visit the Windows Store (itself an app) and download an app to handle the job. *Apps* — small, touch-friendly programs — hail from the world of smartphones. In fact, a Surface works much like a smartphone with a larger screen.

This chapter explains how to get the most from the Start screen and its bundled apps.

Unlocking and Signing In

When you turn on your Surface, the Start screen hides behind the Lock screen, shown in Figure 4-1. Yet even before you move past the Lock screen, your Surface already dishes up useful information.

2:10 Shoot pool
Tony's
6:00 AM-6:00 PM

Saturday, November 3

Figure 4-1:
The Lock
screen
shows
useful
information
in the lower-
left corner.

A glance at the Lock screen's lower-left corner shows the current day, date, and time, as well as the strength of your battery and wireless Internet connection. Plus, you can customize the Lock screen to show your next appointment, your number of unread e-mails, and other bits of information.

To move past the Lock screen, swipe up with your finger, right-click a mouse, or press any key on the keyboard. The screen slides up and off the screen, revealing the Sign In screen, shown in Figure 4-2, listing all your user accounts.

Andy Rathbone   Tina

Figure 4-2:
To sign in
with an
account, tap
its picture.

To sign in, tap your user account and type your password. The tile-filled Start screen appears.

- ✔ When typing any hidden password, you can tap the little eye icon at the end of the password line for a peek at what you've typed. It's a handy way to make sure you're typing the correct password.

- ✔ If necessary, Windows reminds you with the words Caps Lock Is On. That reminds you to turn off the keyboard's Caps Lock feature so you don't mistakenly type your password with uppercase letters.

- ✔ If you see the Guest account listed, feel free to let a friend use it. The Guest account is handy for letting a friend temporarily sign on and check e-mail. I describe how to turn on the Guest account in Chapter 3.

- ✔ I describe how to customize your Lock screen background, icons, and user account photo in Chapter 14.

Managing Windows' Start Screen

If you've used Windows before, you're probably familiar with the Windows desktop. You've seen several open programs, each running inside its own resizable window.

That approach worked fine on desktop PCs with keyboards, mice, and large monitors. You could create spreadsheets and write reports for hours, all the while looking forward to lunchtime.

Tablets like your Surface, by contrast, let you manipulate information in many different situations. You fill out forms at job sites, for example, read books on the couch, or glance at a convention hall map while walking through rows of booths. Your Surface lets you do these tasks quickly, with your fingers, while on the go.

That's where the Start screen comes in, shown in Figure 4-3.

Designed specifically for tablets, the Start screen resembles a personalized billboard. Filled with colorful tiles, the Start screen spreads across your Surface's wide screen, extending off the right edge.

Each tile represents an *app* — a small program — and many tiles constantly percolate to bring up new information. Your Mail app's tile, for example, constantly cycles through your latest unread e-mails. The Weather app displays the ever-changing forecast for your location, and the Calendar app shows the time and location of your next appointment.

Figure 4-3:
The Start
screen
includes
"live" tiles,
which
constantly
update
to show
the latest
information.

That's not to say you *can't* work on a Surface. Your Surface still includes
the traditional Windows desktop — it's an app waiting to be opened. Open
the Desktop app with a tap on its tile, and the Start screen quickly clears to
reveal the desktop, complete with its movable and resizable windows.

✔ To see the portion of the Start screen that disappears off the screen's
right edge, slide your finger along the screen from right to left, just as if
you were sliding a piece of paper. As your finger moves, the Start screen
travels along with it, bringing more tiles into view.

✔ To scroll through the Start screen with your Touch or Type Cover keyboard's trackpad, put two fingertips on the trackpad. Slide your two fingers
to the left or right, and the Start screen follows them. (Your keyboard's
arrow keys also scroll the screen: They let you jump from tile to tile.)

✔ Having trouble finding things on the Start screen? I explain how to organize your screen into neatly labeled groups later in this chapter.

✔ Need a new app to meet a particular need? I explain how to download
and install new apps from the Windows Store in Chapter 7.

✔ I cover the Desktop app in Chapter 12. Microsoft worked hard to make
the desktop finger-friendly. But if you're looking for the same level of
productivity you had on a desktop PC, attach your Surface keyboard. (A
mouse works wonders on the desktop, as well.)

Although the Desktop app is certainly convenient to have around, you
probably won't load it too often. The Start screen apps serve most needs
quite well.

Finding, Opening, Closing, and Switching between Apps

The Start screen heralds a new way of working with Windows and its eco-system of small, inexpensive apps rather than large, expensive desktop programs.

To help you figure out this new world, these sections cover app basics: how to find them, open and close them, switch between them, and find their menus when they need a few tweaks.

Finding and opening an app

Your Surface's Start screen, shown earlier in Figure 4-3, doesn't show much organization. Your apps appear in a haphazard mess that sprawls out of view beyond the screen's right edge. As you slide your finger along the Start screen from right to left, the tiles move, bringing more into view.

If you spot the app you'd like to open, tap it with a finger: The app fills the screen, ready for action.

However, the bigger task may be simply *finding* the app you want to open. The sprawling Start screen doesn't alphabetize your apps or organize them into manageable groups. That leaves way too many hiding places.

When your sought-after app is lost in a sea of tiles, bring the app to the surface by following these steps:

1. **Slide your finger up from the middle of the Start screen.**

   The Start screen displays an alphabetical list of all your apps, shown in Figure 4-4, followed by a list of your desktop programs, organized alphabetically by category. Still don't spot the app you're after? Move to Step 2.

   The lower half of the Start screen normally sorts the apps alphabetically; to change that order, tap the words By Name next to the word Apps in the screen's upper-left corner. There, you can choose to sort them by their installation date, by how often you use them, or by category.

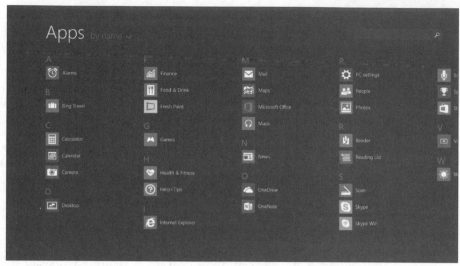

Apps by name

Figure 4-4:
Sliding your
finger up
from the
middle of
the Start
screen
reveals
all your
installed
apps, alpha-
betized by
name.

2. **Pinch the All Apps screen between two fingers.**

   The app icons disappear, and Windows lists the alphabet, from A to Z,
   shown in Figure 4-5. Tap the first letter of your lost app — J, perhaps —
   and Windows redisplays all the apps. This time, though, apps beginning
   with J are placed directly beneath your finger, making them easier to find.

   This trick works best for Start screens with a huge number of apps. If
   you *still* can't find your wayward app, move to Step 3.

Figure 4-5:
Pinch the
list of all the
apps, and
Windows
lets you
jump to
apps begin-
ning with
a certain
letter.

3. **Search for the app.**

   Tap inside the Search box in the screen's upper-right corner. Then begin typing the missing app's name. As you type, Windows lists matching apps, narrowing down the list with each letter you type.

   Spot your app? Tap its icon to launch it.

 If you've added a keyboard to your Surface, just begin typing the app's name directly onto the Start screen. The Start screen quickly transforms into a list of every app matching what you've typed so far. After you spot your app's name on the list, tap it, and it leaps onto the screen. (Or, if your typing has narrowed down the list to one app, press Enter to launch the app.)

 ✔ The Start screen doesn't show *all* of your installed apps. Unless you personally reorganize it, described at this chapter's end, the Start screen shows only the apps Microsoft chose to be listed.

 ✔ Want an unlisted app to appear on the Start screen? Put it there yourself: When looking at the app's tile from the All Apps layout shown in Figure 4-4, tap and hold the app. (A check mark appears to let you know it's selected, and the bottom menu appears.) Then tap the Pin to Start icon from the bottom menu.

 ✔ If an app says it's already pinned to the Start screen, but you still can't find the darn thing, tell Windows to take you there: Tap and hold the app from the All Apps view in Figure 4-4 and then tap the Find In Start icon. Windows returns to the Start screen, pointing out exactly where that app hides on the Start screen.

   ✔ Still don't see an app that meets your needs? It's time to visit the Windows Store, a trip covered in Chapter 7.

Closing an app

Older versions of Windows always wanted you to *close* unneeded programs: You'd click the little X in the program's upper-right corner, and the program disappeared from the screen.

You won't find any close buttons on apps, however: Apps aren't meant to be closed. When they're not being used, apps simply rest in the background, waiting in case you need them again. They consume very few resources, and they don't eat much, if any, battery power.

 When you're done with an app, just head back to the Start screen by pressing the Windows key on the front of your Surface. (You can also swipe in from the screen's right edge and touch the Start icon on the Charms bar, covered later in this chapter.) Then load a different app to move on to another task.

But if you *want* to close an app, perhaps one that's making annoying noises in the background, it's not difficult:

To close the app currently filling your screen, slide your finger from the screen's top edge all the way down to its bottom edge. As you slide, the app follows your finger, shrinking and then disappearing completely when your finger reaches the screen's bottom edge.

It's oddly empowering to watch your finger pull that unwanted app off the screen. It's an easy trick to remember, and you'll find yourself wanting to do it again and again.

If you've attached a mouse or trackpad to your Surface, you can also close an app by pointing the mouse arrow at the app's top edge. When a tiny strip appears along the app's top edge, click the X in the strip's right corner, and the app closes.

Switching between apps

When they're not in use, apps slumber in the background. Your Surface ignores them, devoting its full attention to the app currently filling the screen.

But if you want to awaken a previously used app, you can summon it with this easy trick:

To switch back to the app you've just used, swipe your finger inward from the Surface's left edge.

As your finger moves inward from the screen's edge, it drags your last-used app along with it. When the app begins to appear onscreen, lift your finger: The app grows to fill the screen.

Keep repeating the same trick, sliding your finger in from the left, and you'll eventually cycle through *all* your currently open apps.

Can't remember whether an app is already open? To see a list of your last six open apps, follow these steps from any screen on your Surface:

1. **Slowly slide your finger inward from the screen's left edge.**

2. **When you see an app begin to slide into view, slide your finger back to the left edge.**

   All of your opened apps appear in a column clinging to the screen's left edge, shown in Figure 4-6.

Figure 4-6:
Swipe
your finger
inward, and
then back,
from the
screen's left
edge to see
your open
apps.

After you see the apps' thumbnails clinging to the screen's left edge, you can
perform a few other circus tricks:

- **Return to an open app.** Tap an app's thumbnail from along the screen's
  left edge, and the app fills the screen. Simple.

- **Close an app.** With your finger, slide the app slightly to the right and
  then down and off the screen. This one takes practice because the app
  tries to muscle its way onto the screen. (If you're using a keyboard/
  trackpad or mouse, you can right-click the unwanted app's thumbnail
  and choose Close from the pop-up menu.)

- **Remove the app column.** Because that column of recently used apps consumes some real estate, it closes by itself after you open one of its apps. But
  if you want to close it manually, just tap the currently open app. That brings
  Windows' attention back to your current app and closes the column of apps.

Windows considers the desktop to be a single app, no matter how many programs are running in their own windows. Consequently, this app-switching
trick won't let you jump back to a particular program on the desktop; it only
returns you to the desktop, where you can see all of the windows you happen
to have left open.

Installing and uninstalling an app

You install apps through the Windows Store app. I describe how to install and
uninstall apps in Chapter 7.

Understanding the Charms Bar

Although it sounds like something dipped in milk chocolate, the Charms bar is simply a menu. More than that, it's a tool that unites every portion of Windows. The all-powerful Charms bar lives *everywhere:* on the Start menu, within every app, and even on the Windows desktop.

However, the Charms bar remains out of sight until you summon it with this trick:

Slide your finger inward from any screen's right edge, and the Charms bar appears, shown in Figure 4-7. The Charms bar also fetches a helpful message in the screen's bottom-left corner, showing the current time and date, as well as the strength of your wireless signal and battery.

The Charms bar displays five handy icons, each described in the following sections.

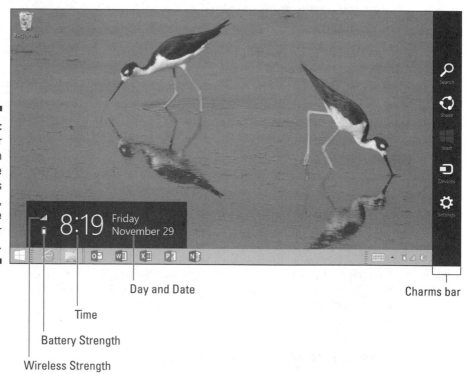

Figure 4-7: Swipe your finger in from the screen's right edge, and the Charms bar appears.

Day and Date

Time

Battery Strength

Wireless Strength

Charms bar

All of the Surface click-on keyboards include keys dedicated to the Charms bar's all-important icons. Look along the top row for keys dedicated to Search, Share, Devices, and Settings. The fifth icon, the Windows key, lives to the left of your keyboard's spacebar.

Search

When you need to find something in the sea of text you're currently viewing, fetch the Charms bar with a finger swipe inward from the screen's right edge. Then tap the Search icon, shown in the margin.

The Search pane appears along the screen's right edge, with a Search box ready for you to type what you'd like to find. The Search icon provides a quick way to find just about anything: an app, a long-lost file on your Surface, a particular song or album, a hidden setting, or a sought-after e-mail in your Mail app.

If you're already on the Start screen, tapping the Search icon in the Start screen's upper-right corner also fetches the Search pane, saving you some time.

But Search isn't restricted to your Surface itself. It searches *everything*, including the Internet. As you type, the Search pane lists matches found on your Surface, shown in Figure 4-8. Below those matches, it lists items found on the Internet, as well.

Figure 4-8:
The Search command lists matches found on your Surface, followed by a list of matches from the Internet.

Fine-tuning your search

True to its name, the Search box normally searches *everywhere:* your Surface as well as the Internet. If that turns into information overload, you can target your search to a specific area by tapping the word Everywhere. A menu drops down, letting you direct your search to one of these specific areas:

✔ **Everywhere:** The default search, this searches both your Surface and the Internet for matches.

✔ **Settings:** A search in this box looks through every setting found in Windows' two control panels: the Start screen's PC Settings area and the desktop's Control Panel. It's handy for finding a helpful-but-rarely-used setting that's hidden deeply in the Control Panel's crevices.

✔ **Files:** Choose this to search through every file on your computer, as well as files you've

stored on OneDrive, Microsoft's new name for its SkyDrive online storage space (covered in Chapter 6). Searching for files turns up songs, videos, documents, and photos, bringing a list of matching names to the forefront. When you spot the one you want, launch it with a tap.

✔ **Web Images:** Don't know what a *Buff-Collared Nightjar* looks like? Choose Web Images for your search, and Windows displays Internet-posted photos of this oddly named bird.

✔ **Web Videos:** Similar to the previous search, this finds videos, which is helpful when you're tracking down movie trailers or YouTube videos.

The next time you open the Charms bar and tap the Search icon, the Search pane resumes to its normal Everywhere search.

If a match appears even before you finish typing, tap the matching item; Search will show it to you, be it a setting, file, or web page plucked from the Internet.

✔ When you open Search, a list of things you've previously sought appears along the bottom of the Search pane, saving you from retyping the app's name. Tap an item's name to search for it again.

✔ The Search pane won't search for files on your *homegroup* — other computers on your home network. You need to search those computers individually.

✔ The Search command will find apps stored on your Surface, and it even finds matches for apps available in the Windows Store. However, it can't search for information you've stored inside your *apps*. To search inside a particular app, open it; most apps include a Search box in their upper-right corner.

✔ To clear your search history or change your current Search settings, slide a finger in from the screen's right edge, tap Settings, and then tap Change PC settings. Tap Search and Apps and then tap Search; the Clear button appears so that you can wipe away your past search history.

✔ When you need to do more advanced searches — finding files created on a certain date, perhaps — open the Desktop app. Every desktop folder includes a Search box in its upper-right corner. To fine-tune your searches, tap the Ribbon menu's Search tab and tap the type of search you need.

Share

Computers excel at sharing information. There's little point in creating something unless you want somebody else to see it. That's where the Charms bar's Share icon comes in.

When you're viewing something you want to share, fetch the Charms bar with a swipe of your finger inward along the Screen's right edge.

 When the Charms bar appears, tap the Share icon, shown in the margin. The Share pane appears, listing different ways you can share what you're currently viewing. You'll almost always see at least one universal sharing mechanism: the Mail app. Choose the Mail app to e-mail what you're seeing to a friend.

Choose the Share icon while viewing a website, for example, to e-mail its link to a friend, shown in Figure 4-9. It also lets you post the link onto your social networks, such as Facebook. You can add the link onto your Reading List app, a handy way to revisit reading material in your spare time.

Figure 4-9: Tap the Share icon while viewing a website, and then tap Mail to e-mail its link to a friend.

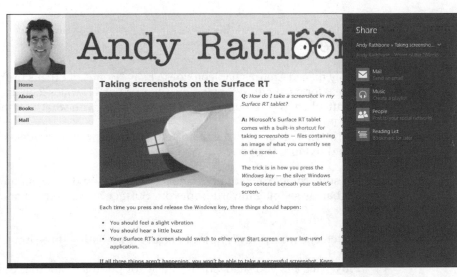

To e-mail a photo to a friend, open the Photo app and open your photo for viewing. Then tap the Charms bar's Share icon and tap Mail. (I describe the Photo app in Chapter 10.)

Not all apps support the Share command, unfortunately. If an app doesn't support it, there's no way to share that app's contents.

The Windows desktop lets you share a screenshot of your desktop, a handy way to let tech support people see what you're experiencing. To send a desktop screenshot, open the Charms bar from the desktop, tap Share, and tap Mail. Your Surface takes a screenshot and attaches it to the e-mail, ready to be sent.

Start

When you want to return to the Start screen, slide your finger inward from the screen's right edge to fetch the Charms bar, then tap the Start icon, shown in the margin.

If you're already on the Start screen, a tap of the Start icon returns you to your last-used app, making it a handy way to toggle back and forth between the two.

However, touching the Windows key on the front of your Surface does the same thing, and it's often faster. (You can also tap the Windows key on any keyboard to toggle between the Start screen and your last-used app.)

Devices

This oddly named Charms bar icon doesn't say "Print," but that's probably what you'll use it for most often. Tapping the Charms bar's Devices icon lists all the devices attached to your computer that can interact with what's on the screen.

Most of the time, that device will be your printer (or your *printers* if you're connected to more than one).

To send something from your Surface to a connected device, summon the Charms bar by swiping inward from your Surface's right screen and then tap Devices.

The Devices pane appears, shown in Figure 4-10, listing three items:

✔ **Play:** This lets you send videos, music, or photos to another device, such as an Xbox. It you don't see your device listed, though, it's not supported, unfortunately. And some videos prohibit playing them on another screen.

✔ **Print:** Tap this to see any connected printers able to print your currently viewed item. (I cover printers in Chapter 6.)

✔ **Project:** Tap this to send your Surface's screen to another screen, usually a projector or monitor attached with a video cable. (I cover projectors and second monitors in Chapter 6.)

Figure 4-10:
The Devices icon lets you play music, print files, or project your screen to an attached TV or monitor.

When you tap Play, Print, or Project, Windows shows a list of connected devices able to receive your information. To print, for example, tap your printer's name, adjust any settings the printer offers, and tap the Print button.

Settings

The Charms bar's Settings icon lets you tweak the settings of the app you're viewing, a perk when you're desperately looking for an app's menus, or need to adjust its boorish behavior. But this often-overlooked icon also serves as a gateway for tweaking many of your Surface's most common settings.

 To change your currently viewed app's settings, summon the Charms bar by sliding your finger in from the screen's right edge. When the Charms bar appears, tap the Settings icon. The Settings pane appears, shown in Figure 4-11.

Figure 4-11:
The top of
the Settings
pane lists
settings
for your
currently
viewed app;
the bottom
lists short-
cuts to other
popular
settings.

Atop the Settings pane, you see the settings available for the app you're currently viewing onscreen. And along the pane's bottom, you see these quick
shortcuts to your Surface's most-tweaked settings:

✔ **Networks:** This five-bar icon represents your wireless signal strength,
as well as the name of the wireless connection that's currently pouring
the Internet into your Surface. (Tap the icon to find the Airplane Mode
toggle, which turns off wireless when you're on an airplane.)

✔ **Volume:** Tap here to fetch a sliding volume control. Slide the bar up to
increase the sound; slide it down to lower it. The Volume toggle on the
Surface's top, left side does the same thing. (The dedicated Volume keys
on the Surface's Touch and Type Cover keyboards also do the same
thing.)

✔ **Screen:** Tapping here brings a sliding control for screen brightness. Slide
it up for a brighter screen; slide it back down to dim it slightly. (Tap the
monitor icon atop the sliding control to lock your Surface's rotation control, keeping it from constantly moving right-side up.)

✔ **Notifications:** Designed for people tired of seeing notifications about
instant messages and other informational tidbits popping up onscreen,
this button lets you hide them for one, three, or eight hours so you can
get some work done.

✔ **Power:** Tap here to sleep, shut down, or restart your Surface. (If you
have updates waiting, you may also see Update and Restart.)

✔ **Keyboard:** This lets you switch between different keyboards or languages, as well as call up the onscreen keyboard, which is listed as Touch Keyboard and Handwriting Panel. I explain keyboard intricacies like that in Chapter 5.

✔ **Change PC Settings:** Tap here to visit the Start screen's PC Settings area, a goldmine of settings for tweaking the Surface to meet your particular needs. (Visit the PC Settings area's PC and Devices section, for example, to customize your Lock screen, Start screen, and account picture.) I cover the PC Settings area in Chapter 14.

Organizing the Start Screen

Windows doesn't bother to organize your Start screen. When you download new apps from the Windows Store, they don't appear on the Start screen. No, they're tossed onto the All Apps area, which keeps them hidden.

Combine that with the fact that the Start screen was designed to look nice on the showroom floor, and you can see the problem: The Start screen doesn't reflect the way *you* want to work.

So, follow this six-step plan to transform the Start screen into something that serves your own needs. It organizes your Start screen only as much as you'd like.

If you prefer working with a messy desk, stop after the first step or two. If you sort your pens by color in separate trays, follow these steps to the very end. When you're through, your Start screen will transform into an array of neatly labeled groups with icons for all of your favorite apps in easy-to-find places.

Follow these steps to organize your Start screen into something you can live with:

1. **Remove tiles for apps you don't want.**

    When you spot an app you don't want to see on the Start screen, get rid of it: Hold your finger down on it until a menu bar appears along the screen's bottom. Then lift your finger, noticing the check mark that appears on that app's icon.

    Now, tap any other unwanted icons; check marks appear on them, as well, showing that they're selected for further action.

     When you've selected all of your unwanted apps, tap Unpin from Start (shown in the margin) from the App bar along the screen's bottom. Presto! The apps disappear from the Start screen. (Tap the Windows key to remove the App bar and return to the normal Start screen.)

Choosing Unpin from Start doesn't *uninstall* the app or program; it only removes the tile from the Start screen and returns it to the All Apps area. If you accidentally remove a tile for a favorite app or program, you can easily put it back in the next step.

Don't *ever* want to see an app again? Then choose the adjacent Uninstall icon (shown in the margin) instead. Windows uninstalls the app, freeing up some valuable storage space. (I explain how to reinstall mistakenly uninstalled apps in Chapter 7.)

2. **Add tiles that you *do* want.**

   Slide your finger upward from the middle of the Start screen; the Start screen slides upward with your finger to reveal the All Apps screen lurking below. There, you find icons for *every* installed app, listed in alphabetical order.

   When you spot an app that you want to appear on the Start screen, hold your finger down on it until the App bar appears along the screen's bottom. That selects the app; tap any others to select them, as well.

   Then tap the Pin to Start icon from the Start screen's bottom menu. Windows tosses a tile for each of your selected apps onto the Start menu's far right end. A press of the Windows key removes the App bar and returns to the Start screen.

   At this point, you've weeded out unwanted tiles and added the ones you like. To move related tiles closer together, move to the next step.

3. **Move related tiles closer to each other and resize them if necessary.**

   When related tiles appear next to each other, they're easier to find on the Start screen. For example, I like to keep my people-oriented apps — Mail, People, and Calendar — next to each other on the left edge for easy access.

   To drag a tile from one place to another, select it first by holding your finger down on it until the App bar appears along the screen's bottom edge. Then drag the tile to its new location. Lift your finger, and the tile remains in its new home.

   If a tile is too big or too small, change its size: Select the tile by holding your finger down on it. When it's selected, tap the Resize icon from the App menu along the Start screen's bottom and then choose the size: Large, Wide, Medium, or Small.

   Remember, some apps have room to show live updates only on wide tiles.

4. **Move related tiles into groups.**

   Placing related tiles into separate groups makes them easier to relocate. For example, you may want to create one group for tiles you use at home, another for work-related tiles, and a third for tiles that play media — choose whatever groups work for you.

To begin creating new groups, look closely at your Start screen: It comes set up in two groups. (See that empty spot separating the two groups?)

To create a new group, select a tile with a long finger press and then drag that tile into the empty space that separates two groups. As your dragged tile reaches that empty space, the groups move farther apart, shown in Figure 4-12, and a bar appears between them. Lift your finger, and the tile drops into place, forming the start of a new group.

Repeat this step; keep rearranging tiles and creating new groups until your related tiles live together in their own groups.

Each group of tiles would be easier to identify if it had a name, though. To do that, move to the next step.

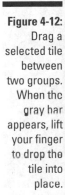

Figure 4-12:
Drag a selected tile between two groups. When the gray bar appears, lift your finger to drop the tile into place.

5. **Name the groups of related tiles.**

In the first few steps, you may have noticed that something odd happened whenever you selected a tile: A strip with the words Name Group appeared over each group of tiles.

So, to name a group, select any tile. Then tap the Name Group strip over the group you'd like to name. When the strip turns white, type the group's name and press Enter.

The new name appears above the group. Repeat until you've named all your groups.

At this point, you may be organized enough. But if you want to move the groups into a different order, perhaps keeping your most important groups on the far left, where they're always in view, move to Step 6.

6. **Move your most important groups to the far left, where they're always visible.**

   Start by pinching the Start screen tiles between two fingers; as you slide your two fingers closer together, the tiles shrink until you're looking at all of your groups onscreen, shown in Figure 4-13.

   While you're still looking at your groups as miniatures, shown in Figure 4-13, rearrange the groups by dragging them into new positions.

Figure 4-13:
Pinch the Start screen with your fingers to shrink the tiles, bringing all your groups into view.

When you finish dragging, dropping, and naming tiles and groups, your Start screen is customized to the way *you* use your Surface. (I've shown mine in Figure 4-14.) Your tiles live in their own neatly named groups, and your most frequently accessed tiles appear first on the screen.

You can add favorite desktop folders to the Start screen, as well. While on the desktop, hold down your finger on a desired folder or library; when a square appears, lift your finger. Then, from the menu that appears, tap Pin to Start.

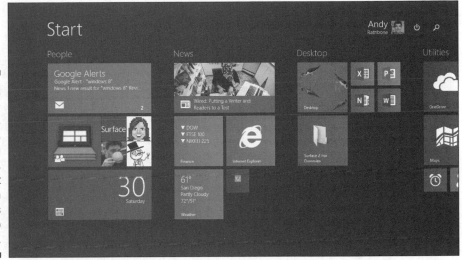

Figure 4-14:
After rearranging, organizing, and naming your groups, your Start screen becomes easier to manage.

Browsing Files from the Start Screen

Eventually, you'll need to browse through some files with your Surface. For example, you may need to grab some files off of that flash drive you just inserted into the USB port. Or perhaps you want to find and view a photo stored on OneDrive.

When you need to access files stored in some computer crevice, turn to the OneDrive app. Despite its name, the OneDrive app lets you browse files stored on your Surface, as well as on OneDrive.

To browse files and folders without leaving your Surface's Start screen, follow these steps:

1. **From the Start screen, tap the OneDrive app.**

    Press the Windows key to return to the Start screen, if needed, and then tap the OneDrive app. (Can't find it? Open the Charms bar, tap Search, and type **OneDrive**. When the Search pane lists the OneDrive app, tap its name to bring it to the screen.)

2. **Choose whether you want to browse files on your PC or on OneDrive.**

   The OneDrive app opens to show your folders and files stored on OneDrive, your storage space on the Internet. To see files stored on your *Surface,* tap the word OneDrive in the screen's upper-left corner, shown in Figure 4-15, and choose This PC from the drop-down menu.

When you tap the words This PC, the app lists all the storage areas available on your Surface: your Documents, Pictures, Music and Videos folders, for example, as well as your Desktop and Downloads folder. (The Downloads folder contains all the files you download from websites.)

The OneDrive app's This PC section also lists places *outside* of your Surface. For example, you can access files shared on your homegroup from other networked PCs. (I cover networking in Chapter 6.)

If you've added a memory card, OneDrive lists it as "Secure Digital Storage Device." Flash drives, by contrast, usually appear with the name "Removable Disk (D:)" or "Removable Disk (E:)."

Tap here, then choose between viewing files stored on OneDrive or on your Surface.

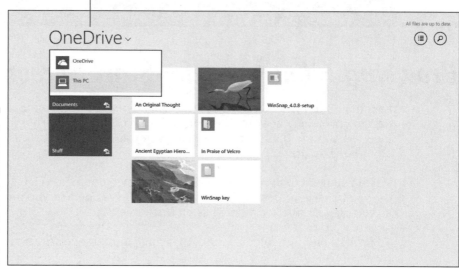

Figure 4-15:
Tap the word OneDrive and choose This PC to browse files on your Surface.

3. **Tap the folder or storage area you'd like to browse, or tap the file you'd like to open.**

   When you tap a storage area, OneDrive displays all of that storage area's folders and files.

   If you see your file's name, tap it and you're through: Your app opens it for action.

    Tapped the wrong folder by mistake? Tap the Back arrow (shown in the margin) in the upper-right corner to return to the previous screen.

   If you don't see your desired file, keep tapping folders, opening different ones to keep looking.

Still can't find your file? Summon the Charms bar and tap the Search icon, described earlier in this chapter. The Windows Search feature can find your file fairly quickly. After you find it, remember its location so you can return to it with OneDrive.

I explain more about OneDrive, as well as how to transfer files to and from OneDrive, in Chapter 6.

Using the Start Screen with a Mouse and Keyboard

If you plan on using the Desktop app to crank out some serious work, you'll want to attach your Surface's keyboard or plug in a mouse and keyboard, as I describe in Chapter 6. The mouse and keyboard feel right at home on the desktop, of course, but the Start screen is a different world.

Yet, the mouse and keyboard still let you navigate the Start screen, although a little more awkwardly. If you wish, you can simply use your fingers while navigating the Start menu; plugging in your keyboard or a separate mouse and keyboard won't disable the touch controls.

But if you'd prefer to leave your hands on your keyboard, trackpad, or mouse, Table 4-1 shows how to control the Start screen with a mouse and keyboard.

Table 4-1   Controlling the Start Screen with a Mouse or Keyboard

How to . . .	With a Mouse	With a Keyboard
Open the Charms bar.	Point at the screen's top- or bottom-right corners.	Win+C
Return to last-used app.	Point at the screen's top-left corner and click.	Win+Tab, Enter
Return to Start menu.	Point at screen's bottom-left corner and click.	Win
See currently running apps.	Point at screen's top-left corner and then slide the mouse downward.	Win+Tab (Keep pressing Tab to cycle through open apps.)
View the Power menu.	Right-click in the Start screen's bottom-left corner.	(None)

Poking at the Power menu

The Power menu, shown in Figure 4-16, offers quick shortcuts to some oft-used locations in Windows. Some destinations are familiar; others are cherished only by network administrators. Here's the rundown behind some options you may find useful:

✔ **Programs and Features:** Tap this, and the Control Panel opens to the spot where you can uninstall unloved desktop programs.

✔ **Mobility Center:** Introduced back in 2002, this panel helps old-timers find shortcuts to commonly used laptop settings. (Your Surface already lets you reach most of these from the bottom of the Charms bar.)

✔ **Power Options:** Head here to adjust your Surface's battery life. You can tell the screen to blank every five minutes instead of every two, for example, sacrificing a little battery life for more convenience.

✔ **System:** This lifts the hood of your Surface, letting you see its make and model, amount of memory, processor type, exhaust manifold, and similar hardware specs.

✔ **Device Manager:** A powerful troubleshooting tool, this lists all of the parts inside of and attached to your Surface. You need to head here to update *drivers,* pieces of software that determine how your Surface talks to its parts.

✔ **Control Panel:** Click this for a quick visit to the *desktop's* Control Panel, rather than the Start screen's PC Settings area.

✔ **File Explorer:** When the Start screen's OneDrive isn't enough to manage your files, choose this to call in the desktop's powerhouse file manager.

✔ **Search:** This simply calls up the Charms bar's Search box.

✔ **Desktop:** This not only takes you to the desktop but also minimizes any open windows, letting you start a new project without clutter.

The shortcuts I've left out appeal mostly to hardcore techies. They're safely ignored.

Chances are good, though, that you'll still use your fingers on your Surface's screen even after plugging in a mouse and keyboard. You'll probably use the keyboard only for typing text, and the mouse for pointing at small items on the desktop.

Don't forget the dedicated Charms bar keys atop the Surface's Touch and Type Cover keyboards. They let you jump quickly to the Charms bar's Search, Share, Devices, and Settings features.

Power users take note: If you right-click any screen's bottom-left corner, a Power menu appears, shown in Figure 4-16. That menu places many oft-used settings a mouse-click away. (If you've attached a keyboard, summon the Power menu by pressing Win+X.) On the desktop, hold down your finger on the Start button; when a square appears, lift your finger to see the Power menu.

Figure 4-16: Right-click the Start screen's bottom-left corner to summon the Power menu's many shortcuts.

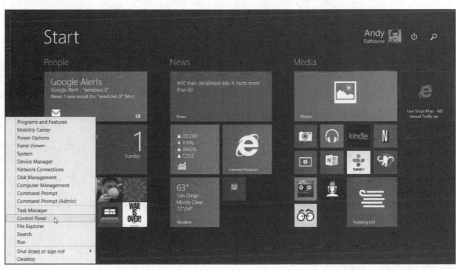

Chapter 5

Typing, Touching, and Drawing on the Surface

· ·

In This Chapter

▶ Controlling a touchscreen with your fingers

▶ Typing with the click-on keyboards

▶ Typing on the onscreen keyboard

▶ Typing on a detachable keyboard

▶ Speeding up your typing

▶ Selecting and editing text with your fingers

▶ Writing on the Surface

· ·

Chances are good that you know how to click a mouse or manipulate a laptop's trackpad. A touchscreen adds a third dimension: Now, your *fingertips* tell your Surface how to behave. This chapter covers the touch control tricks stashed inside every Surface warrior's arsenal.

Here you discover your Surface's seven main touch commands. Although these may sound complicated as you read them, envision your Surface's display as a piece of paper: Most of the finger commands are as intuitive as manipulating a sheet of paper as it lies flat on a table.

This chapter also explains the Surface's Touch and Type Cover click-on keyboards, letting you know the special finger commands and gestures built into the touchpad. I also cover the newer Touch Cover 2 and Type Cover 2 keyboards and their variants.

I explain how to write on the screen with a stylus, which comes bundled with both the Surface Pro and Surface Pro 2. (I also explain which type of stylus works with the Surface RT and Surface 2 models.)

And because you may not have a keyboard, or your keyboard cover may be wrapped behind your Surface, I explain the mechanics of typing on the onscreen keyboard. Although unwieldy for most things, it's a handy skill to have when you need it.

Controlling a Touchscreen with Your Fingers

Controlling a touchscreen sounds easy enough. You just touch it, right? Complicating matters, though, is that your Surface's screen lets you touch it in *seven* different ways. And each type of touch does something very different.

The following sections describe the seven main ways to touch your Surface's screen, as well as examples of when to use each one.

Tap

The equivalent of a mouse click, this is a quick tap and release of your finger. You can tap any item on the screen, be it a button, an icon, or some other bit of computer viscera. When in tight quarters, a fingertip often works better than the pad of your finger.

Example: Tap the Next button to move to the next step; tap the Charms bar's Start button to return to the Start screen. Tap an app's tile on the Start screen to open the app.

Double-tap

The equivalent of a mouse's double-click, a double-tap is two quick taps of your finger. Double-tap any item on the screen that you'd like to double-click.

Example: Double-tap a desktop folder to open it. Double-tap a web page to make it larger.

On a Surface, many things can be opened by merely tapping. But if a tap doesn't open an item, try the double-tap instead.

Press and hold

To achieve the equivalent of a mouse's right-click on the Windows desktop, tap the item but *hold down your finger.* A second or two later, the screen changes slightly: A square appears onscreen, or a check mark appears on your selected item. Lift your finger, and more options appear, just as if you'd right-clicked the item with your mouse.

Example: Press and hold your finger on a blank portion of the Windows desktop. When the square appears, lift your finger; a menu appears, letting you choose your desktop's settings.

Pinch and/or stretch

A handy way to zoom in or out of a photo or website, pinch the screen between two fingertips (usually your thumb and index finger). The photo, text, or window shrinks as your fingers move inward. (Lift your fingers when you've found the right size.)

To enlarge something, spread your two fingers across the screen. As your fingers spread, the object beneath them grows along with their movements.

Example: Stretch your fingers across hard-to-read items such as web pages, photos, and documents until they reach a suitable level of size or detail. Pinch them to reduce their size and to fit more of them onto the screen.

Rotate

Press and hold the screen with two fingers and then rotate your fingers. The item turns as if it were paper on a table.

Example: When viewing maps or photos, rotating your two fingers repositions them according to your fingers' movements.

Slide

Press your finger against the screen and then, without lifting your finger, slide your finger across the glass. When you lift your finger, the item stays in its new location.

Example: To reposition a window across the desktop, press your finger on the window's *Title bar* — that colored strip along its top edge. Slide your finger to the window's desired position and then lift your finger to drop the window in its new place.

Swipe

A swipe is a short slide. For example, slide the finger a short distance in a certain direction, usually inward from one of the screen's edges. You'll constantly find yourself swiping inward from your Surface's edges because that summons hidden menus.

Example: Swipe across a digital book to turn its pages. Swipe across a web browser's screen to scroll up or down a web page. Swipe across the Start menu to see tiles hidden along the left or right edges. Swiping almost always seems natural, like you were flipping a magazine's pages.

Note: You can sometimes swipe to *select* items. To do that, swipe in the opposite direction the item usually moves. For example, you normally swipe *downward* on your list of e-mail to scroll through the subjects. So, to select a particular piece of e-mail, swipe it *sideways* and release. Windows highlights the e-mail and adds an adjacent check mark, meaning you've selected it for further action. (I describe the Mail app in Chapter 9.)

Typing with the Click-On Covers

Part of the Surface's attraction comes from its detachable keyboard, which doubles as a screen cover. Thin and lightweight, the keyboard clicks onto the Surface with magnets. The connectors also let the keyboard draw power from the Surface, so it doesn't need batteries.

After you attach the keyboard, you can fold it in different directions to handle different tasks:

- ✔ Fold the keyboard down flat on a table, and you're ready to type. (Flip your Surface's kickstand back to keep it upright.)

- ✔ Fold the keyboard up to protect the screen, and you're ready to travel. (The Surface automatically goes to sleep.)

- ✔ Fold the keyboard around the back of your Surface, and it's out of the way, letting you control the Surface with your fingers. (The keyboard automatically turns off.)

A sensor embedded in the keyboard lets the Surface know its position so it can behave correctly. When flat on the table, the keyboard turns on, ready for you to type. When folded back behind the screen, the keyboard turns off. And when you close the keyboard, the Surface goes to sleep to preserve battery life.

Both the Touch and Type Cover keyboards also include a thin trackpad that lets you control a mouse pointer, clicking, double-clicking, and right-clicking.

The two keyboards both offer the usual typewriter keys, Function keys, and dedicated keys that bring up the Charms bar icons, mute the volume, and pause or resume your music and video.

The Type Cover 2 and Touch Cover 2 keyboards

With the arrival of the Surface 2 and Surface Pro 2, Microsoft released updated snap-on keyboards: the Type Cover 2 and Touch Cover 2. For the most part, they're identical to their counterparts, the Type and Touch Cover keyboards. They have the same number of keys, and the same layout.

The two new keyboards differ from their older cousins in these main ways:

✔ **Cost:** They're more expensive than the older keyboards, especially now that that the old keyboards have been marked down in stores.

✔ **Back-lighting:** When attached, a glow rises from below the keys, making them easier to see in the dark.

✔ **Size:** Both keyboards are a tiny bit thinner than their older counterparts. On the Type Cover 2 keyboard, the keys don't travel down as far, increasing your typing speed.

✔ **Function keys:** The first generation keyboards included dedicated keys for raising or lowering the volume. The Touch Cover 2 and Type Cover 2 keyboards now make those F1 and F2 keys raise or lower the screen brightness. Also, the first Touch Cover keyboard didn't label its Function keys; the Touch Cover 2 keyboard adds the labels.

✔ **Sensitivity:** The Touch Cover 2 keyboard includes more sensors, making for more accurate typing.

✔ **Trackpad:** The trackpad on both new keyboards is a little wider.

Other than those differences, all four keyboards are almost identical; every keyboard works with every Surface model.

So, to keep things simple, I refer to both the new and old keyboards as simply Touch and Type Cover keyboards.

When you attach either keyboard, the screen's rotation lock automatically kicks in, keeping your Surface locked in *landscape mode:* The screen no longer rotates. Fold the keyboard behind the screen, and the rotation lock turns off, letting the screen rotate "right-side up" as you carry it around.

The following sections describe how the covers differ and how to best put them to work.

Typing on the Touch Cover keyboard

The Touch Cover keyboard cover lacks mechanical keys. But its pressure-sensitive keys, shown in Figure 5-1, work surprisingly well. A mere touch won't trigger the keys, so you can rest your fingers on the keys without typing. But when you start tapping on the keys, the keyboard translates your taps into typing.

Figure 5-1:
The Surface
Touch Cover
and Touch
Cover 2 key-
boards don't
move when
touched.

The Touch Cover keyboard feels almost like fabric or cardboard more than a keyboard, and typing on it is an eerie feeling at first. You can start typing on it immediately with good results, but your speed won't pick up until you've used it for a few days.

Don't try to type too quickly — you'll need to grow used to typing without feeling anything in response. But after you grow used to it, you'll find it faster than the onscreen keyboard. And unlike the onscreen keyboard, it doesn't fill half your screen.

Basically, the Touch Cover keyboard works much like any other keyboard, but these tips will save you some time:

✔ The F and J keys have slight indentations on them to help you position your fingers correctly. Feel for them with your index fingers, and your other fingers will stay aligned more correctly.

✔ The Touch Cover keyboard isn't waterproof enough to toss into the dish-washer, but a damp rag removes most spills.

✔ The 12 dedicated keys across the keyboard's top edge double as Function keys. To turn a Function key into a dedicated key, hold down the Fn key while pressing it. (The Fn key is to the right of the space bar.)

✔ The first Touch Cover keyboard didn't label its Function keys, so you need to remember which one is which; the Touch Cover 2 includes the labels, thankfully.

✔ On the first Touch Cover keyboard, the trackpad's left- and right-click buttons are just *beneath* the trackpad, separated by the little vertical line. On the Touch Cover 2 keyboard, those buttons are along the bottom of the trackpad rather than beneath it.

✔ If the mouse pointer or cursor disappears while you use the scroll pad, detach the keyboard, wait a few seconds, and reattach it. The pointer or cursor should reappear.

✔ The Touch Cover keyboard comes in different colors: black, white, purple, cyan, and magenta. (Not every country carries every color.) And no, snapping a colored keyboard onto your Surface won't automatically change your screen's background color to match. (I explain how to change your background color manually in Chapter 14.)

Typing on the Type Cover keyboard

The Surface's Type Cover keyboard, shown in Figure 5-2, contains mechanical keys. Designed for people who prefer movable keys, this makes the keyboard slightly thicker than the Touch Cover keyboard, a compromise readily accepted by many touch typists.

Figure 5-2: The Surface Type Cover and Type Cover 2 keyboards offer mechanical keys that move when touched.

The Type Cover keyboard outweighs the Touch Cover by less than an ounce and costs only a few dollars more. If you feel hesitant about the immobile Touch Cover, opt for the Type Cover keyboard.

In addition to its movable keys, the Type Cover keyboard differs from the Touch Cover keyboard in a few other ways:

✔ Both the Type Cover and Type Cover 2 keyboards include labels on their Function keys.

✔ The F and J keys have standard bumps rather than indentations to help you position your fingers.

Using Surface trackpad gestures

Both the Touch and the Type Cover keyboards include a trackpad below the keys. Chances are good that you won't use it much: It's usually easier to touch the screen to do what you want.

However, it comes in handy if you spend much time on the desktop. There, the trackpad controls your mouse pointer, bringing the pinpoint precision needed to navigate the desktop's crowded menus.

Table 5-1 explains how to mimic mouse clicks, drags, and scrolls with your Surface's trackpad.

Table 5-1	Trackpad Gestures for all Surface Keyboards
To Do This . . .	*. . . Do This*
Move the onscreen pointer.	Drag your finger anywhere on the trackpad.
Left-click.	Tap one finger anywhere on the trackpad or press the left trackpad button.
Right-click the Windows desktop.	Tap two fingers anywhere on the trackpad or press the right trackpad button.
Left-click and drag.	Hold down the left trackpad button and then tap and slide your other finger on the object you want to drag.
Scroll.	Slide two fingers horizontally or vertically, a handy way to navigate the Start screen.
Show a Start screen app's App bar.	Tap two fingers anywhere on the trackpad.

Pay particular attention to these tips, which work equally well on both the Touch and Type Cover keyboard's trackpads:

- ✔ When reading a website or browsing an app like the News app, put *two* fingers on the trackpad and then slide them back and forth or up or down, depending on how the page flows. That sometimes scrolls the page more smoothly than touching the screen with your fingers.

- ✔ Tapping with two fingers brings up the right-screen menu on the desktop. That's often faster and easier than right-clicking by tapping on the trackpad.

- ✔ The Touch Cover 2 and Type Cover 2 covers also let you pinch and zoom with two fingers on the trackpad. Also, swiping in from the left or right sides of the trackpad mimics doing the same on the screen. (That lets you fetch the Charms bar or see the currently open applications.)

- ✔ Tapping with two fingers quickly brings up an App's menu. But because you still need to tap the menu item with a finger or well-placed mouse click, it rarely saves time.

Typing on the Onscreen Keyboard

Your Surface isn't really complete without a Touch or Type Cover keyboard. Combined with the Surface's built-in kickstand, a keyboard cover transforms your Surface into a desktop PC whenever you sit down.

But whether or not you own a keyboard, this section describes how to use the free keyboard built into every Surface: the *onscreen keyboard,* also called the virtual or glass keyboard.

Typing on glass has its challenges. First, the keyboard covers the bottom half of your screen, hiding half of your workspace. Second, you can't feel whether you've hit the right key.

On the positive side, each key clicks and lights up when tapped, offering positive reinforcement that you've hit the right one. And your Surface auto-corrects fairly well; when your fumbling fingers type *thw,* your Surface automatically corrects the word to *the.*

The onscreen keyboard will never outperform a *real* keyboard for speed. But with practice, your typing speed will improve. The following sections help you make the most out of the keyboard built into every Surface tablet.

Don't like the autocorrect feature? I explain how to both tweak and disable it in Chapter 14. (Look for the Typing section in the PCs and Devices area of PC Settings.)

Summoning the onscreen keyboard

If you've attached your Touch or Type Cover keyboards, the onscreen keyboard stays hidden. But when your keyboard is detached or folded behind your Surface, the onscreen keyboard is ready for action.

In fact, the onscreen keyboard pops up automatically when you stay on the Start screen side of things. Tap inside the Charms bar's Search box, for example, or inside an app that accepts text.

As you tap, the onscreen keyboard automatically fills the screen's bottom half, shown in Figure 5-3, ready for you to begin typing.

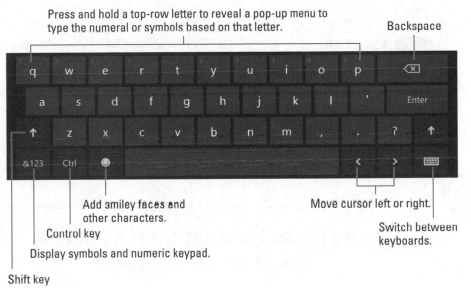

Press and hold a top-row letter to reveal a pop-up menu to type the numeral or symbols based on that letter.

Backspace

Figure 5-3: While working within a Start screen app, tap where you'd like to type, and the onscreen keyboard appears.

Add smiley faces and other characters.

Control key

Display symbols and numeric keypad.

Shift key

Move cursor left or right.

Switch between keyboards.

The Windows desktop isn't as friendly, unfortunately; tapping in a text box doesn't automatically summon the onscreen keyboard. You must *manually* summon the keyboard by tapping the desktop's keyboard icon (shown in the margin) on the taskbar along the bottom edge.

The keyboard looks and behaves much like a real keyboard, with many of the same keys. Position your fingers over the keys the best you can and start typing. As you type, the letters appear onscreen.

Typing on glass is completely foreign to many people, and it's an oddly unsettling experience. Try these tips when typing for the first few days:

✔ Tap the Shift key to type an uppercase letter. (The Shift key automatically turns off after you've typed that first letter.) To turn on the Shift Lock, tap the Shift key twice. When you're through typing uppercase letters, tap the Shift key again to turn off Shift Lock.

✔ If you're accustomed to pressing keyboard commands like Ctrl+V for Paste, press the Ctrl key, and some of the keyboard's keys will change. The word *Paste* appears on the V key, for example. Other keys sprout labels, as well, letting you know which key you need to press to Select All, Undo, Cut, Copy, or Paste.

✔ Need a numeric keypad? Press the &123 key in the bottom-left corner, and the keypad appears, along with a Tab key and the brackets and symbols usually found on most keyboards' top row.

✔ When you're through typing, press Enter, and the keyboard enters your text and disappears. If you called up the keyboard mistakenly, just tap anyplace away from the text box to remove the keyboard. Or, tap the Keyboard icon (shown in the margin) in the screen's bottom-right corner; when the pop-up menu appears, press the keyboard icon with the downward-pointing arrow beneath it.

✔ On the desktop, the pop-up keyboard has a little X in its upper-right corner, like all the other windows. Click or tap the little X, and the keyboard disappears.

Typing on the Start screen without an attached keyboard

To search for files, apps, or settings on your computer, you can type directly into the Start screen itself: The Charms bar's Search box automatically appears to accept your keystrokes.

Typing directly into the Start screen is easy when you've attached a keyboard. But what if you're simply holding your Surface, with no keyboard attached?

You can fetch the onscreen keyboard at any time by following these steps:

1. **Summon the Charms bar by sliding your finger inward from the screen's right edge.**

2. **When the Charms bar appears, tap the Settings icon.**

3. **When the Settings pane appears, tap the Keyboard icon in the bottom-right corner.**

4. **When the Keyboard icon pop-up appears, tap the words Touch Keyboard and Handwriting Panel.**

The onscreen keyboard rises from the bottom of the Start screen, ready for you to type the name of your sought-after item, be it a file, a setting, an app, or something on the Internet.

Switching between the different onscreen keyboards

The onscreen keyboard normally looks like the one shown earlier in Figure 5-3. But the onscreen keyboard can morph into several other keyboards, as well.

 To switch to a different keyboard, press the Switch Keyboards button in the onscreen keyboard's bottom-right corner. A pop-up menu lets you choose among your Surface's different keyboards, shown in Figure 5-4. (If you install keyboard layouts from other languages, those other layouts also appear.)

Figure 5-4:
Tap the keyboard-switching button to choose how to enter text.

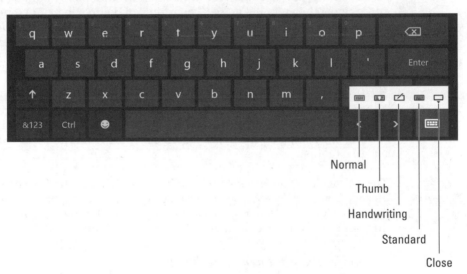

Normal

Thumb

Handwriting

Standard

Close

I explain your other keyboard choices in the next three sections.

Typing with the Thumb keyboard

Built for a generation raised on smartphones, the Thumb keyboard lets you hold your Surface vertically, like a giant phone. Shown in Figure 5-5, the keyboard appears split into three sections, each clinging to a bottom edge.

Your thumbs can then poke at the letters while typing, letting you whip out e-mails beneath the dinner table at family gatherings.

Figure 5-5:
The Thumb
keyboard
works best
when you
hold your
Surface
in portrait
mode.

 Adjust the Thumb keyboard for different-sized thumbs by holding down the three dots (shown in the margin) near the keyboard's left side. A pop-up appears, letting you slide your thumb over the words Small, Medium, and Large. As your thumb slides, the keyboard reshapes itself to the new size. When you're satisfied, lift your thumb to lock in the new setting.

Writing on the Handwriting panel

Your Surface also recognizes your handwriting, translating it into text as you write on the screen. To write on the screen, choose the Handwriting panel. Writing or drawing on the panel requires a *stylus* — a type of pen with a special plastic tip.

 The Surface Pro and Surface Pro 2 include a stylus, but the Surface RT and Surface 2 don't. However, any *capacitive* stylus (the cheap kind) works on those models. I explain how to use a stylus on the Handwriting panel in this chapter's "Drawing and Writing with a Stylus" section.

Adding a Standard keyboard layout

If you need a full-sized, standard keyboard, complete with numbers and Function keys across the top, choose the Standard keyboard. Shown in Figure 5-6, it's the real deal, complete with the Windows key, the Alt key, and even four arrow keys for navigating menus.

Figure 5-6:
The
Standard
keyboard
contains
characters
found only
on full-sized
keyboards.

However, the Standard keyboard is normally turned off. To add it as an option on the keyboard menu, follow these steps:

1. **Slide your finger inward from the screen's right edge to summon the Charms bar and then tap Settings.**

2. **When the Settings pane appears, tap Change PC Settings from its bottom edge.**

3. **When the PC Settings screen appears, tap the PC and Devices category.**

4. **When the PC and Devices screen appears, tap the Typing category.**

5. **Tap the On toggle switch next to the last option, which is labeled Add the Standard Keyboard Layout as a Touch Keyboard.**

The Standard keyboard then appears as a keyboard option along with the other three.

The Standard keyboard doesn't include a PrintScreen key. To take a screenshot on your Surface, hold down the Windows key on the Surface's front and press the Volume Down switch in your Surface's upper-left corner. The screenshot appears as a PNG file in your Pictures library's Screenshots folder.

Typing special characters

Your Surface's onscreen keyboard simplifies typing symbols and foreign characters, something quite difficult on other keyboards, including the Surface's Type and Touch Cover keyboards.

To add the little accent mark on the letter *é,* for example, press and hold the onscreen keyboard's **e** key. A little pop-up appears around the letter, shown in Figure 5-7, showing possible foreign characters based on the *e* key. Slide your finger in the direction of the key you want and let go. The desired character appears.

Holding down the question mark key lets you choose among eight other common symbols missing from the keyboard, including brackets, hyphens, slashes, ampersand, and the exclamation point.

Press the &123 key to bring up a Numeric keypad and mathematical symbols. When the Numeric keypad appears, press the arrow keys directly above the &123 key to toggle between even *more* characters, including symbols for copyright, advanced mathematics, and popular currencies.

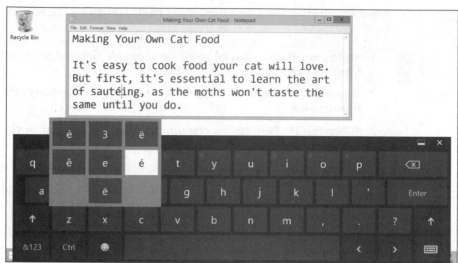

Figure 5-7:
Press and
hold a letter
to see the
possible
variations
and then
slide your
finger
toward the
character
you want.

Typing smileys (emoticons)

Whether they're called smileys, emoticons, or *emoji,* these little characters grew from the simple smiley face created from a colon, a dash, and a right parenthesis — :-).

 Your Surface embraces the smiley tradition by supporting *dozens* of emoticons. To insert an emoticon, press the smiley key shown in the margin. The Emoticon keyboard appears, as shown in Figure 5-8.

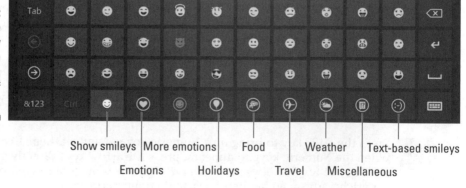

Figure 5-8:
Press the
smiley key
to choose
from among
dozens of
characters.

Show smileys | More emotions | Food | Weather | Text-based smileys

Emotions | Holidays | Travel | Miscellaneous

The Emoticon keyboard begins by showing the smiley faces shown in Figure 5-8. To see more, press any of the keys along the bottom. There, you can choose among other symbol categories: Holiday, Food, Travel, Weather, Miscellaneous, and Text. (The Text category is a quick way to add text-based smiley faces when sending text-based e-mail.)

Unfortunately, emoticons don't translate well between different programs, computers, and e-mail systems. They'll work most reliably if you're sending them between computers running Windows 8 or 8.1.

However, if you're sending them to somebody using a different operating system, stick with the Text emoticon category, which lets you insert the always-compatible text-based smileys — :-).

Emoticons are resizable, so they work well as clipart when creating flyers and newsletters. After you insert them into your document, enlarge their font size until they're the size you need.

Predictive typing

As you type in some apps, Windows watches over your shoulder and tries to predict your next word. If Windows feels particularly prescient, it lists words beneath your cursor, as shown in Figure 5-9.

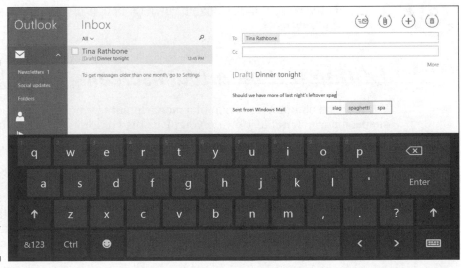

Figure 5-9: If Windows guesses your intended word correctly, tap it, and Windows fills in the rest of your word.

If Windows has guessed correctly, tap the word, and Windows quickly finishes typing it. If you notice that Windows has guessed incorrectly, simply ignore it and breathe a sigh of relief, knowing that computers won't be smart enough to overthrow us within our lifetimes.

The prediction accuracy rate differs for different people; teenagers type more predictably than scientists, for example. Your Surface will never guess correctly 100 percent of the time. But when Windows offers to fill in the word *serendipity* after you type *seren,* the help is quite welcome, especially when you're typing directly onto the screen.

The Windows keyboard also changes its key layout as you type in different situations, adding particularly handy keys:

- ✔ When you begin typing a web address into Internet Explorer, a .COM key appears to the right of the spacebar. Tap that to insert **.COM**, saving you from typing in those four characters. (A backslash key appears right next to it, handy when typing long web addresses.)

- ✔ Tap and hold the .COM key, and a pop-up menu appears, letting you choose to insert the .us, .net, or .org characters, instead.

- ✔ When you type an e-mail address into the Mail app, the keyboard sprouts the .COM key, as well as the @ key, speeding up your e-mail address entry.

- ✔ Typing a logon password? If strangers are nearby, tap the keyboard's Hide Keypress key that appears just to the left of the spacebar. That prevents the keys from lighting up when tapped, protecting your password from prying eyes.

Editing text on a touchscreen

Without the pinpoint precision of a mouse pointer, editing a few lines of text seems insurmountable. How do you place the cursor in the exact location necessary to excise the unwanted text?

Like nearly anything else on your Surface, it starts with a strategically placed tap.

Double-tap a word near where you want to edit. Windows highlights the word, surrounding it with a small marker on each side. To extend the selection, drag the first marker to the selection's beginning; drag the second marker to the section's end, as shown in Figure 5-10.

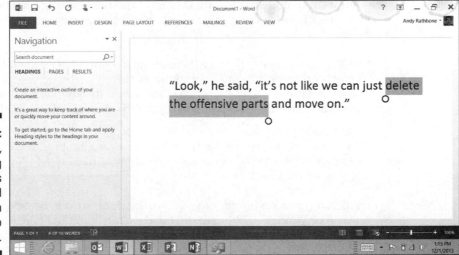

Figure 5-10:
Tap a word, then drag the markers to surround the portion you'd like to delete.

Some apps and programs differ in how they treat a tap of your finger:

✔ Sometimes double-tapping a word highlights it but doesn't place the markers on each side. If this happens, hold down the Shift key: As you slide your finger, Windows highlights adjacent words. When you've highlighted the unwanted words, lift your finger and press Delete to delete them.

✔ Sometimes a tap simply places a cursor on the screen, which is handy when you need to position the cursor in *just the right spot.* When the cursor appears, drag it to the right or left until it's at the position where you'd like to begin typing.

✔ Having trouble putting the cursor where you want it? Try zooming in with your fingers: Straddle the words with your fingertips and then spread your fingers. In many programs, the text increases in size, making it much easier to touch *exactly* where you want to begin typing or editing.

✔ If your Surface came with a stylus, keep it handy. You can quickly and easily mark text for changes by drawing over it with your stylus, much like using a highlighter.

Typing on a Detachable Keyboard

Not everybody has a Surface Touch or Type Cover keyboard. (They're very cool but more than a little pricey.) Luckily, every Surface model works with a variety of other keyboards.

The Surface Pro models will work with *any* type of detachable keyboard. The Surface RT and Surface 2 work well only with these types of detachable keyboards:

- ✔ **USB:** Because every Surface includes a USB port, it works with USB keyboards commonly found on desktop PCs. USB keyboards work on the Surface RT and Surface 2, as well, but only if the keyboards don't require special software. (Many gaming keyboards do, unfortunately.)

- ✔ **Bluetooth:** Every Surface includes *Bluetooth*, a common way of connecting a wireless keyboard. I explain how to attach Bluetooth gadgets in Chapter 6. (Most iPad keyboards use Bluetooth, so most iPad keyboards also work on a Surface.)

When looking for a keyboard for your Surface, look for one designed with Windows 8 or Windows 8.1 in mind. Those usually include dedicated keys for the Charms bar.

Drawing and Writing with a Stylus

When Microsoft released its first tablets a decade ago, the company thought people would treat them as digital notepads: Doctors would carry them from room to room, scribbling notes, consulting charts, and viewing x-rays taken minutes before. That dream never quite caught on.

Instead, people today think of tablets as easy ways to watch movies, read books, or browse websites. Yet, all of Microsoft's pioneering "digital notepad" work isn't lost. Your Surface still accepts your handwriting when you draw on it with a *stylus* — a specially designed, plastic-tipped pen.

As you write in either cursive or block letters, your Surface recognizes your scrawls, automatically converting your word into text. In some programs, Windows saves your handwritten text but indexes it. That not only makes your notes easy to relocate but also preserves any drawings you've added along with the text, a handy perk for Chemistry students.

These sections explain how to turn your expensive Surface into a pad of paper.

Opening the Handwriting panel

Because all models of Surface accept a stylus, you can write by hand anywhere that Windows accepts typing. You can handwrite a letter in Microsoft Word, for example, or write the name of a newly created folder.

As you write, Windows converts your handwriting to words and drops them into the appropriate place.

The key is to call up the Handwriting panel by following these steps:

1. **Tap where you'd like to enter text.**

   Tap any place that accepts text — an e-mail, a Word document, an entry in a calendar, or even the name of a new file you're saving.

   If the keyboard doesn't appear (it doesn't appear automatically on the desktop), summon it by tapping the taskbar's keyboard icon, shown in the margin.

2. **If a keyboard doesn't display its Handwriting panel, tap the keyboard switching key and tap the Stylus option, shown in the margin.**

   The Handwriting panel appears.

3. **Begin writing in the Handwriting panel, in cursive, block letters, or a combination.**

   As you write, Windows quickly begins recognizing the separate words, listing them in order along the panel's left edge. After you've written a short phrase, tap the Insert button. Windows inserts the words as text, shown in Figure 5-11.

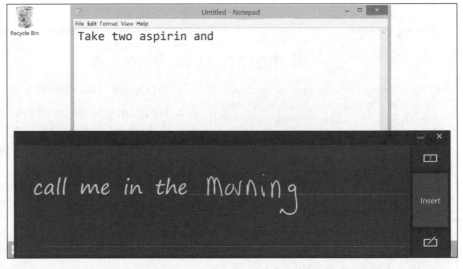

Figure 5-11:
Tap the Insert button to insert your recognized words as text.

If all goes according to plan, you'll write your words, insert them, and move on. To bring yourself up to speed, tap the little question mark inside the rectangle (shown in the margin). Tiny visual tutorials show how to correct, delete, split, and join handwritten words.

✔ After you call up the Handwriting panel, it automatically appears as your preferred keyboard until you manually choose a different type of keyboard.

✔ The Surface RT and Surface 2 require a *capacitive* stylus, the inexpensive type of stylus sold nearly anywhere. The ones sold for an iPad work fine.

✔ The Surface Pro and Surface Pro 2 include a bundled *digitizer* stylus. More expensive than the capacitive stylus, the digitizer stylus allows finer, pressure-sensitive control when drawing. Those Surface models also include a special screen with palm-blocking technology that makes it easier to take notes.

✔ Both types of styli work also in drawing programs.

Correcting handwritten mistakes

A mistake will inevitably creep onto the Handwriting panel. It won't recognize one of your words correctly, for example, or it will turn an inadvertent keystroke into a period.

To correct mistakes in the Handwriting panel before you've touched the Insert button, draw a strikeout line through the misspelled words, word, or letters, as shown in Figure 5-12. When you lift the pen, the unwanted word disappears.

Calibrating your stylus

Handwriting recognition works quite well in the Surface, perhaps because Microsoft has been perfecting it since its introduction in 1992. However, to make Windows recognize your writing style the most accurately, calibrate it: Let Windows watch as you tap a set of crosshairs on the screen. Windows compares your onscreen touch with the actual location of the crosshairs and behaves more accurately.

To calibrate your tablet, follow these steps:

1. **From the Desktop, swipe in from your tablet's right edge to fetch the Charms bar; then tap the Settings icon.**

2. **From the Settings pane, choose Control Panel at the top.**

The Control Panel appears.

3. **Tap the Hardware and Sound category; then tap the Tablet PC Settings section.**

4. **From the Tablet PC Settings window, tap the Calibrate button.**

5. **Follow the instructions, repeatedly tapping the onscreen crosshairs; then tap the Yes button to save the data.**

Windows saves your calibration data, tracking the touch of your stylus that much more accurately. Feel free to repeat these steps anytime you feel Windows doesn't correctly recognize your stylus.

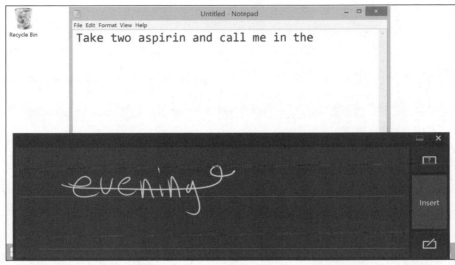

Figure 5-12:
Draw a
strikeout
line through
mistakes,
and
Windows
removes
them from
the panel.

Spot a mistake in text that's already entered? Then run your stylus over the text that needs correcting, just as though you were highlighting it with a marker. As you highlight the text, it appears in the Handwriting panel for editing, as though you'd just written it by hand.

When the text appears in the Handwriting panel, draw a line through the words you'd like to remove, just as though you'd written them there, and the unwanted words disappear. Then tap the Insert key to put the corrected version back in place.

You can correct mistakes several other ways inside the Handwriting panel:

✔ To correct a single letter within a word in the Handwriting panel, tap the word. Windows spaces the word out, letter by letter. Write the correct letter over the incorrect letter, and Windows replaces the wrong letter with the newly corrected letter.

✔ To add a symbol, tap in your document where the symbol should appear. When the Handwriting panel appears, tap the &123 key (shown in the margin). Tap it to see the available symbols and then tap the one you'd like to place into the document.

✔ For more tips on how to correct items in the Handwriting panel, tap the question mark icon (shown in the margin) in the Handwriting panel's upper-right corner. Detailed animations show exactly how to correct, delete, split, and join letters and words.

Part II
Connections

Visit www.dummies.com/extras/surface for a step-by-step tutorial on how to add web pages to your Surface's Reading List app for reading later at your leisure.

In this part . . .

- ✔ Get connected to the Internet, networked PCs, printers, portable accessories (like flash drives), monitors, TVs, as well as projectors for giving presentations.

- ✔ Find out about available storage spaces, including flash drives, portable hard drives, networked PCs, and online spaces such as SkyDrive.

- ✔ Get comfortable with browsing the web and reading e-mail, as well as managing your social connections, such as Facebook, Twitter, and other services.

Chapter 6

Connecting to the Internet, Printers, Monitors, Storage, and More

. . . .

In This Chapter

▶ Connecting to the Internet

▶ Connecting to networked PCs

▶ Connecting to a printer or other accessory

▶ Connecting to a monitor or an HDTV

▶ Connecting to flash drives and portable hard drives

▶ Connecting with OneDrive

. . . .

*Y*our Surface tablet strips computing down to the bare essentials: Your most important files, a screen, and your fingers to control it all. You end up carrying a package weighing less than two pounds.

Yet your Surface can still adapt to meet your needs. Need to leave a paper trail? Plug in a printer. The Surface Pros automatically recognize most of them; the Surface RT and Surface 2 recognize many.

Need to crank out some Excel spreadsheets or a Word document but don't have a Surface keyboard? Plug in a desktop PC mouse and keyboard and fire up the Desktop app. Screen too small? Plug in an external monitor.

Need more storage space? Slip in a memory card, plug in a flash drive, or even attach a portable hard drive. The list goes on: To watch high-definition movies in style, plug in an HDTV.

When you're through with all the accessories, unplug them and walk away. You've returned to minimalist mode, carrying all of your data with you.

That's the beauty of a Surface tablet.

Connecting to the Internet

Windows lives and breathes through the Internet, and if you're not connected, your programs will start to complain. Some Internet-starved programs send scolding messages like "You're Not Connected." Other apps simply freeze, hoping you'll notice the tiny word *Offline* in their upper-right corners.

All Surface tablets connect to the Internet *wirelessly* — they already contain a built-in wireless network adapter. To connect, you and your Surface need only be within range of a wireless network.

Today, that's easier than ever. You can find Wi-Fi networks — sometimes called *hotspots* — waiting for you in airports, coffee shops, hotels, and many homes. (I describe how to set up your own home's wireless network in *Windows 8.1 For Dummies.*)

These steps explain how to know when you're within range of a Wi-Fi network, as well as how to connect to it and start browsing the Internet:

1. **From any screen, summon the Charms bar by sliding your finger inward from the screen's right edge.**

   When the Charms bar appears along the screen's right edge, look at the dark rectangle that appears near the screen's bottom left. A glance at the icon in the rectangle's upper-left corner, shown in Figure 6-1, shows when you're within range of a wireless network.

   If you're within range, move to Step 2. Not within range? Move to another spot, probably the place where clusters of people huddle over their tablets and laptops.

Figure 6-1:
When you summon the Charms bar, this icon lets you know whether you're within range of a Wi-Fi signal.

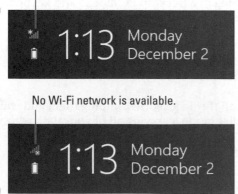

A Wi-Fi network is available.

No Wi-Fi network is available.

2. **Tap the Charms bar's Settings icon. When the Settings pane appears, tap the Network icon.**

   The bottom of the Settings pane, shown in Figure 6-2, shows six icons. The icon in the top left represents networks. The icon toggles between Available and Unavailable depending on whether you're currently within range of a wireless network.

   • **Available:** When the icon says Available (shown in the margin), you're within range of a wireless network. Move to Step 3 to begin connecting.

   • **Unavailable:** When the icon says Unavailable (shown in the margin), you're out of range and out of luck. (Wi-Fi signals rarely reach more than 300 feet from their transmitter.) Try moving to a different location or ask somebody whether a Wi-Fi signal is available. Then return to Step 1.

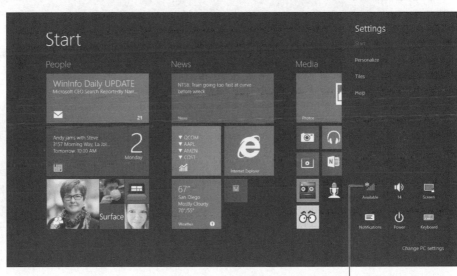

Figure 6-2:
To connect, tap the wireless network available icon in the bottom top-left corner.

Tap this icon to connect to a wireless network.

3. **Tap the Available icon if it's present.**

   The Settings pane turns into the Networks pane, shown in Figure 6-3, listing the names of all the wireless networks around you. Depending on your location, you may see several listed. Windows ranks the wireless networks by signal strength, placing the strongest (and usually closest) network atop the list.

   A wireless network's name is known as its *SSID* (Service Set Identification). The SSID represents the name that you (or the network's owner) chose when originally setting up the wireless network.

Figure 6-3:
Your
Surface lists
all the Wi-Fi
networks
within
range. To
connect to a
network, tap
its name.

4. Tap the name of the network you'd like to connect to and tap the Connect button that appears.

If you'll be connecting to this network frequently, select the Connect Automatically check box before tapping the Connect button, both shown in Figure 6-4. That tells your tablet to connect automatically whenever you're within range, a convenience you'll enjoy in your home, office, or favorite coffee shops.

If Windows connects to the network, you've finished: You've connected to an *open network,* meaning it's unsecured and requires no password.

Don't do any shopping or banking on an unsecured network. Unscrupulous bystanders can snoop on your connection to discover your username and passwords as you sign into websites.

If Windows asks you to enter a password, however, move to Step 5.

5. Enter the password for the wireless network and tap the Next button.

If Windows asks you to Enter the Network Security Key when you tap the Connect button, you're trying to connect with a *secured,* or password-protected, network. So, you must type the network's password, shown in Figure 6-5.

If you're in your own home, here's where you type the password you created when setting up your wireless network. (On some wireless routers, you can simply press a button on the router at this point. That proves you're in the same room and not trying to break in from outside.)

Figure 6-4:
When your
Surface lists
names of
all the Wi-Fi
networks
within
range, con-
nect to one
by tapping
its name
and tapping
the Connect
button.

If you're connecting to somebody *else's* wireless network, you need to ask the network's owner for the password (or whisper "What's the Wi-Fi password?" to the person next to you at the coffee shop).

Windows hides the password as you type it, keeping it secure from nearby eyes. Think you've made a typo? Then tap and hold the eyeball icon on the right side of the password field, shown in Figure 6-5, and Windows displays your password. (That handy eyeball icon appears whenever you type hidden passwords into a Start screen app.)

Tap and hold the eyeball icon
to see the password you've
typed.

Figure 6-5:
Type in the
network's
password
and tap
Next.

6. **If asked, choose whether you want to share your Surface's files on the network and search for other networked devices such as PCs, TVs, and printers.**

How you handle this important choice, shown in Figure 6-6, depends on whether you're connecting in a private or public location:

- **Yes:** If you're in a private setting, such as your home or office, tap Yes. That lets you connect with networked printers and swap files with other people on the network.

- **No:** If you're in a public place, such as a hotel or coffee shop, tap No because you don't want strangers to access your files. That lets you access the Internet but keeps other people on the network away from your files.

Figure 6-6:
Turn on sharing only if you're connecting to your own network.

When you finish the steps, Windows connects to the network, and your Internet connection begins flowing into your Surface. If the Internet connection remains dry, however, try these tricks:

✔ **Move closer to the transmitter.** This often-difficult maneuver cures 90 percent of Wi-Fi connection problems. Ask somebody where the Wi-Fi transmitter is located, or look around the room for a small plastic box with two or three pencil-sized antennas sticking up from it. (They're often mounted on walls or atop cabinets.)

✔ **Try connecting to an unsecured network.** Such networks are fine for casual browsing.

Disconnecting for Airplane mode

Airplane mode is shorthand for disconnecting completely from the Internet. To put your Surface into Airplane mode before a plane flight, follow these steps:

1. **Summon the Charms bar by swiping your finger in from the screen's right edge and then tap the Settings icon.**

2. **When the Settings pane appears, tap the Network icon.**

3. **When the Network pane appears, tap the Airplane Mode toggle switch along the pane's top edge.**

The Settings pane's Network icon shows that you're in Airplane mode. (Bluetooth wireless gadgets, covered later in this chapter, also stop working in Airplane mode.) To turn off Airplane mode and return to a lifestyle of searching for Internet connections, repeat the three steps.

✔ **You can also connect to a wireless network from the Windows desktop.** When the taskbar's right corner shows a wireless network available icon (shown in the margin), tap it. That takes you to Step 4 in the previous list for you to choose a network and tap the Connect button.

Only have wired network access? You can buy an USB-to-Ethernet adapter from the Microsoft Store. (The adapter works on all four Surface models.)

To disconnect from a wireless network, simply walk out of range; Windows disconnects automatically. Or, if you want to disconnect while still in range, summon the Charms bar, tap the Settings icon, tap the Network icon, tap the network's name, and tap the Disconnect button.

Connecting to Networked PCs

Your Surface's hard drive may always seem too small, at least by desktop PC standards. Because you probably can't fit all of your information onto your Surface, keep an eye out for other places to stash files, storing a few videos in one spot and a few music files someplace else.

One of the easiest places to stash your files might be on your home or office network. To browse the files on those huge-hard-drive-stuffed PCs, you first need to connect to their wireless network.

To connect to PCs on a home or office network, follow the steps in the previous section to connect to the wireless network. In the last step, though, make sure to tap the button labeled Yes, Turn On Sharing and Connect to Devices.

But what if you forgot to tap that Sharing and Connect button?

You can turn it on by following these steps. These steps also let you connect to a *homegroup* — a simple way for Surface tablets, Windows 7, Windows 8, and Windows 8.1 computers to share files.

1. **Summon the Charms bar by sliding your finger in from your Surface's right edge and then tap the Settings icon.**

2. **Tap the Change PC Settings link at the bottom of the Settings pane.**

3. **When the PC Settings screen appears, tap the word Network in the left column and then tap your network's name.**

   The Network screen appears, listing your network connections. Tap your connected network's name, probably the only one listed in the Wi-Fi category. The settings for that network appear, shown in Figure 6-7.

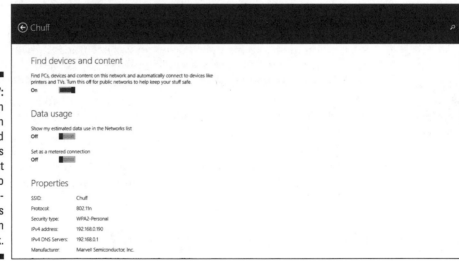

Figure 6-7:
Tap the On toggle in the Find Devices and Content section to find available devices and files on the network.

4. **Tap the On toggle in the Find Devices and Content section, shown in Figure 6-7.**

   That screen offers other technical tidbits about your connection, including your network's SSID, protocol, type of security, and IP address. It also lists the type of network adapter you're using and its driver version, which is handy for troubleshooting.

5. **Tap the Start screen's Desktop app and then tap the File Explorer icon.**

   You can find the icon for File Explorer (shown in the margin) near the left end of the *taskbar* — the strip along the bottom of the desktop. (I cover File Explorer in Chapter 12.)

6. **When File Explorer appears, tap the word Homegroup in the Navigation pane that clings to every folder's left edge.**

   The Homegroup window appears, shown in Figure 6-8.

Figure 6-8:
Tap the Join Now button and follow the steps to enter the homegroup's password.

7. **Tap the Join Now button and follow the steps to enter the homegroup's password.**

Don't know the homegroup's password? To find it, visit any computer on your network's homegroup, open any folder, and right-click the word *Homegroup* from the Navigation pane. When the pop-up menu appears, choose View the Homegroup Password. That's the password you need to enter into your Surface. Type the password, and you've connected to the homegroup.

✔ In Step 7 in the preceding list, tapping Next at each window lets you connect to the homegroup and access the contents of the Pictures, Videos, and Music libraries on other computers in the homegroup.

✔ Although the Surface RT and Surface 2 can *connect* to an existing homegroup and access files from those computers, they can't *create* a new homegroup, nor will they let other homegroup computers access their own files.

✔ Unlike the Surface RT and Surface 2, the Surface Pro and Pro 2 tablets *can* share the contents of their pictures, videos, and music libraries. Unless the settings are changed, the Documents folder on all homegroup computers remains private and not shared.

✔ Joining a homegroup also lets you connect with many networked devices (usually, printers).

✔ Store things you want to share from your desktop PC in your libraries: Music, Pictures, and Videos. That makes them available to your Surface, as well as any Windows 7, Windows 8, and Windows 8.1 PCs on the network's homegroup.

✔ Although Windows Vista and Windows XP PCs can't join homegroups, you can access their files from your Surface in another way. Tap the word Network at the bottom of any folder's Navigation pane. The Network window appears, listing every networked PC. Tap any PCs name to open it and browse its shared files.

Connecting to a Printer

Surface Pro and Surface Pro 2 tablets can connect with just about any printer that works with your desktop PC.

Surface RT and Surface 2 tablets, by contrast, are much pickier about their printers. They can't run a printer's installation software, for example. Many newer printers will work, but you may have trouble connecting with older printers.

Most printers connect either through a USB port or through a wired or wireless network. Here's how to set them up:

✔ **USB:** The simplest way to connect with a USB printer is to plug the printer's USB cable directly into your Surface's USB port, and turn on your printer. Your Surface should recognize and install it automatically. (If you have a Surface Pro or Surface Pro 2, try installing the printer's software.) If the printer still doesn't work, it probably isn't compatible with your Surface.

✔ **Network and wireless:** After you connect to a network, described in a previous section, your Surface has access to all the compatible printers shared on that network.

To see whether your Surface recognizes a networked printer, follow these steps:

1. **Open the Charms bar by sliding your finger inward from the screen's right edge.**

2. **Tap the Settings icon; when the Settings pane appears, tap the words Change PC Settings.**

   The PC Settings screen appears.

3. **Tap PCs and Devices from the PC Settings screen, and when the PCs and Devices screen appears, tap Devices from the left column.**

   The Devices screen shows every device attached or available to your Surface, including printers. They're listed alphabetically, and available printers have the icon shown in the margin.

Not every Start screen app can print, and there's no way to know if your app is printable until you try. So, to try and print from any Start screen app, open it and follow these steps:

1. **From within any app, open the Charms bar by sliding your finger inward from the screen's right edge and then tap the Devices icon.**

   The Devices pane appears, listing three categories: Play, Print, and Project.

2. **Tap Print.**

   The Print pane appears, listing your available printers.

3. **Tap the desired printer's name and make any final adjustments.**

   The Start screen's Printer window, shown in Figure 6-9, sums up exactly what's going to the printer. It shows a preview and the number of pages required. To see all of the pages you're printing, slide your finger across the preview image from right to left.

   To see even more options, tap the miniscule More Settings link, right above the Print button. There, you can sometimes choose the type of printer paper you're using, an essential step when using photo paper on a color printer.

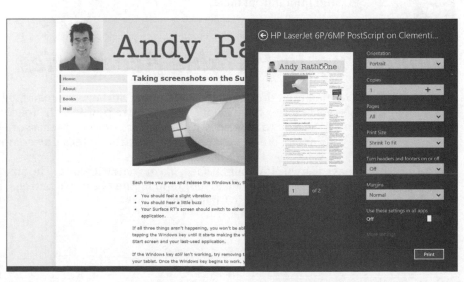

Figure 6-9: The Start screen's Printer window offers minimal adjustments to your print job.

4. **Tap the Print button.**

   Your Surface sends your information to the printer.

But the Start screen's emphasis on speed leaves out some details:

- Many apps can't print. You can't print a day's itinerary from your Calendar app, for example, or even a monthly calendar.

- When printing from the Start screen's Internet Explorer app, you're stuck printing the entire web page — advertisements, comments, and everything in between. There's no way to print selective portions.

- If you need more control over your print jobs on a Surface Pro or Pro 2, head for the desktop and its cadre of more full-featured programs. Surface RT and Surface 2 tablets, unfortunately, don't offer much more in the way of printer controls on the desktop.

- The printer listed as "Microsoft XPS Document Writer" is *not* a printer. It's Microsoft's way of storing information in a file, much like Adobe Acrobat's PDF files. You can then share the file with others, letting *them* print it instead. (The Surface RT and Surface 2 also offer a Send to OneNote option, which sends the information to the OneNote note-taking program.)

- If your Surface RT or Surface 2 tablet can't print to a networked printer, try plugging the printer directly into your Surface. If the Surface recognizes the printer when plugged in directly, your Surface may also recognize the printer when it's plugged back into the network.

- Stuck with a printer that's incompatible with your Surface RT or Surface 2? You can copy the file to a flash drive, plug the flash drive into a desktop PC, and print it from there.

Connecting to Portable Accessories

After you finally sit down at a desk with your Surface, you can plug in a few strategic accessories to give your Surface extra powers. The following sections describe how to connect with whatever computer accessories you may find in your home, office, gadget bag, or even the hotel's tiny computer room.

If you have a stylus for your Surface, *always* carry it along. The size of a pen, the stylus comes in really handy for tapping the desktop's buttons, as well as editing text, as I describe in Chapter 5.

Connecting to a USB hub

Every Surface model includes one USB port. Chances are good, though, you have more than one USB accessory. The solution is a *USB hub*. Similar to a power strip, the USB hub plugs into your lone USB hub and offers several more USB ports in exchange.

Portable hubs are inexpensive, often costing less than ten dollars. Small, flat hubs pack easily into your Surface's case. Buy a hub with a protruding USB cable; when inadvertently knocked, the cable softens the impact, saving your Surface's lone USB port from damage.

Choose hubs with the newer and faster USB 3.0 ports because they work best with all Surface models. (The lone Surface RT lives in the slow lane of USB 2.0 speeds, but it can still use a USB 3.0 hub.)

Powered USB hubs include an AC adapter, so you can plug in power-hungry gadgets like portable DVD players. However, powered hubs cost more and take up more space in your gadget bag. They're overkill for plugging in mice, keyboards, and flash drives.

Connecting a mouse or keyboard

When you reach for your Surface's Desktop app, you'll probably want to reach for your Surface's click-on keyboard, which I describe in Chapter 5. But if you don't have a Surface keyboard, nearly any mouse and keyboard will do. Mice and keyboards come in two types:

- **Wired:** These plug straight into your USB port. In fact, any two-button mouse or standard keyboard also works with your Surface.

- **Wireless:** Both Surface tablets include *Bluetooth* — a way of connecting to nearby gadgets without wires. You can find plenty of Bluetooth mice and keyboards on the market.

When shopping for a mouse and keyboard for your Surface, keep these tips in mind:

- Because you may want to pack your mouse and keyboard when traveling, look for flat, lightweight models. For example, Microsoft's Surface Arc mouse flattens completely for storage and then curls up into a mouse shape when needed. (I describe portable mice and other handy accessories in Chapter 17.)

- Before buying a mouse or keyboard, try one out in your own hands. They're highly personal items, and only you can tell whether it feels right for you.

- Choose a Bluetooth keyboard with dedicated Windows 8 or 8.1 keys, giving you one-key access to your Surface's volume, Charms menu, brightness control, and other features.

Connecting Bluetooth accessories

When you're running out of room to plug in USB accessories, Bluetooth is your friend. Bluetooth works much like Wi-Fi, but it specializes in connecting gadgets that live just a few feet apart. You can add both a Bluetooth mouse and Bluetooth keyboard to your Surface, leaving your USB port free for other items.

To add a Bluetooth item to your Surface, follow these steps:

1. **Turn on your Bluetooth device and, if necessary, make it discoverable.**

   Most Bluetooth devices automatically turn themselves off to save power. Sometimes turning it on is as simple as flipping a neatly labelled On/Off switch; other devices sense their own movement, automatically turning on and off when needed.

   Making a device *discoverable* makes it available to be detected by a computer, usually for a period of at least 30 seconds. Some devices automatically become discoverable when turned on. Others make you hold down a button until their light begins blinking.

   If you're having trouble making your particular device discoverable, you may need to check its manual.

2. **On your Surface, fetch the Charms bar by sliding your finger inward from the screen's right edge. Tap the Settings icon to fetch the Settings pane and then tap the words Change PC Settings.**

   The Start screen's PC Settings screen appears.

3. **Tap the PCs and Devices category and then tap Bluetooth from the left column.**

   The PC Settings' Manage Bluetooth Devices screen appears, shown in Figure 6-10, and immediately begins searching for nearby Bluetooth gadgets in discoverable mode.

   If Windows doesn't find and list your device by name, head back to Step 1 and make sure your Bluetooth gadget is still turned on and discoverable. (If it's been longer than 30 seconds, your device may have given up.)

4. **When your Bluetooth device's name appears in the Devices list, tap the device's name so Windows knows to connect to it.**

5. **Type in your device's code if necessary and, if asked, tap the Pair button.**

Everything usually works pretty smoothly until Step 5, where Bluetooth's security measures kick in. Windows sometimes needs you to prove that you're controlling both your Surface *and* your Bluetooth device, and that you're not somebody sitting three rows back on the bus trying to break in.

Figure 6-10: When you see your Bluetooth gadget listed, tap its name to introduce it to your Surface.

To clear that security hurdle, different Bluetooth devices offer slightly different tactics. Sometimes you need to type a *passcode* — a secret string of numbers — into both your device and your computer. (Pull out the device's manual to find the passcode.) Adding to the tension, if you don't type the passcode quickly enough, both gadgets stop waiting, forcing you to start over.

Some Bluetooth gadgets let you press or hold in a little push button at this step, if you're holding it in your hand. Some blindly accept the tapping of the Pair button and simply start working.

After your new gadget successfully pairs with your Surface, its name and icon remain in the Bluetooth category of the PC Settings screen, shown earlier in Figure 6-10.

To remove a device shown in the Bluetooth list in Figure 6-10, tap its name and then tap the Remove Device button that appears below its name.

Connecting a digital camera and importing your photos

Nobody likes viewing photos on a camera's tiny screen. Thankfully, Windows makes it easy to import your camera's photos onto your Surface, where they shine on the big screen. And you can do it all from the Start screen, making it an easy task to perform while in the field.

Best of all, you needn't install any of the software that came with the camera; Windows handles it all.

To import your camera's photos into your Surface, follow these steps:

1. **Turn off your camera and then plug the camera cable's USB connector into your Surface's USB port.**

   Plug the small end of your camera's cable into your camera. The cable's larger end plugs into your Surface's USB port, shown in Figure 6-11, found on the Surface's right side (Surface 2 and Surface RT) or left side (Surface Pro and Surface Pro 2).

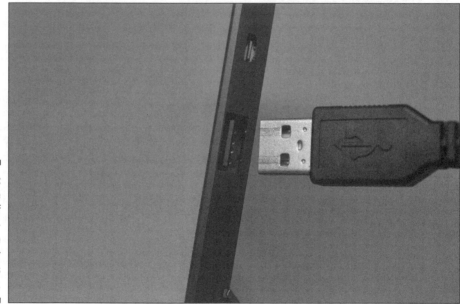

Figure 6-11:
Plug the large end of your camera's cable into your Surface's USB port.

2. **Turn on your camera and wait for your Surface to recognize it.**

   Wait for a little announcement in your computer screen's top-right corner. The announcement, called a *toast* in some manuals, lists your camera's name and, if you've plugged in a camera for the first time, asks you to Tap to Choose What Happens with This Device.

   Tap the announcement and then move to the next step. (If the announcement disappears before you can tap it, turn off your camera, wait a second, and then turn it on again; the announcement reappears.)

3. Choose how to import your photos.

The next announcement, shown in Figure 6-12, offers several options for how to handle your newly recognized digital camera. These three options always appear:

- **Open Device to View Files:** If you prefer to import your files from the desktop, choose this option. The desktop offers more control but works better with a mouse and keyboard than your fingers. This option fetches File Explorer (see Chapter 12), where you can manually copy the photos from the camera to a folder of your choosing.

- **Import Photos and Videos:** The easiest method, this imports your photos with the Start screen's Photos app. Then move to Step 4.

- **Take No Action:** An option to avoid, this cancels the importing process and tells your Surface to no longer recognize your camera when plugged in.

After you've chosen an option, Windows remembers it, automatically taking the same route the next time you plug in your camera.

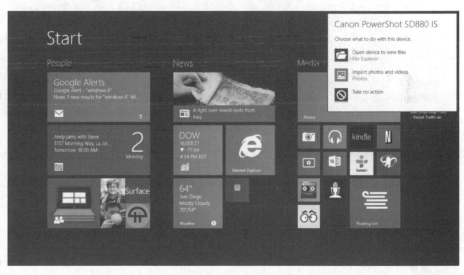

Figure 6-12: Choose Import Photos and Videos to import your photos with the Start screen's Photos app.

4. When the Photos app appears, choose your options; tap the Import button to import your all camera's photos and videos.

The Start screen's Photos app, shown in Figure 6-13, tries to keep things simple: It offers to import all your camera's photos and videos into a folder named after the current date. To make a quick and easy transfer, tap the Import button in the screen's bottom-right corner to copy all the camera's photos and videos onto your Surface. (You can safely unplug your camera from your Surface after importing your photos.)

But if you don't want to import every photo, choose the Clear Selection option from the screen's bottom menu to deselect *all* the photos. Then tap just the photos you want to import. (If you have too many photos to fit on one screen, scroll to the right to see the rest.) Finally, tap the Import button to import your selected photos.

Figure 6-13: Tap the Import button to copy *all* of your camera's photos into your Surface.

When you tap the Import button, the Photos app imports your camera's photos and videos. When the Photos app announces that it's finished importing the photos, tap the announcement box's Open Album button to see your photos.

 The Photos app only *copies* your camera's photos onto your Surface; it doesn't delete them from the camera. Your camera's own menu offers an option to delete the photos or format its memory card. I'd love to tell you how, but different cameras have different menus.

 If your Surface stops recognizing your camera when plugged in, open the Charms bar, choose Settings, choose PC Settings from the Settings pane, and tap PC and Devices from the PC Settings screen. When the PC and Devices screen appears, tap AutoPlay in the left column. Then tap your camera's model number from the right pane; when the drop-down menu appears, choose Ask Me Every Time.

Connecting to a scanner

When you need to send somebody a copy of a paper document, the Surface gives you two options: You can simply take a photo of it with your Surface's built-in camera, as I describe in Chapter 10. Or, if the Accounting Department requires higher-quality images for your Las Vegas expense receipts, you can scan them with a scanner.

Your Surface's Scan app, found on the Start screen, ignores many older scanners, unfortunately. But if your scanner is relatively new, the Scan app is a refreshing change from complicated scanner menus.

Follow these steps to transform a sheet of paper into a computer file:

1. **From the Start screen, open the Scan app.**

   Shown in the margin, the Scan app appears on the screen. Don't see the Scan app's icon on the Start screen? Slide your finger upward from the middle of the Start screen to see the All Apps screen, then tap it from there.

   If the Scan app complains that your scanner isn't connected, make sure you've connected the USB cord between your computer and the scanner and that the scanner is turned on.

   The Scan app, shown in Figure 6-14, lists your scanner's name and the file type used for saving your files. (The default PNG file type is widely accepted by most programs.)

   If the app doesn't recognize your scanner, your scanner is too old. You're stuck with the scanner's bundled software — if it works — or, unfortunately, buying a new scanner.

Figure 6-14: Tap the Show More link for additional options. Tap the Preview button at the bottom to test a scan.

2. **(Optional) To change the settings, tap the Show More link.**

The app's default settings work fine for most jobs. But tapping the Show More link lets you customize your options for scanning certain items:

- **File Type:** If somebody requests a scan using a particular file type, like TIFF, Bitmap, OpenXPS or XPS, chose it here. Otherwise, stick with the default PNG.

- **Color mode:** Choose Color for color items, including color photos and color magazine pages. Choose Grayscale for nearly everything else. Only choose Black and White for line drawings or black-and-white clip art; grayscale works better for everything else.

- **Resolution (DPI):** The default resolution of 300 dots per inch works fine. Higher resolution scans (larger numbers) bring more detail but consume more space, making them difficult to e-mail. Lower resolution scans show less detail but create smaller file sizes.

- **Save File To:** The Scan app normally creates a Scans folder in your Surface's Pictures folder, where it stores your newly scanned images. If you prefer a different folder, tap this to choose it.

3. **Tap the Preview button to test your scan.**

The Scan app makes a first pass and shows you the results, as shown in Figure 6-15.

If the preview doesn't look right, make sure you've made the right choice for your job. If you need to make different choices, go back to Step 2. If the preview shows a blank white page, make sure you've unlocked the scanner as described in the scanner's bundled instruction sheets. (Unlocking usually requires sliding a switch or turning a knob.)

If you're scanning a smaller item that doesn't fill the entire scanner bed, look for the circle markers in each corner of the preview scan. Drag each circle inward to surround the area you want to copy, shown in Figure 6-15. That crops your scan to remove the boring white space.

4. **Tap the Scan button.**

The Scan app scans your image with the settings you've chosen in the previous steps and then saves your image in your Pictures folder's Scan folder. Then it places a menu atop the screen with two options, View and Close.

5. **Tap View to see the scan; tap Close to close the menu.**

View splits the screen, showing your Scan app on the screen's left side, while the Photo app displays your scanned item on the right side. (I describe how to manipulate two apps on the same screen in Chapter 7.)

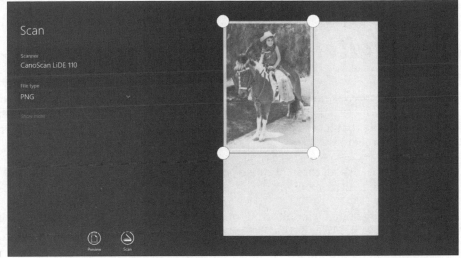

Figure 6-15: Tapping the Preview button shows you the results of your scan.

 To rotate a photo in the Photos app, slide your finger up from the screen's top or bottom edge to fetch the Photo app's menus. Then tap the Rotate button, shown in the margin, until the photo faces the way you want. (I cover the Photo app in Chapter 10.)

 To close the preview window, find the three little dots separating the Scan app's window from the Photo apps window. Then slide the dots to the right, pushing the Photo app off the screen. That leaves the Scan app on the screen, ready for more photos. (I describe more about putting two apps on one screen in Chapter 7.)

The Scan app works well for fast, easy scans. But it relies on the simple, built-in Windows software, which doesn't understand a scanner's built-in control buttons like PDF, or AutoScan.

If you want your scanner's buttons to work or you need finer control over your scans, skip the Scan app, head for the desktop, and install the scanner's bundled software. (On some scanner models, Windows Update installs the scanner's bundled software automatically as soon as you plug in the scanner.)

 You can only install the scanner's bundled software on a Surface Pro or Surface Pro 2. It won't work on a Surface RT or Surface 2.

Connecting to a Monitor, an HDTV, or a Digital Projector

The screen on your Surface is larger than an iPad, but it's probably smaller than your desktop PC's monitor. That doesn't mean you're stuck with your Surface's small screen, though. Your Surface includes a high-definition video port that lets you plug in desktop monitors, HDTV sets, and video digital projectors.

Because all three of those potential monitors plug in the same way, I refer to them all as *monitors*.

Plugging in a monitor not only gives you a larger screen, it gives you *two* screens: Your Surface's screen stays active, as well, if you want.

This section explains how to connect a monitor to your Surface, as well as how to tell the monitor to begin displaying your Surface's input. Finally, I explain all four ways your Surface can send its signal to your monitor.

Connecting your Surface to a monitor

In theory, connecting your Surface to a monitor is quite simple: Connect a cable between your Surface's video port and your monitor's input port.

The challenge is finding the *right* cable. No single cable works in every situation. That's because Surface tablets and monitors contain different types of video connectors. And your cable needs the correct connector on each end, or it won't fit.

All of the Surfaces connect using HDMI (High-Definition Multimedia Interface), although they do it in slightly different ways:

- The Surface RT and Surface 2 contain a *micro-HDMI* port.
- The Surface Pro and Surface Pro 2 contain a *Mini DisplayPort* port.

TVs and monitors also include one or more types of video adapters:

- **HDMI:** Shown in Figure 6-16 (right), this port is the same as the ones found on many computers, but it's *full-size* — more than twice as large. HDMI cables also carry the sound as well as the video, a perk when watching movies on a big screen.

Figure 6-16:
Plug the
small end
of the cable
into your
Surface RT
or Surface 2
(left); the
cable's large
end plugs
into the
monitor's
HDMI port
(right).

Figure 6-16: Plug the small end of the cable into your Surface RT or Surface 2 (left); the cable's large end plugs into the monitor's HDMI port (right).

- ✔ **DVI:** The next most popular, this connector appears mostly on PC monitors rather than TVs.

- ✔ **VGA:** This oldster has graced the backs of monitors for more than 20 years, so it still exists as a last-resort connector. Cables and adapters with VGA connectors often cost more because they need more circuitry to translate between the types of signals flowing through the cable.

Matching your Surface's video port with your monitor's port leaves you with three ways to connect the two:

- ✔ Buy Microsoft's customized adapters. At $40 apiece, Microsoft's stylish adapters contain the correct jack for your Surface on one end, and a VGA or HDMI port on the other. Buy the adapter you need and then plug in your own standard VGA or HDMI cable.

- ✔ Buy a cable with the correct plug for your Surface on one end and the correct plug for your monitor on the other end. This might be your least expensive option for HDMI connections.

- ✔ If you already have a cable that fits into the video port on either your Surface or your monitor, head to Amazon (www.amazon.com), Newegg (www.newegg.com), or your local electronics store to buy an *adapter* for the cable's other end. For example, an adapter can turn a standard HDMI plug into a micro-HDMI plug that fits into a Surface RT or Surface 2.

Depending on the variety of external monitors you plan to connect to your Surface, you may need to collect several types of cables or adapters.

The Surface's sloped edges pose a challenge for many flat-faced adapters, especially those bought from third parties. If your adapter doesn't reach far enough into your Surface's video port, look closely at where the cable meets the Surface's sloped case. You may be able to shave away some of the cable's plastic end with a pocket knife, allowing the cable's end to reach more deeply into the Surface's port.

When shopping for HDMI cables, be aware that the higher-priced ones don't make the video signal any better. The cables either work, or they just lie there like soggy noodles.

Sending the display to the attached monitor

After you've connected your Surface to a monitor with the right cable, you need to tell your Surface exactly *how* to send its image. Windows offers you four options, and you can see them by following these steps:

1. **Swipe your finger inward from any screen's right edge to fetch the Charms bar and then tap the Devices icon.**

2. **Tap the Project icon to connect with an attached monitor, a TV, or a digital projector.**

   I explain how to connect a cable between your Surface and the second monitor in the previous two sections.

   The Project pane offers four choices, shown in Figure 6-17:

   • **PC Screen Only:** This option recognizes the second monitor but keeps it blank, displaying only your Surface's screen. It's handy mostly when connecting to a projector at a meeting or conference. You can set up everything on your Surface without everybody having to see your busywork on the projector. Then, when you're ready to wow the crowd, switch to one of the other modes, described next.

   • **Duplicate:** Perhaps the easiest way to use two monitors, this option simply duplicates your Surface's screen onto the second monitor or projector. It's great for presentations, and it lets you control what you see on both screens. When your fingers touch the Surface, you see the effect on both screens.

   • **Extend:** Meant mostly for office work, this option extends your Surface's Desktop app across your second monitor, giving you an extra wide desktop. Or, you can keep the Start screen on your Surface and run your Windows desktop on the larger, second screen.

- **Second Screen Only:** This option blanks the Surface's screen, sending the display only to your second monitor. It's a simple way to connect a larger monitor, but you lose the benefits of your touchscreen tablet. Unless you're trying to mimic a desktop computer, complete with a mouse and keyboard, use the Duplicate option instead.

Figure 6-17: Choose how your Surface should handle your newly connected monitor.

After you tap your choice, your Surface may blank its screen as it looks for and connects to the second screen. A moment later, your Surface's screen appears on the second screen.

Working on two different monitors simultaneously may be confusing at first. These tips help you adjust to this strange new configuration:

✔ When setting up the second monitor for the first time, choose the Duplicate option. That makes it a lot easier to see if your monitor is recognizing your Surface.

✔ Your Surface's sound piggybacks along with its video through both an HDMI and a Mini DisplayPort cable. However, the sound plays through the speakers built into your monitor or TV set. If you want better sound, route the HDMI cable to your home stereo. Then have the stereo send the video to the monitor through a second HDMI cable.

✔ When you choose Extend, Windows makes the screen extend off your Surface's *right* edge and onto the second monitor. To change that, visit the Desktop app's Control Panel. There, in the Appearance and Personalization category's Adjust Screen Resolution section, you can tell Windows which way to extend the desktop: left, right, up, or down.

 ✔ That same Adjust Screen Resolution section's Detect and Identify buttons help you figure out which monitor is which. Then you can position the two screens to meet your needs.

 ✔ If you're accustomed to using a mouse, the mouse-clickable corners on your Surface's screen work on both monitors. Point and click in either monitor's lower-left corner to fetch the Start menu, for example.

Making your monitor recognize your Surface

After you've connected the correct cable between your Surface and the monitor and told the Surface to send its signal to the monitor, you face one last challenge: You must convince the monitor to *recognize* your newly plugged-in Surface.

Some monitors recognize your Surface's connection immediately, filling their screens with the colorful Surface tiles. Others require more coaxing.

The solution here works a little differently depending on whether you're connecting your Surface to a HDTV or a PC monitor.

 Make sure your Surface is turned on and set to Duplicate mode, described in the previous section, so your Surface sends a constant video signal to your monitor. When you see the Surface's screen on the monitor, you'll know you've found the right combination.

 ✔ **HDTV:** On your TV's front panel or handheld remote control, look for a button for switching between video inputs. Keep slowly pressing the remote's Video Input button, switching between inputs if necessary, until your Surface's screen eventually appears.

 ✔ **Monitor:** If your monitor is already connected to another PC, take time to unplug the monitor from the second PC. (You can plug it back in when you're through.) Your monitor should sense your Surface's signal and automatically begin displaying it. (Sometimes turning the monitor on and off again helps it switch to the right signal.)

It might take a little fiddling, but you eventually see your Surface appear on the big screen.

Adding Portable Storage

Your Surface's drive is speedy but tiny, especially when compared to today's desktop PCs, which usually include more than 300GB of storage space.

Because apps can be installed only on your Surface's internal drive, that doesn't leave you much space for your own files.

If you need more storage, your Surface offers you several options, each serving different needs:

- ✔ **Memory slot:** This slot in your Surface, hidden beneath the kickstand, accepts a tiny memory card that holds up to 128GB. You can swap memory cards to access different batches of files. However, memory cards are tiny, expensive, easy to lose, and cumbersome to move between computers.

- ✔ **Portable hard drive:** Essential for people who collect a lot of information in the field, portable hard drives let you tote a huge amount of files. Today's portable hard drives can hold more than 4TB of information: That's about *4,000GB*, which should be more than enough space until you return to your desktop PC.

- ✔ **Flash drives:** Also known as *thumb drives,* these tiny drives make it easy to transfer files between your Surface and other PCs. (If you can't find a printer that's compatible with your Surface RT or Surface 2, copy those files from your Surface to a flash drive and then print them from your desktop PC.)

The following sections describe these storage spaces in more detail. And if that's still not enough room, drop by the later section, "Connecting to the Cloud with OneDrive."

Connecting to built-in memory cards

Your Surface includes a special slot for sliding in a tiny memory card. Many cell phones accept the same type of memory card, a fingernail-sized bit of plastic called *microSD* (micro Secure Digital), *microSDHC* (micro Secure Digital High Capacity), or *microSDXC* (micro Secure Digital eXtended Capacity).

To insert a memory card into a Surface, first locate your Surface's memory card slot. The tiny slot lives behind the kickstand on the Surface RT and Surface 2, and on the right edge of the Surface Pro and Surface Pro 2. (If you can't find it, flip back to Chapter 2.)

The card fits into the slot only one way — the right way, as shown in Figure 6-18. Push the card into the slot until you hear it lock into place. (It will slide back out just a bit when locked into place.) Your Surface makes a joyous beeping sound as it recognizes the card.

Figure 6-18:
Push the card into the slot until it locks into place.

To remove a card from your Surface, push it back into the slot until it unlocks and then pull it out. (Be careful, though: They're spring loaded and sometimes shoot out.)

I explain how to copy information to and from cards and other storage spaces in Chapter 12.

- ✔ The microSDHC cards can hold up to 32GB, whereas the newer microSDXC cards currently come in capacities up to 128GB, with higher-capacity microSDXC cards arriving soon.

- ✔ You can't store apps on the memory card, but you can store the biggest space hogs: videos, music, and photos.

- ✔ For easy file transfers, buy a memory card reader that accepts micro SDXC cards. Insert your memory card into the reader and copy files onto it with your desktop PC. Then remove the card and insert it back into your Surface to enjoy the card's files.

Connecting to portable hard drives

If you own a large music, photo, or video collection, your Surface's hard drive may not be large enough. Only one gadget can handle the job: a portable hard drive like the one shown in Figure 6-19.

Figure 6-19:
Plug a
portable
hard drive
into your
tablet to
carry huge
amounts of
files, songs,
or videos.

Photo image provided by Western Digital

Plug the cable from one of these small hard drives into your Surface's USB port. After a few moments, the drive shows up in File Explorer, covered in Chapter 12.

Newer portable hard drives draw their power directly from your Surface's USB port. Some older drives won't work because they need more power than your Surface can give.

Portable hard drives typically hold up to 4TB of information, which is about 4,000GB. That should be enough to last most people while on the road.

Connecting to flash drives for file transfers

An essential addition to your gadget bag, flash drives are tiny memory sticks that plug into the USB port on your Surface's side. After they're inserted, the drive appears in File Explorer. (If you're working from the Start screen, you can also reach its files with the OneDrive app, covered in Chapter 4.)

Flash drives are the simplest and fastest ways to copy files to or from your Surface. In fact, they're why your Surface beats many competing tablets: Few other tablets even include a full-sized USB port, much less let you copy files to and from a flash drive.

I explain how to copy files to and from drives with the Start screen's OneDrive app in Chapter 4.

Connecting to the Cloud with OneDrive

Today, it seems every company wants you to save your files on the *cloud.* The word *cloud* is technospeak for an online storage place — a personal cubbyhole on the Internet. Microsoft, Amazon, Google, and a host of other companies offer free Internet storage spaces where you can keep your files. All Surface tablets include an app to access Microsoft's brand of cloud, called *OneDrive.* (Microsoft renamed its SkyDrive service to OneDrive in early 2014.)

Storing files on the cloud brings several advantages, especially for a storage-starved Surface:

- ✔ After you stash files on OneDrive, you can access them from *any* Internet-connected tablet, computer, or smartphone.

- ✔ When you edit a OneDrive-stored file — update a document with the latest information, for example — it's automatically updated for *all* of your other devices, as well.

- ✔ Should you ever lose your Surface, your OneDrive files remain safe and password-protected in the cloud. And you can still access them from any web browser.

Just signing up for a Microsoft account gives you 7GB of free OneDrive storage space, and if you bought a Surface 2 or Surface Pro 2, Microsoft gives you another 200GB of storage for a year.

Should you ever fill up your allotted OneDrive storage space, Microsoft offers you two choices:

- ✔ **Pay up:** Microsoft charges an annual fee that increases according to your allotted storage space.

- ✔ **Pare down:** Delete some of your OneDrive files to make room for your newer, incoming files.

But whether you live with 7GB of space or splurge for extra, your Surface lets you access your OneDrive-stashed files any of three ways:

- ✔ **OneDrive app:** The OneDrive app lets you manage your files from the touchscreen — no mouse needed. But it's designed mostly for copying a few files back and forth. The app can't copy folders, for example, just files.

- ✔ **Desktop:** The traditional Windows desktop in Windows 8.1, covered in Chapter 12, embeds OneDrive directly into the File Manager. OneDrive appears as a location in every folder's Navigation pane along the left edge. If you use OneDrive a lot, you'll probably want to access it from there: On the desktop, OneDrive behaves much like any other folder.

> ✔ **Internet Explorer:** You can access your OneDrive files from any computer's web browser, including Internet Explorer. To visit, head to `http://onedrive.live.com` and log in with your Microsoft account.

The next two sections explain how to upload files from your Surface to OneDrive and how to download files from OneDrive to your Surface.

Uploading files from your Surface to OneDrive

Uploading files to OneDrive makes them accessible to any computer you use, as well as your smartphone. If you're connected with the Internet, OneDrive provides an easy way of overcoming your Surface's limited storage space.

To upload files from your Surface to OneDrive, follow these steps:

1. **From the Start screen, tap the OneDrive app.**

   The OneDrive app fills the screen, shown in Figure 6-20, showing all of your folders and files uploaded to your OneDrive account.

   The OneDrive app shows your stored files' names even if you're not connected to the Internet. You can even view your photos. However, you can't *download* or *edit* files without an Internet connection. (I describe how to overcome that obstacle in the next section, "Making OneDrive files available offline.")

Figure 6-20:
Shown here in Thumbnails view, the OneDrive app lets you upload or download files to or from your OneDrive storage space.

2. **Navigate to the OneDrive folder where you'd like to upload the files.**

Tap any OneDrive folder (it looks like a tile), and OneDrive opens it to display the files and folders stored inside. To back out from a folder, tap the back arrow in the screen's upper-left corner.

To create a new folder on OneDrive, fetch its menus by sliding your finger up from the screen's bottom edge. Then tap the New Folder icon (shown in the margin), type a name for your new folder, and tap the Create button.

When you're peering inside the OneDrive folder you'd like to stuff with files, move to the next step.

3. **To upload files from your Surface, fetch the OneDrive app's menu bar and tap the Add Files icon.**

To fetch the OneDrive app's menu bar, slide your finger up from the screen's bottom edge or down from the top. When the App bar appears, tap the Add Files icon.

The OneDrive's File Picker appears, shown in Figure 6-21, showing your Surface's available files and folders.

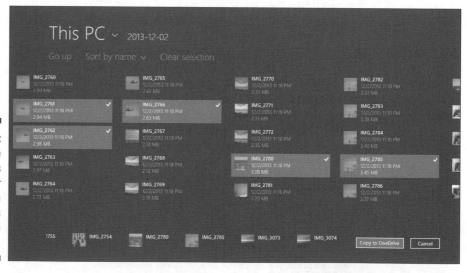

Figure 6-21: The OneDrive's File Picker lets you select files to upload to OneDrive.

4. **Browse to the files you want to upload, select them with a tap, and then tap the Copy to OneDrive button.**

You navigate through the File Picker just as you did through OneDrive: Tap a folder to see what's inside; tap the Go Up link to back out and delve into a different folder.

When you've found the folder containing the files you want, select the ones you want to send into OneDrive: Select them all by tapping Select All along the window's top. Or, cherry-pick the ones you want by tapping on them individually.

Finished? Tap the Copy to OneDrive button to send them to the OneDrive folder you picked in Step 2.

The OneDrive app grabs the files you've selected and copies them to your folder on OneDrive. Depending on the size and number of files, OneDrive can take from anywhere from a few minutes to a few hours to copy the files.

Making OneDrive files available offline

Your OneDrive cubbyhole lives on the Internet — *the cloud,* as the computing world calls it. And when your Surface is connected to the Internet, OneDrive files open just as if they were stored on your Surface.

But what if you're *not* connected to the Internet? Surprisingly, not much changes. You can still *browse* your OneDrive files. You can see their folder and filenames, for example, although their icons are fainter than usual. (That faintness provides a visual clue that you're not connected to the Internet.)

You can even fill the screen with your photos, scrolling through them like they were actually stored on your Surface.

But here's the clincher: If you want to *open* or *edit* those OneDrive files without an Internet connection, you're stuck.

So, if you want the luxury of editing your OneDrive files at any time, tell OneDrive to make those files or folders available offline. That way you can access them *without* an Internet connection.

To make some or all of your OneDrive files available offline, follow these steps:

1. **From the Start screen, tap the OneDrive app.**

   The OneDrive app fills the screen, as shown earlier in Figure 6-20, displaying all of your folders and files uploaded to your OneDrive account.

2. **Navigate to the OneDrive folder containing your folders and files.**

3. **Select the folders or files you'd like to make available offline by swiping down on them with your finger.**

   Swipe down on the Documents folder, for example, shown in Figure 6-22. A check mark appears next to it, and the App bar appears as a strip below it.

Figure 6-22: Swipe down on each file or folder you want to make available offline, and tap the Make Offline icon.

4. **Tap the Make Offline icon.**

    Tap the Make Offline icon (shown in the margin) from the App bar along the screen's bottom, and the OneDrive app copies the file to your Surface. (To return the files to online only status, repeat these steps, but choose Make Online Only in Step 4.)

   Making files available offline comes with a few peculiarities. The key is to remember that OneDrive *always* keeps the files in sync:

   ✔ Whenever you edit an offline file or folder on your Surface, OneDrive automatically updates its own copy, as well, as soon as you reconnect to the Internet.

   ✔ If you use another PC to update OneDrive's copy of that file, then OneDrive will automatically update your *Surface's* copy the next time you connect to the Internet.

   ✔ If you're editing a OneDrive file on one PC, and somebody else tries to open that file on another PC, he'll be able to open the file. But he won't be able to edit it. Instead, he'll see a Locked message that lists who is currently editing that file. When the other person closes the file, you'll be able to edit it.

✔ Making OneDrive files available offline consumes storage space, and most Surface models don't come with much storage space to spare. To keep from filling up your Surface, choose only your most important files or folders to make available offline.

✔ If your Surface has oodles of storage space, however, you can easily make your entire OneDrive contents available offline: Open the OneDrive app, fetch the Charms bar, and tap Settings. When the Settings pane appears, tap Options at the top and then tap the toggle called Access All Files Offline. (Tap the toggle again to delete the copies, leaving the originals on OneDrive.)

Chapter 7

All About Apps

*T*he latest version of Windows brings many changes, but one of the most baffling is that it no longer likes the word *program.* As a result, *programs* — software that runs on the Windows desktop — are now called *apps* in the new world of Windows. Confusingly, Windows also uses the word *apps* to describe programs running on the Start screen.

This odd nomenclature causes some confusion. For example, the Surface RT and Surface 2 can run *only* Start screen apps. The Surface Pro and Surface Pro 2, by contrast, can run both apps *and* desktop programs. But if you look at Microsoft's website, it simply says both types of Surface run *apps,* as if the word *programs* no longer exists.

It's way too early to retire the word *program* — it still appears on all your old software boxes, installation discs, and manuals, so this book refers to Windows desktop software as *programs.*

Mini-programs that run on the Start screen are called *apps.*

With that bit of linguistics taken care of, this chapter tackles a more important topic: Just what can you *do* with the darn things on your Surface?

Mini cheat sheet for apps

The Start screen serves up a smorgasbord of apps, each built to handle a specific task. But no matter how much the apps differ, every app shares the same basic commands. These tips work in *every* app, whether they came bundled with your Surface, or you downloaded them from the Windows Store:

✔ **Open an app.** From the Start screen, tap the app's tile with a finger. (You can return to the Start screen with a press of your Surface's Windows key.)

✔ **Close an app.** Apps needn't be closed, as I explain in Chapter 4. But if you *really* want to close your currently viewed app, slide your finger all the way down the Surface's screen, from the top edge to bottom edge.

✔ **Change an app's settings.** After opening the app, fetch the Charms bar by sliding your finger inward from the screen's right edge.

Then tap the Charms bar's Settings icon to see every setting your app allows to be changed.

✔ **Print from an app.** Fetch the Charms bar, tap the bar's Device's icon, tap Print, and tap your printer's name. (Not all apps can print.)

✔ **View an app's menus.** Slide your finger up a bit from the screen's bottom edge or down a bit from the top edge.

✔ **Return to your last-used app.** Slide your finger inward from the screen's left edge; your finger drags your last-used app into view.

✔ **See currently running apps.** Slide your finger in slightly from the screen's left edge and then back to the left edge. A strip appears along the left edge, displaying thumbnails of your currently running apps. To return to an app, tap its thumbnail.

Making the Most of Apps

You can download and install new apps, covered later in this chapter, but your Surface comes with more than a dozen built-in apps. Most of them live right on the Start screen for easy access.

Others aren't listed on the Start screen but hide in the Start screen's All Apps area. To see *all* of your installed apps, slide your finger upward from the middle of the Start screen. A formerly hidden screen comes into view, showing alphabetically organized icons for all of your apps.

But whether they're listed on your Start screen or hiding in the All Apps area, the following apps appear on every Surface tablet:

 ✔ **Alarms:** New in Windows 8.1, this lets you set a wakeup alarm, a timer, or a stopwatch.

 ✔ **Bing Travel:** Designed around people who keep their suitcase packed, this app caters to impulse buyers. Formerly called just Travel, the app is filled with tempting panoramic photos of travel hotspots, maps, reviews, and, of course, links for booking flights and hotels.

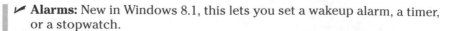

✔ **Calculator:** Another app introduced in Windows 8.1, Calculator offers standard, scientific, and conversion modes to meet the needs of students, cooks, and budding physicists.

✔ **Calendar:** This handy app lets you enter your upcoming appointments, of course. But it can also automatically fetch appointments you've made in online calendars. The app then blends appointments from several sources into one calendar. I cover the Calendar app in Chapter 9.

✔ **Camera:** Your Surface's front camera works best for vanity shots, whereas the back camera is more suited for scenic vistas (if you don't mind looking dorky while holding up your tablet to frame the wonders of nature). I explain how to use your Surface's camera in Chapter 10.

✔ **Desktop:** A tap of the Start screen's Desktop tile fetches the traditional Windows desktop, covered in Chapter 12. There, you find several of the usual Windows accessories, such as Paint and Notepad, as well as the robust File Manager. The Desktop app lets you run all of your old, traditional Windows programs. (Surface RT and Surface 2 tablets include the Desktop app, but they can't install your older Windows software.)

✔ **Finance:** In the U.S., this tile shows a 30-minute delay of the Dow, NASDAQ, and S&P. (You can set it to display indexes of markets in other countries, as well.) Tap the tile to open the Finance app, filled with charts, indexes, news, rates, and stocks you've added to your personalized Watchlist.

✔ **Food and Drink:** Another new app for Windows 8.1, this helps you plan meals and catalog your recipes. Look for the hands-free mode, which automatically turns pages with a wave of your batter-spattered hand.

✔ **Fresh Paint:** This drawing program, added for Windows 8.1, lets you create art several ways: from scratch, based on a photograph, or based on an existing drawing or image. Budding digital artists should take the tutorial, because digital watercolor brushes work quite differently.

✔ **Games:** A tap of the Games app brings the Xbox Games app, a link to your Xbox game console. Here, you can see your Xbox friends and gaming achievements, as well as view game trailers and buy Xbox games. (The app also lists a few free games to play on your Surface.)

✔ **Health and Fitness:** New for Windows 8.1, this offers not only exercise tips but also information about nutrition, well-being, and prescription drug interactions.

✔ **Help + Tips:** Missing from Windows 8, this app finally tries to explain how to use this drastically new version of Windows.

✔ **Internet Explorer:** This no-nonsense browser site fills the screen with your currently viewed website, with no messy menus or tabs to get in the way. To see the app's menus, slide your finger up from the screen's bottom edge. (I cover this stripped-down version of Internet Explorer in Chapter 8.)

✔ **Mail:** Described in Chapter 9, this simple app lets you send and receive files and e-mail. It works in conjunction with your People app, automatically filling in e-mail addresses as you begin typing a person's name.

 ✔ **Maps:** A tap of the Maps app brings up Microsoft Bing Maps and a view of your current city. Because current Surface models lack a GPS *(Global Positioning System)* chip, the Maps app won't pinpoint your exact location or offer turn-by-turn navigation. However, it can dish up accurate directions when you type in two addresses.

 ✔ **Music:** This music player, covered in Chapter 11, plays music stored on your Surface or stashed away on OneDrive (covered in Chapter 6). It's also a gateway to Xbox Live Music, which offers an array of streaming music options to owners of an Xbox game console.

 ✔ **News:** Drop by here to read news pulled from a wide variety of news sources, customized according to your interest or geographical location.

 ✔ **OneDrive:** This app lets you stash files online, where you can share them with other people and access them from other computers. OneDrive also serves as a convenient way to add storage to a space-deprived Surface. I cover OneDrive and other storage solutions in Chapter 6.

 ✔ **OneNote:** This finger-friendly digital notebook app works fine on its own, or it syncs with the full version, which runs on the desktop. OneNote lets you collect and organize notes, either typed or handwritten. You can also toss in photos and recordings when needed.

 ✔ **PC Settings:** This simply opens the PC Settings screen, saving you from a trip to the Charms bar.

 ✔ **People:** The People app, covered in Chapter 9, contains your friends' contact information. You can enter or edit the details yourself or let the app automatically harvest your friends' information from your Facebook, Twitter, Google, or other online networks.

 ✔ **Photos:** The Photos app, covered in Chapter 10, lets you show off photos stored on your Surface or OneDrive. It can also import photos from your digital camera.

 ✔ **Reader:** Many downloadable documents and manuals come stored in Adobe's *Portable Document Format* (PDF), and this app opens them for easy reading.

 ✔ **Reading List:** Don't have time to read that extraordinary Internet article? Fetch the Charms bar, choose Share, and toss the article onto the Reading List app. When you open the Reading List app, all of your articles will be waiting for you.

 ✔ **Scan:** Covered in Chapter 6, this Windows 8.1 app finds your attached scanner and lets you scan documents right from the Start screen.

✔ **Skype:** Covered in Chapter 9, this app lets you chat, swap instant messages, or hold face-to-face meetings over the Internet.

 ✔ **Skype WiFi:** Also covered in Chapter 9, Skype WiFi lets you connect with wireless Internet networks across the globe.

 ✔ **Sound Recorder:** This simple recorder works well for recording classes or recording short bursts of inspiration.

 ✔ **Sports:** Sports fans drop by here to see the latest team scores and game news. Open the App bar and tap Favorite Teams to create a mini-newspaper devoted to your favorite team's news and statistics.

 ✔ **Store:** To download new apps, visit the Windows Store, covered later in this chapter.

 ✔ **Video:** This plays videos from your Surface and its storage areas, as well as providing a portal to Xbox Video, covered in Chapter 10.

 ✔ **Weather:** This personalized weather station grants you a weeklong glimpse into your city's future weather patterns. (Load the App bar and tap Places to add other cities to the app's crystal ball.)

I explain the mechanics of the Start screen in Chapter 4, including tips on adding, removing, and organizing apps on the Start screen.

Customizing apps to meet your needs

Microsoft's built-in apps come preset to cater to the widest audience. But once they're living on *your* Surface, take some time to make them cater to your own needs instead. Tell the Weather app to display your own city, for example; add your favorite newspapers to the News app and add your favorite sports teams to the Sports app.

The customization tricks described here apply to most apps, whether they came bundled with your Surface or you downloaded them from the Windows Store app.

To customize any open app, follow these steps:

1. **Fetch the App menu, called the *App bar,* by sliding your finger up slightly from the screen's bottom, or down slightly from the screen's top.**

   Different apps treat their App bar differently. Some place their menu along the bottom, others drop them down from the top, and some do both.

2. **When the App bar appears, tap its buttons to customize the app to your needs.**

Fetch the App bar in the News app, for example, shown in Figure 7-1, and the top App bar offers three options:

- **Bing News:** The equivalent of a browser's Home button, a tap of this button returns you to the News app's front page. (It's called Bing News because Microsoft's search engine, Bing, constantly stocks the News app with the latest news.)

- **Topics:** Tap here to personalize your news with topics of interest to you. To start, tap the plus sign within the Add a Topic box; when the Add a Topic screen appears, type a favorite topic. Tap the Add button, and the Bing News section collects stories on that topic. Revisit Topics to see the latest news about that specific subject.

Place quotes around your search term to find results that contain that exact phrase. For example, type **"brussels sprouts"** to see news only about today's trendy vegetable. Type **brussels sprouts**, by contrast, and the app fetches news about Belgium *and* salad toppings.

- **Sources:** Want to read information from one favorite source? Tap the Sources option to read news from a particular news outlet, including the *New York Times, The Wall Street Journal, Time,* and many of your favorite websites.

- **Video:** Many news outlets include videos with their stories, and this button takes you directly to the hour's most popular news videos. (If a video doesn't hold your interest, tap the screen; then tap the Back arrow that appears in the upper-left corner.)

Figure 7-1: To customize an app, swipe your finger up from the screen's bottom or down from the top edge to fetch that particular app's App bar.

After customizing the News app to meet your own interests, try these other tips to personalize your Surface's other apps:

✔ Traveling to a new city? Prepare yourself by opening the Bing Travel app, typing your destination into the Search Destinations box, and tapping the Magnifying Glass icon. When the travel guide shows your destination, swipe up from the screen's bottom edge and tap Pin to Start; that places a travel guide to that city on your Start screen.

✔ Add your stock portfolio to the Finance app by fetching its App bar, tapping the Watchlist button, and tapping the plus sign to add stocks symbols. After you've added your portfolio, tap any of the stock's symbols to see detailed information about the stock's historical value.

✔ If you click the Allow button when the Weather app first asks your location, the app automatically updates its Start screen tile with your city's weather forecast. To add other cities, fetch the App bar, tap Places, tap the Favorites button, type another location, and tap the Add button.

✔ Several other apps ask permission to use your location to tailor their information. To see the list of apps you've approved — and revoke their access, if you want — fetch the Charms bar, tap Settings, and choose Change PC Settings from the Settings pane. When the PC Settings screen appears, tap Privacy and then choose Location from the Privacy screen. There, you find toggle switches for every app that requests location information.

✔ If you don't see any way to customize an app on its App bar, fetch the Charms bar and tap the Settings icon. When the Settings pane appears, check the list near the top edge. Some options let you change or personalize your app's behavior.

Organizing your apps

Microsoft sets up your Surface's Start screen in a pretty boring way. And as you begin adding apps, it changes from boring to a sprawling mess that creeps out of sight past the screen's right edge.

To make your Surface *yours,* take control of your Start screen, personalizing it to fit your lifestyle. As I explain in Chapter 4, you can remove tiles for apps you don't use, add tiles for apps you *do* use, move related tiles into groups, and move favorite tiles to the front so they're easy to tap.

After you've done that, Microsoft's Surface will start looking a lot more like *your* Surface.

Downloading new apps from the Windows Store

Your Surface comes with plenty of built-in apps, described in the previous section. But sooner or later, those won't be enough. When you need to beef up your Surface with more features, there's an app for that: It's called the Windows Store app.

The Store's apps let you mold your Surface around your own interests. Birdwatchers can download bird-watching tools. Sailors can download tide-prediction apps. Cooks can download recipe collections. You'll even find music and video playing programs that compete with Microsoft's built-in offerings.

As programmers write more apps to fill in more niches, the Store's wares keep growing. And best of all, most of the apps are free.

Because the Surface RT and Surface 2 tablets can't run desktop programs, they're limited to apps downloaded from the Store app. In fact, you won't even see apps that run on Surface Pro or Surface Pro 2.

To add new apps to your Surface, follow these steps:

1. **Open the Store app.**

   If you're not already on the Start screen, head there with a press of the Windows key. Tap the Store app's tile, and the Store app fills the screen, shown in Figure 7-2.

Figure 7-2: Your Surface can download apps only from the Windows Store.

2. **Browse for apps, tapping interesting apps to read their description, details, and reviews left by others.**

   You can search for a specific app, as I describe in the next step. But if you feel like browsing, the Store app offers several ways to window shop its app collection.

    As you browse, watch for the left-pointing arrow in the screen's top-left corner. Tap that arrow to return to the Store page you just left.

   When you first open the Store, Microsoft displays "featured" apps — apps that pay to appear first. So, to see apps ranked by their merit rather than their marketing money, keep scrolling to the right until you see these categories:

   - **Picks for You:** As your Surface learns about your interests, it places apps you may like in this category.

   - **Trending:** These apps are creating a buzz, either through Internet chatter or other media attention. Give these a look to see what everybody's talking about.

   - **New & Rising:** Newly released apps that have made an impression appear here. Some are long-awaited apps that recently appeared in the store — Facebook's app, for example. Others come from popular websites that finally took the plunge and created a Windows app to display their information.

   - **Top Paid:** High-quality games, in particular, tend to appear here. Give these a close look because people are finding them worth buying.

   - **Top Free:** Be sure to tap the Top Free tile to see the most popular free apps. Chances are good that you'll want to grab the top five.

   You can also browse by category by sliding your finger up from the screen's bottom or slightly down from the screen's top. The App bar appears along the top, shown in Figure 7-3, letting you tap the category of apps you want to browse.

   If you spot the app of your dreams, head to Step 4 to install it onto your Surface. If you still can't find the right app, move to the next step and search for it.

3. **Search for an app.**

   When you can't find what you want by browsing, try searching: Type a keyword or two that describes your app in the Search box, located in the top-right corner of every screen. After typing your keywords, press Enter or tap the Magnifying glass icon on the right side of the Search box.

    In Windows 8, searching within apps took place through the Charms bar's Search icon. Windows 8.1 drops that approach, and now you search within apps from the Search box built directly into the app, usually in its upper-right corner.

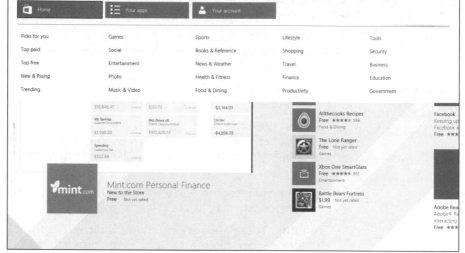

Figure 7-3:
Tap a category from the App bar to browse apps in that category.

Windows searches the Store app for your key word, shown in Figure 7-4, showing all the apps that match. Drop-down menus along the top let you sort the matching apps by their category, price, rating, and more.

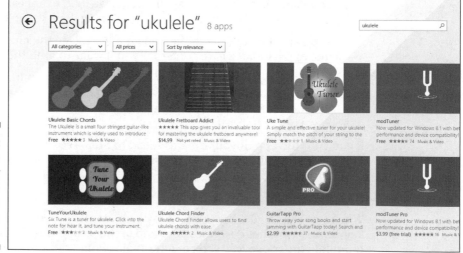

Figure 7-4:
Search the Store app by keyword to see all the matching apps.

4. **Tap an app's name to read more about it.**

The app's page in the Store appears, shown in Figure 7-5, and offers three ways to see more about the app.

- **Overview:** The app displays this page by default, as shown in Figure 7-5. Here, you see a picture and description of the app, its features, and ways to see more information: the app's website, for example, as well as the app's support page and legal terms.

   Slide your finger up and down on the app's picture to see additional photos. Most apps offer two or more photos of how the app will look on your Surface.

- **Details:** Although boring, this page may be the most important. It elaborates on the details shown in the app's far-right pane, lists what bugs were fixed in the latest release, what processors the app supports, and the permissions it requires.

- **Reviews:** Here, owners leave comments based on their experience. Judge by the consensus rather than individual reviews: Different people have different expectations.

Looking at an app's pictures and reading an app's Overview, Details, and Reviews pages let you know whether the app is right for you or whether you should continue browsing.

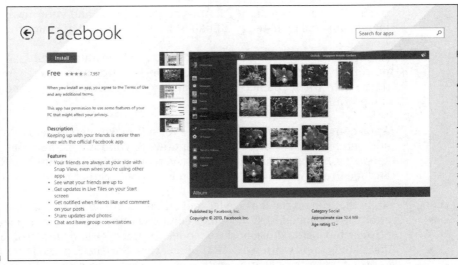

Figure 7-5: Scroll to the right to see more information about an app, including reviews left by users.

5. **Install or buy the app.**

   When you find an app you want to place on your Surface, the app's page (shown earlier in Figure 7-5) displays any of three buttons:

   - **Install:** Found on free apps and purchased-but-uninstalled apps, tap this button to install the app onto your Surface. A minute or so after you tap the Install button, the app appears on your Start screen's All Apps area. (To see the Start screen's All Apps area, slide your finger upward from the middle of the Start screen.)

- **Try:** Found on paid apps, tap this to try out the app for a week. After a week, the app expires unless you tap the Buy button, opening your wallet for the app's full price.

- **Buy:** Paid apps cost anywhere from $1.49 to $999.99, but most cost less than $5. Tapping the Buy button lets you purchase the app immediately if you've already linked a credit card with your Microsoft account. No credit card link? Then the Buy button takes you to a secure website to enter that information.

If you don't see a button, the words You Own This App appear, meaning you've already downloaded the app. If it's missing from your Start screen, visit the Start screen's All Apps screen just below the Start screen. That presents an alphabetical list of *all* the apps installed on your Surface.

6. **Wait for the app to download.**

   Most apps download in less than two minutes. When the app finishes downloading, a notice pops up in the screen's upper-right corner, telling you the app was installed.

There's one oddity, though: Your downloaded app won't appear on the Start screen. Instead, it's in the screen *below* the Start screen. Slide your finger up the Start screen to pull the All Apps screen in view, and your newly downloaded app will be listed in alphabetical order with all of your other apps.

As the Store's number of apps increases, you'll be able to add many extra powers to your Surface quickly, and easily — a welcome change from the days of old when you needed to slide discs into your computer, hoping everything would work.

Apps constantly change. Companies release newer versions to add features and patch security holes. Unlike Windows 8, Windows 8.1 automatically keeps your apps up-to-date. If you haven't upgraded your Surface RT or Surface Pro to Windows 8.1, you're missing out on that handy feature.

 Apps that run on the Surface RT and Surface 2 are known as *ARM* apps, named after the Advanced RISC Machines company that created the special low-power chip inside those Surface models. Surface RT and Surface 2 tablets can install only apps written for ARM processors. Surface Pro and Pro 2 tablets, by contrast, can run only apps written for x86, x64 processors. (As you browse the apps, the Store helps out by showing only apps that run on your particular Surface model.)

Uninstalling or changing an app

Before you can uninstall or change an app, you need to *select* its tile on the Start screen. Oddly enough, selecting an app's Start screen tile is a task rarely stumbled upon on your own. So, here's the secret:

REMEMBER

To select an app on the Start screen, hold your finger down on its icon until the App bar appears along the bottom.

After you select an app, a check mark appears in the app's top-right corner, like the Bing Travel app shown in Figure 7-6. The App bar also appears along the bottom, listing everything you can do with your newly selected app.

Figure 7-6: After you select an app, the App bar appears along the screen's bottom, letting you choose how to change that app.

TIP

✔ To uninstall an app, tap the Uninstall button from the App bar.

✔ You can also uninstall apps that came pre-installed on your Surface. If you're not using one of your Surface's bundled apps, feel free to uninstall it. (It can always be reinstalled from the Windows Store.)

✔ App bar icons also let you change the size of an app's tile, start or stop the app's live updates, or unpin (remove) the app from the Start screen.

✔ Selecting the Start screen tile of a traditional Windows desktop program brings a slightly different set of icons to the App bar. You can open the program in a new desktop window, pin it to the desktop's taskbar, or view its location in the desktop's File Explorer program.

✔ The Windows 8.1 Spring Update, released through Windows Update in April, lets you pin Start screen apps to the desktop's taskbar, making them easy to access without a trip to the Start screen.

✔ You can select more than one app at a time, which is handy when weeding out a batch of unwanted tiles from the Start screen.

Working with Two Apps on One Screen

Windows lets you place two apps side by side. In fact, it will probably happen when you don't expect it: You click a link that somebody mailed you, and all of a sudden the Mail app shrinks to fill half the screen, and Internet Explorer fills the screen's other half to display the linked page.

Windows calls that "snapping an app" because you're snapping one app next to another on the same screen. You can snap Start screen apps next to each other, and you can even snap a Start screen app next to your traditional Windows desktop. To snap an app, follow these steps:

1. **Open an app that you'd like to use and snap it to the screen's left or right.**

    Tap an app from the Start menu to open it. When it fills the screen, slide your finger down from the screen's top until the app turns into a small window on a blank screen, as shown in Figure 7-7.

Figure 7-7:
Drag your finger down from the screen's top edge until the app shrinks into a small window.

Then, drag the app to the screen's left or right side; when a horizontal line appears, lift your finger; the app "snaps" to the closest edge, as shown in Figure 7-8.

If you're using a mouse, point at the top of the app and, while holding down the right mouse button, drag the app downward. When the app shrinks, drag it to the left or right side of the screen to snap it into place.

Figure 7-8:
The app snaps to the screen's closest edge.

2. **Return to the Start screen and open a second app; it snaps to the opposite side of the screen.**

   When you open the second app, it automatically snaps to the empty side of the screen, leaving both apps onscreen, as shown in Figure 7-9.

Figure 7-9:
The second snapped app fills the empty space next to the first app.

3. **To resize the apps, drag the divider between them.**

Find the three dots (shown in the margin) on the line separating the two snapped apps. Then drag those three dots to the left or right side, depending on which app you want to enlarge.

To close a snapped app, drag the three dots all the way toward the app you want to close; when your finger reaches the edge, the app disappears from the screen. (It stays running in the background, though, so you can return to it later.)

4. **If desired, replace a snapped app with a different one.**

If you revisit the Start screen and open a third app, that app opens as a small window on top of the other two, as shown in Figure 7-10. Tap the app you don't want, and the hovering third app jumps in to replace it.

Figure 7-10:
Open a third app and it hovers, waiting for you to tap the snapped app it should replace.

By opening and snapping apps, dragging the divider between them, and replacing snapped apps with others, you can make the most of the Start screen's formerly full-screen apps.

Want to snap an app that's already open? Reveal all of your open apps by sliding your screen in about an inch from the left edge and then back again. A row of thumbnail-sized apps appears, representing your open apps. Drag any of those thumbnails to the screen's left or right edges, and it snaps to that side.

You can also snap apps alongside the Windows Desktop app, a handy way to keep an eye on e-mail while working.

Installing Desktop Programs

Surface RT and Surface 2 tablets include a traditional Windows desktop, but with one big restriction: They won't let you install any programs onto the desktop. Instead, Surface RT and Surface 2 tablets are limited to downloads from the Windows Store app.

Surface Pro and Surface Pro 2 tablets, by contrast, include a fully functional desktop, just like the one found on desktop PCs. But because your Surface lacks a CD or DVD drive, how do you install a desktop program?

You have several options:

- ✔ **Windows Store:** When you browse the Windows Store app with a Surface Pro or Surface Pro 2 tablet, many desktop programs appear along with the Store's list of apps. When looking at a program you want, tap the Go to Publisher's Website link. The software publisher's website appears, and you can buy the program if required, download the program, and install it by double-tapping its download icon.

- ✔ **Website:** Desktop programs not listed in the Windows Store can still be downloaded directly from the Internet, just as in previous versions of Windows.

- ✔ **Flash drive:** All Surface tablets include a USB port. You can copy or download a program's installation file onto a flash drive with another computer, and then insert the flash drive into your Surface and install it from there.

- ✔ **OneDrive:** Described in Chapter 6, this online cubby hole works well for swapping files between your Surface and desktop PC. From your desktop PC, copy a program's installation file to any folder in OneDrive. Then, open the Start screen's OneDrive app, visit the OneDrive folder, and tap the program's installation file to install it.

Chapter 8

Browsing the Web

Your Internet-hungry Surface includes *two* web browsers. The Start screen's nimble browser works easily with your fingers. The old-school browser on the Desktop app provides extra power but works best with a keyboard and trackpad or mouse.

Although the two browsers behave quite differently, they're oddly intertwined: They share your home page, login passwords, browsing history, and your list of favorites sites, among other things. Adding to the confusion, both browsers bear the same name: Internet Explorer.

Chances are good that you're fairly familiar with the desktop version of Internet Explorer. And, on a touch-screen service, you'll find yourself poking the Start screen's browser much more often.

The following sections explain everything you need to know about the Start screen's nimble browser: how to find and open its menus, quickly load your favorite sites, simultaneously browse several sites, share and download files and information, and adjust your browser's settings — all with your fingertips.

Not yet connected to the Internet? Flip back to Chapter 6, where I explain how to connect your Surface with the Internet.

Opening Internet Explorer

Your Surface contains two versions of Internet Explorer, each opened in a slightly different way. These sections explain how to open each, and when to choose one browser over another.

Opening the Start Screen's Internet Explorer app

You'll find yourself using the Start screen browser much more often than the desktop browser. Unlike the desktop browser, the Start screen browser is designed for your fingers, and its icon lives directly on the Start screen.

 To open the Start screen's browser, tap its icon (shown in the margin) on the Start screen. The browser opens, filling the screen as shown in Figure 8-1.

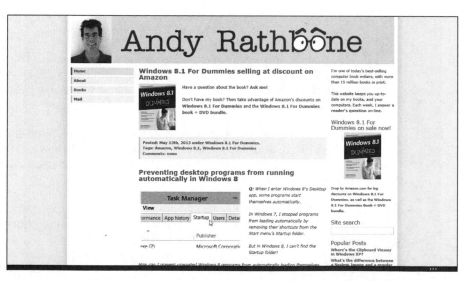

Figure 8-1: Like all Start screen apps, the Internet Explorer app hides its menus, filling the screen with your website.

When opened, the Start screen's browser displays one of these three things:

 ✔ **Your home page:** When opened for the first time, the Start screen's browser displays your *home page:* a favorite site you've chosen to display whenever you open Internet Explorer. If you haven't chosen a home page, as I describe later in this chapter, Microsoft fills the screen with one of its own websites.

✔ **Your last-visited site:** Unless you specifically *closed* the browser after your last visit, the browser displays the same site you last visited. (I explain how to close apps in Chapter 4.)

✔ **You're not connected:** When the browser displays this alarming error message, it means your Surface lacks an Internet connection. (I explain how to connect with the Internet in Chapter 6.)

But no matter which page your browser displays upon opening, notice how the page completely fills the screen. That makes the page easier to read, but it also highlights the Internet Explorer app's greatest weakness: The browser hides all of its menus.

You may not miss the menus, though. The browser loads quickly, works very well with your fingers, and you can easily tap one site's links to jump to another site. The fast-loading browser excels at serving up quick bits of information, which is what most people need from the Start screen.

Windows 8.1 adds a lot of power to the Start screen's browser, and it's often all a Surface owner needs.

Opening the desktop's Internet Explorer

Opening the Desktop app's version of Internet Explorer on the Surface takes more effort: You won't find an icon for it on the Start screen. That's actually a good thing because the desktop's browser is very difficult to use with your fingers.

If you have a mouse and keyboard and need to run the desktop's browser in a window, follow these steps:

1. **From the Start screen, tap or click the Desktop app's tile.**

   The traditional Windows desktop appears.

2. **From the taskbar along the desktop's bottom, tap or click the Internet Explorer icon next to the Start button in the screen's bottom-left corner.**

Internet Explorer leaps to the screen in its own window.

If you plan on working with your Surface's desktop more often than the Start screen, I cover the desktop version of Internet Explorer — as well as the desktop itself — in my 420-page book, *Windows 8.1 For Dummies.*

Opening the Start Screen Browser's Menus

Like most Start screen apps, the browser app hides its menus. That lets you concentrate on the picture rather than the frame. When you need the menus, you can reveal them using the same trick that summons the menus from any Start screen app:

Slide your finger inward from the screen's top or bottom edges.

As you slide your finger, the App bar comes into view, snapping along the screen's top or bottom edges, as shown in Figure 8-2.

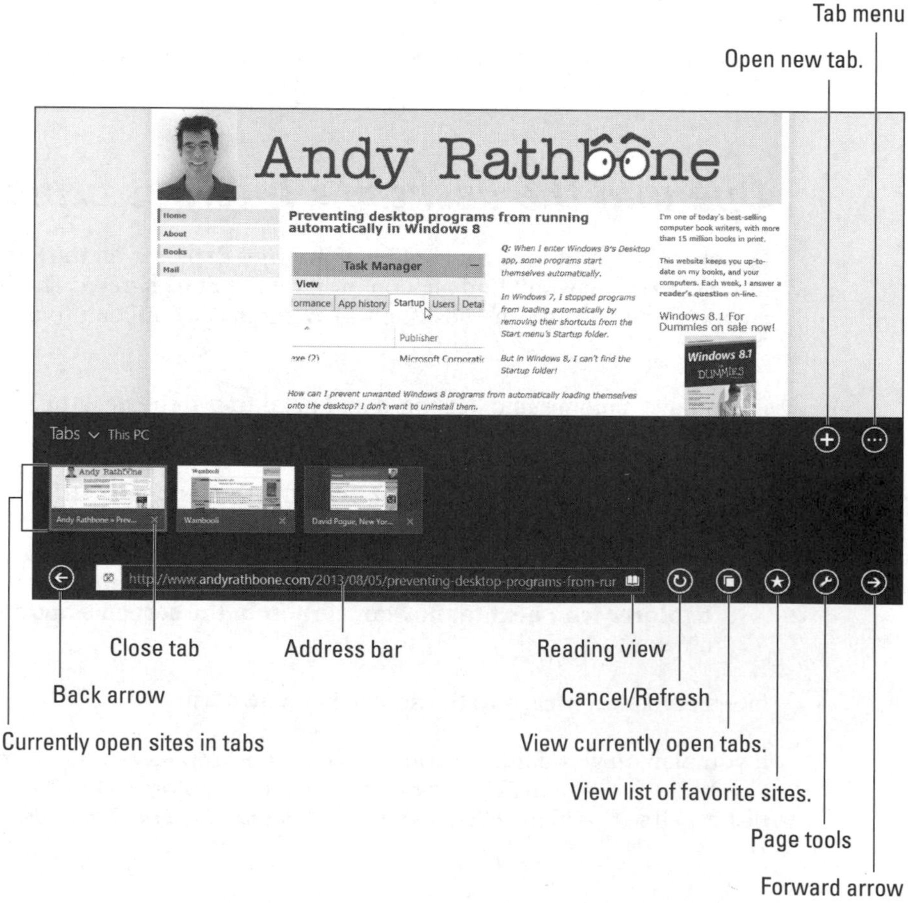

Figure 8-2:
To see the browser's menu, called an *App bar,* slide your finger slightly inward from the screen's top or bottom edge.

Tab menu

Open new tab.

Andy Rathbone

Home
About
Books
Mail

Preventing desktop programs from running automatically in Windows 8

I'm one of today's best-selling computer book writers, with more than 15 million books in print.

Task Manager

View

ormance | App history | Startup | Users | Detai

Publisher

ype (2)   Microsoft Corporatio

Q: When I enter Windows 8's Desktop app, some programs start themselves automatically.

In Windows 7, I stopped programs from loading automatically by removing their shortcuts from the Start menu's Startup folder.

But in Windows 8, I can't find the Startup folder!

How can I prevent unwanted Windows 8 programs from automatically loading themselves onto the desktop? I don't want to uninstall them.

This website keeps you up-to-date on my books, and your computers. Each week, I answer a reader's question on-line.

Windows 8.1 For Dummies on sale now!

Windows 8.1
DUMMIES

Tabs ∨ This PC

Andy Rathbone   Wambooli   David Pague, New Yor...

Andy Rathbone » Prev...   Wambooli   David Pague, New Yor...

http://www.andyrathbone.com/2013/08/05/preventing-desktop-programs-from-rur

Close tab

Address bar

Reading view

Back arrow

Cancel/Refresh

Currently open sites in tabs

View currently open tabs.

View list of favorite sites.

Page tools

Forward arrow

Each icon on the App bar performs a different task with a tap of your finger:

 ✔ **Back arrow:** Tap this to revisit your previously viewed web page.

✔ **Address bar:** To type a new web address, tap inside the address bar. If no keyboard is attached, the touch keyboard appears, ready for you to type the address of the website you'd like to visit. (As you type, the area above the address bar lists matching names of previously visited sites. Spot the name of the site you want to visit? Tap its name to load it.)

 The address bar also doubles as a Search box. Type a few keywords and press Enter, and Microsoft's Bing search engine lists websites matching your search.

 ✔ **Cancel/Refresh:** As you view a site, this is a *Refresh* icon; tap it to reload the page, retrieving the latest details. While a web page loads, this icon becomes a *Cancel* button; if the site loads slowly, tap the Cancel icon to stop trying to load the sluggish site.

 ✔ **Favorite:** Tap this icon, and a list of sites you've marked as Favorites appears above the address bar. This makes them much easier to launch from within the browser, as I explain in this chapter's "Visiting websites" section.

 ✔ **Add to Favorites:** Displayed when viewing your Favorites list, this icon lets you add your currently viewed site to your Favorites list.

 ✔ **Pin to Start:** Seen when viewing your Favorites list, this icon places a shortcut tile on the Start screen that launches your currently viewed site.

 ✔ **Share:** Displayed when viewing your Favorites list, this icon opens the Charms bar's Share icon, where you can share the site with others, place it on your Reading List app, post to social networks, or e-mail the site to friends.

 ✔ **Tabs:** Tap this icon to replace the Favorites list with a view of your currently open tabs.

 ✔ **Page Tools:** When a page doesn't load properly, tap this little wrench icon. When the pop-up menu appears, choose View on the Desktop. That opens the site in the *desktop* version of Internet Explorer. (If the wrench icon sprouts a plus sign, that means that site offers an app for easier access.)

 ✔ **Forward arrow:** After clicking the Back arrow to revisit a site, click the Forward arrow to return to the site you just left.

 ✔ **Tab Menu:** Displayed when viewing a list of your currently open tabs, this icon brings a pop-up menu with two options: Close tabs, which closes all the open tabs, and New InPrivate tab, which opens a new tab for browsing in private (covered in the "Browsing in private" sidebar).

✔ **Open New Tab:** A tap of the plus sign icon in the top right lets you open a blank new tab. That tab lets you open a new web page, which is handy when you want to compare two websites. (You can jump between the sites by tapping their thumbnails on the Tab menu.)

 ✔ **Reading View:** Tap this little book icon, shown at the end of the address bar, to strip the web page of cluttering ads and formatting and display the page's content full screen. You can then read it by paging from left to right rather than scrolling down. (To return to normal view, tap the icon again.)

The Start screen browser may look lightweight, but it provides everything you need for casual browsing. As shown in Figure 8-2, the browser lets you open several sites simultaneously, each in its own tab.

I describe how to close the Internet Explorer app in Chapter 4, but there's really no need to close Internet Explorer or any other Start screen app. They're designed to stay open constantly, letting you switch between them as needed, also described in Chapter 4.

Browsing in private

Most websites leave lasting impressions long after they've left your eyes. Days or months later, the sites' names can still pop up in your address bar as you begin typing a few letters. They also linger in your browser's history of visited websites. Some even leave behind *cached* photos — copies of viewed photos — on your Surface's hard drive. And they leave behind *cookies* — small files that help websites track your visits.

When you want to visit a website without leaving a trace, head for the Start screen browser's InPrivate mode from the Tab menu. InPrivate mode lets you shop for holiday presents, visit controversial websites, or browse on a public computer without letting others know your business.

To turn on InPrivate mode on the Start screen's browser, follow these steps:

1. **From the Start screen's Internet Explorer app, slide your finger down slightly from the screen's top edge to reveal the menu.**

2. **Tap the Tab menu (it looks like three dots) and, when the pop-up menu appears, tap New InPrivate tab.**

A blank InPrivate window appears in the browser, ready for you to browse without leaving a trace on your PC.

The desktop version of Internet Explorer requires different steps to enter InPrivate mode:

1. **Tap or click the browser's Tools icon in its upper-right corner. (The icon resembles a gear.)**

2. **When the drop-down menu appears, choose Safety.**

3. **When the Safety pop-out menu appears, choose InPrivate Browsing.**

A new version of Internet Explorer opens, showing a window that says *InPrivate Is On*.

To leave InPrivate mode in either program, just close Internet Explorer or close the browser's InPrivate window.

Navigating a Website with Your Fingers

Being designed specifically for your fingers, the Start screen's version of Internet Explorer works quite well with touch controls. When you're browsing a website, a well-placed finger lets you perform any of these tasks:

- ✔ **Scroll through a web page.** When viewing a web page, remember the "sliding a piece of paper" rule: Slide your finger up or down the page, and the web page travels along the screen with your finger. By sliding your finger up or down the page, you can read the entire page, skipping up or down a few paragraphs at your own pace.

- ✔ **Enlarge tiny text.** When the text is too small to read, place two fingertips on the screen and spread them. As your fingers move, the information expands, enlarging the text. Pinching the screen between two fingertips shrinks the page. By stretching and pinching, you find the sweet spot for easy visibility of both text and photos. (A quick double-tap makes the page fill the screen, letting you pinch or stretch it to your preferred size.)

- ✔ **Fetch menus.** Slide your finger up slightly from the screen's bottom or down slightly from the screen's top. A menu pops up along the screen's bottom edge, as shown earlier in Figure 8-2.

- ✔ **Open a link in a new tab.** Hold your finger down on the link until a menu appears along the screen's bottom. From that menu, tap the Open in New Tab icon. (Choosing the Open in New Window icon splits the screen, snapping a second version of Internet Explorer to the right of your current version. I explain snapping apps side-by-side in Chapter 7.)

Using the Start screen's Internet Explorer with a trackpad or mouse

Most of the time, the Start screen's Internet Explorer works just fine with your fingertips. But armed with your Surface keyboard's trackpad or a mouse, the app tosses these new moves your way:

- ✔ **Back/Forward:** As you browse between a string of websites, hover your mouse pointer over the currently viewed page's left or right edges. An arrow appears along the edge, letting you click to move backward or forward, revisiting previously viewed pages.

- ✔ **Opening menus:** To fetch the menus from Internet Explorer and any Start screen app, right-click a blank portion of the web page, away from words and pictures, and the menus appear.

- ✔ **Dragging:** Some, but not all, websites recognize dragging. If you find yourself stuck at a stubborn website, try using your fingers to drag instead.

I explain more about using a trackpad, mouse, and keyboard in Chapter 5.

Visiting Websites

You don't always have to open Internet Explorer to begin browsing. If you spot a web link inside a piece of e-mail in the Mail app, for example, tap the link. Internet Explorer appears automatically, snapping itself alongside the Mail app to display that website. (I describe how to maneuver snapped apps in Chapter 7.)

If you've pinned a favorite site to the Start screen with a tap of the App bar's Pin to Start icon, a quick tap of that site's Start screen tile brings it to the forefront.

When Internet Explorer is onscreen, the app lets you visit sites in other ways, as well:

- ✔ **Return to your last-visited site.** Slide a finger inward from the screen's left edge, as if you're flipping back a page in a book, and the previous page returns into view. You can also slide a finger up from screen's bottom until the App bar appears; then tap the left-pointing arrow. (Conversely, a tap on the right-pointing arrow returns to the site you left.)

- ✔ **Type a site's address.** Slide your finger up the page to fetch the App bar and begin typing the site's name in the address bar, shown earlier in Figure 8-2. Press Enter, and the website opens.

- ✔ **Search for a site.** Type a keyword or phrase directly into the address bar and press Enter. Microsoft's Bing search takes over, listing websites that match your searched item.

- ✔ **Visit a favorite site.** When you fetch the App bar and tap the Favorites icon (shown in the margin), look directly above the address bar. There, Windows lists three categories of sites: Pinned (sites you've pinned to the Start screen), Frequently Visited, and Favorites (sites you've marked as favorites). To scroll through them all, slide your finger from right to left. Tap a site's name to revisit it.

- ✔ **Revisit a previously visited site.** As you begin typing a site's name in the address bar, the browser checks your list of favorite sites, listing sites that match what you're typing. If you spot your desired site's name before you finish typing, tap the site's name for a quick revisit.

Windows remembers quite a bit about what you do in Internet Explorer. It remembers every term you've searched for, as well as every site you've visited. Although that sometimes comes in handy when trying to relocate information, some view it as an invasion of privacy. Should Internet Explorer grow too nosy, read this chapter's sidebar, "Making Internet Explorer forget."

You can also avoid the problem by using InPrivate browsing, covered in this chapter's "Browsing in Private" sidebar, to keep Internet Explorer from remembering secret visits in the first place.

Making Internet Explorer forget

Windows offers two ways to control what your browser remembers about the time you spend online:

✔ **Manage your search history.** To delete your search history from the Start screen's version of Internet Explorer, open the app. Then fetch the Charms bar and tap Settings. When the Settings pane appears, tap Options. Finally, when the Options pane appears, tap the Select in the History section. There, you can tell the App what to remember and what to forget.

✔ **Stop Windows from remembering your searches.** From anywhere within Windows, fetch the Charms bar and tap Settings. When the Settings pane appears, tap Change PC Settings at the pane's bottom. When the PC Settings window appears, tap Search and Apps from the left pane. When the Search and Apps screen appears, look for the Your Search Experience section and tap the toggle switch called Don't Get Personalized Results from Bing.

Changes made here also affect the desktop's version of Internet Explorer. That version offers additional privacy controls, covered later in this chapter.

Managing Several Sites in Tabs

It's not obvious, but the Start screen's version of Internet Explorer often keeps several sites open at the same time. For example, while viewing a website, you might visit the Start screen and tap a link you'd pinned there earlier for easier access.

The Start screen's Internet Explorer reappears, now displaying the pinned website. What happened to the web page you were viewing previously? The browser places it on a hidden *tab* — a storage place the browser uses to juggle several open sites simultaneously.

You can open websites in different tabs, too, a handy trick when you want to visit a page but keep the first page open for reference.

To open a link in a new tab, follow this simple step:

 Hold down your finger on a link. When the App bar appears along the screen's bottom, tap the Open in New Tab icon, as shown in Figure 8-3.

To see your currently open tabs, slide your finger up slightly from the bottom edge of the Internet Explorer app. When the menus appear, you see thumbnails of all the sites currently open in tabs, as shown earlier in Figure 8-2.

 To revisit a site, tap its name; the browser switches to that tab.

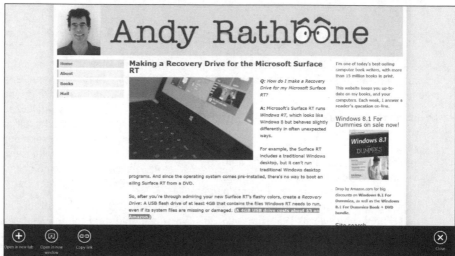

Figure 8-3:
When the pop-up menu appears from a held-down link, tap the Open in New Tab icon.

When a site lives on a tab, it stays there even if you restart your computer. In fact, tabbed sites close only if any of these two things happen:

✓ You manually close a tabbed site by clicking the X in the thumbnail's lower-right corner.

✓ You close the browser manually, usually by swiping your finger from the screen's top edge all the way to the bottom. (The next time you open the browser, only your home page appears.)

Making Sites Available with One Tap

Eventually, you'll run across a site you don't want to forget. When that happens, pin the site to your Start screen. Seeing that tile on the Start screen jogs your memory that you haven't visited for a while. And, it lets you remedy that with a tap on the tile.

To pin a site to the Start screen, follow these steps:

1. **While viewing the site, slide your finger up from the screen's bottom to see the App bar.**

   The App bar rises from the screen's bottom, shown earlier in Figure 8-2.

2. **Tap the Pin to Start button.**

   Don't see the Pin to Start button, shown in the margin? Then reveal it by tapping the App bar's Favorites button, which looks like a star.

When you tap the Pin to Start button, the browser quickly creates a new tile with the website's colors and then sticks that tile on the Start screen's far-right edge. (The tile also bears the website's name.)

When you want to revisit the site, tap its icon from the Start screen. Or, open the browser's bottom menu and tap the address bar; a list of pinned sites appears above the address bar, letting you revisit one with a tap on its name.

 The Start screen always tacks newly pinned sites onto its far-right edge. To manage your Start screen's inevitable sprawl, head for Chapter 4, where I describe how to separate the Start screen into organized groups of tiles. (You may want to create a separate Start screen group for your favorite websites.)

Sharing Sites and Their Information

Eventually, you stumble upon something worth sharing with friends. It may be an entire web page, or it may be just a recipe's ingredients and instructions from a cooking site.

In previous Windows versions, you'd probably have reached for the age old copy-and-paste trick to shuttle the information to your friends.

Windows now updates that maneuver with the easier-to-use Share icon. Sharing items begins with a trip to the Charms bar:

 Fetch the Charms bar by sliding your finger in from the right edge and then tapping the Share icon, shown in the margin.

When the Share pane appears, shown in Figure 8-4, you see every app capable of sharing your screen's current contents. For example, tap the Mail icon, and the Sharing pane shows the Mail app, letting you type an e-mail address and send the page on its way.

The Share pane usually shows these items:

 ✔ **Mail:** Tap this option to e-mail your currently viewed link to a friend.

 ✔ **Music:** In a surreal experiment, the Music app scans the website and creates an Xbox Music playlist based on the site's words. (I cover Xbox Music in Chapter 11.)

 ✔ **OneNote:** On the Surface RT and Surface 2, this option sends the page to OneNote for later reading. (It does the same on the Surface Pro and Surface Pro 2 only if you've installed OneNote.)

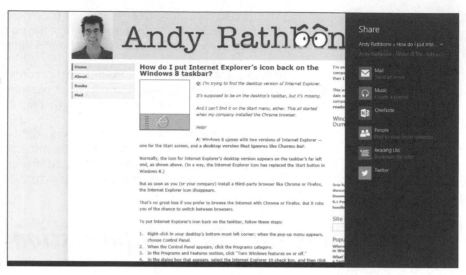

Figure 8-4:
Tap the
Charms
bar's Share
icon to see
how to
share your
currently
viewed or
selected
item.

 ✔ **People:** Tap this option to share the page with your social networks.

✔ **Reading List:** New to Windows 8.1, this option saves the page to your Reading List app, where you can refer to it later, even when away from the Internet.

Tap any app's icon, and the app appears along the screen's right edge, ready to lead you through the steps of sharing the page's information in its own particular way. Tap People, for example, and the app leads you through the steps of sharing the link through a post on Facebook or Twitter.

Tap Reading List, and the Reading List app asks you to list a category for the site and then files it away for later reading.

You may see more apps listed here, depending on how often you've shopped at the Windows Store. However, not all apps can share, and some apps share information in limited ways. If a tap of the Sharing icon doesn't let you share something, the app's creator probably doesn't want that information to be shared.

Downloading Files and Photos

The Start screen's Internet Explorer app can download files and photos, just like its full-sized cousin on the desktop.

For example, to download a file from a website, tap the website's download button. A permission bar appears along the screen's bottom, shown in Figure 8-5.

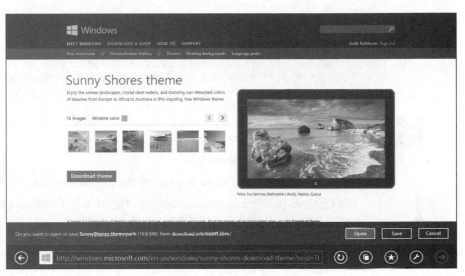

Figure 8-5:
From the menu along the site's bottom edge, tap Run to download and run the file, or tap Save to save the file to run later.

Depending on what you're trying to download, the permission bar offers different options:

- ✔ **Run:** Tap this option if you're downloading a program to install onto your Surface Pro or Surface Pro 2 tablet. The browser downloads the program and then automatically installs it, leaving its icon on the desktop or in the Start screen's All Apps area.

- ✔ **Open:** This downloads and opens the item for viewing or installing.

- ✔ **Save:** This saves the file in your Downloads folder, which is handy when you're downloading something you want to access later.

- ✔ **Cancel:** Tapped a Download button by mistake? A well-placed tap on the Cancel button stops the download.

 To find your downloaded file in the Downloads folder, slide your finger down from the screen's top edge to open the App bar and then tap the Page tools icon, shown in the margin. When the pop-up menu appears, choose View Downloads to see a list of your downloaded files.

If you own a Surface Pro or Surface Pro 2, I explain how to install saved program files in Chapter 12. (Surface RT and Surface 2 tablets can install only programs downloaded from the Store app.)

 To download a photo, hold your finger down on the photo until the App bar appears along the screen's bottom. Then tap the Save Picture icon. The App bar vanishes, and the picture appears in the Pictures folder, visible through the Photos app covered in Chapter 10.

Changing Settings

The Start screen browser, like nearly all apps, lets you tweak its settings to meet your particular needs. And, just as with all apps, opening the settings area begins with a trip to the Charms bar, described in these steps:

1. **Fetch the Charms bar by sliding your finger inward from the screen's right edge. Tap the Settings icon.**

   The Settings pane appears.

2. **Tap the word Options near the top of the Settings pane.**

   The Options pane appears, as shown in Figure 8-6. The Internet Explorer app is built for speed rather than power, so it lets you change only these things:

   - **Appearance:** Head here, and a toggle switch lets you make the App bar stay put so you can always see the menus. The Zoom option's sliding bar lets you choose the magnification level to view sites. If you've set up the desktop to enlarge the screen by 125 percent, as I describe in Chapter 12, this bar will be set at 125. That's fine for most websites — you can always pinch or stretch them to the size that best displays their content.

   - **Home pages:** Tap this section's Customize button to add your currently viewed site or sites to your Home page tabs. Those tabs will automatically load whenever you open the browser.

Figure 8-6: To see Internet Explorer's Options menu (shown here), slide your finger in from the screen's right edge, tap the Settings icon, and tap Options.

Turning on Flip Ahead

Start screen apps usually move their pages across the screen *horizontally*. That lets you swipe your finger in from right to left to move to the next page, much like you do when reading a book.

Websites, by contrast, expect you to move *down* the page, which is contrary to the Windows movements.

The solution? Microsoft's Flip Ahead technology purports to fix things. When you turn on Flip Ahead, Microsoft reformats web pages in the background as they flow onto your screen. To scroll down the page, just flip your finger from right to left, like turning a book's page. Your Surface quickly reformats the website, presenting the portion that dangled off the page as a new page, ready for reading.

Although this makes web browsing more like flipping magazine pages, the cost is a loss of privacy. Turning it on sends Microsoft a link to every web page you visit, which allows them to format the pages in advance. If you're not concerned about privacy, though, it might enhance your web browsing experience.

It can also break the natural flow of some websites, leaving awkward page breaks. To try out Flip Ahead, visit the Internet Explorer app's Settings area, described in the previous section, but tap *Privacy* instead of Options. There, you can toggle on Flip Ahead with Page Prediction.

Beware, however: Even when turned on, the Flip Ahead feature won't work for every site.

- **Reading view:** This lets you customize the browser's Reading View, described earlier in this chapter, to show text at your preferred size and font.

- **History:** Don't want anybody to see websites you've browsed? Tap this section's Select button to delete cached images, cookies, browsing history, download history, and other items.

- **Passwords:** Normally, the browser remembers your usernames and passwords, sparing you from typing them at every visit. This section lets people with perfect memories turn off that feature, as well as manage previously saved passwords.

- **Phone numbers:** This feature lets you detect phone numbers on websites so you can dial them by using your Surface's built-in Skype program.

- **Fonts and Encoding:** Helpful mainly to bilingual Surface owners, this area lets you change how the browser displays sites containing foreign languages.

3. **Tap anywhere on the web page to close the Options pane and return to browsing.**

Your changes to the Internet Explorer app's settings take place immediately.

Sending a Site to the Desktop's Browser

Not all sites display properly in the Start screen's minimalist, finger-friendly browser. Some sites don't show everything, for example; other sites format the page as if you were browsing from a smartphone. Still others protest with cryptic error messages that leave you with frustration rather than solutions.

Instead of giving up and moving on to another site, try routing the site to the desktop's more powerful browser, which specializes in coddling cranky websites.

To route a misbehaving site to the desktop's web browser, follow these steps:

1. **Swipe your finger up from the screen's bottom to fetch the browser menu.**

2. **From the browser's bottom menu, tap the Settings icon.**

Setting your home page in the desktop's browser

Many of the settings made in one browser apply to the other browser, as well. For example, you can set your *home page* — the page your browser shows upon opening — in the Desktop's browser, and the Start screen's version of Internet Explorer will also open to that home page.

To set your home page on the desktop version of Internet Explorer, follow these steps:

1. **With the desktop version of Internet Explorer, visit the site you'd like to see when you first open either browser.**

   Visit your favorite site by typing its address into Internet Explorer or clicking a link.

2. **Click the Tools icon in the program's upper-right corner. (It looks like a gear.)**

3. **When the drop-down menu appears, choose Internet Options.**

4. **When the Internet Options page opens to the General tab, click or tap the Use Current button.**

That sets your currently viewed page as your home page. Once you close and re-open either version of Internet Explorer, it will open to show that page.

Because both browsers can show several sites simultaneously in separate tabs, you can also open different sites in the desktop version of Internet Explorer. When you tap or click the Use Current button in Step 4, it adds *all* of those sites to your home page, and they each open every time you open either version of Internet Explorer.

It's a little wrench with a plus sign, shown in the margin.

3. **Choose View in the Desktop.**

The Desktop app appears, Internet Explorer in tow. Internet Explorer's savvier tools usually help the site display its wares to its fullest capacity.

If the Settings icon's pop-up menu offers the option Get App for this Site, tap that instead. That takes you to the Windows Store, where you can download an app that accesses the site, translating it into a more finger-friendly experience. (After you download the app, the Get App for this Site option disappears.)

Chapter 9

Reaching Out with Mail, People, Calendar, and Skype

*N*obody enjoys typing their friends' names and e-mail addresses into Yet Another New Computer. And the thought of typing them all in on a *glass* keyboard probably makes you give serious thought to buying a click-on keyboard.

Chances are good, though, that you won't have to type them all. Windows *automatically* adds your friends' contact information into your Surface, and it stashes your upcoming appointments into your calendar.

Your Surface works its magic by grabbing your friends' information from your *social networks*. Tell Windows about your Facebook, Twitter, LinkedIn, Google, and other accounts, and your Surface automatically harvests your friends' names and contact information. As your Surface searches your social networks for your friends' information, Windows also grabs your friends' latest status updates for quick reading.

The end result? When you open the People and Calendar apps on your new Surface, your friends already appear. Yes, after several decades, computers are finally making some things easier.

Adding Your Social Accounts to Windows

Before you can run your Surface's core apps — Mail, People, Calendar, and Skype — you need a Microsoft account. (I explain Microsoft accounts in Chapter 3.) Without a Microsoft account, most apps simply display a notice telling you to sign up or switch to a Microsoft account. (Tap those nagging words to sign up for a Microsoft account on the spot.)

Those core apps need something else, too: your username and password information from Facebook, Google, Twitter, LinkedIn, Hotmail, and other accounts you may use.

Although handing over your password sounds fishy, it's actually safe, secure, and quite convenient on your Surface. Armed with your social networking information, the People app dutifully stocks itself with everybody's contact information.

When you open the People app and view people's entries, you see their contact information, as well as their latest posts and photos from Facebook and Twitter.

To let your Surface grab the information that's currently scattered across your social networks, follow these steps:

1. **From the Start screen, open the Mail app.**

   From the Start screen, tap the Mail app's tile, and the Mail app fills the screen, listing any mail you've received from your Microsoft account.

2. **Tell the Mail app about your other accounts.**

    To add your accounts to the Mail app, head for the Charms bar's Settings icon: Summon the Charms bar by swiping your finger inward from the screen's right edge and then tap the Settings icon (shown in the margin).

   When the Settings pane appears, tap the word Accounts, and the Accounts pane appears, listing your Microsoft account. From the Accounts pane, tap the Add an Account link, and the Mail app lists the accounts you can add, as shown in Figure 9-1.

   When you enter the username and password for some mail accounts, the Mail app simply collects any waiting mail. For other mail accounts, such as Gmail, the Mail app takes you to a secure area on the Google website where you authorize the transaction.

   Repeat these steps for other e-mail accounts you want to add to the Mail app.

   Don't see your e-mail account listed? I explain how to add missing e-mail accounts in this chapter's sidebar, "Adding other e-mail accounts to Mail."

Unfortunately, the Mail app doesn't accept POP mail servers, which are offered by many ISPs. To add IMAP servers, tap the Other Account option and enter your username, password, and the name of your IMAP servers. Don't know whether your mail account uses POP or IMAP? Contact your ISP and ask which one it uses for your e-mail.

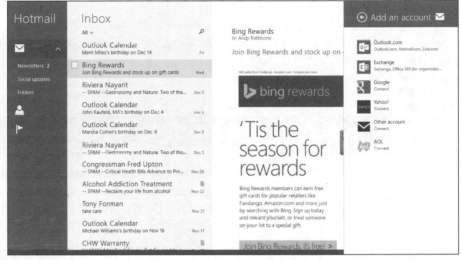

Figure 9-1:
On its right edge, the Mail app's Add an Account pane lets you enter e-mail accounts from different services.

3. **Return to the Start screen, tap the People tile, and enter your other accounts.**

   When the People app first opens, you may already see a few of your friends, grabbed from online contact lists associated with the e-mail accounts you entered in the previous step.

   To stock the app with more of your friends, tell the People app about your social networking sites, like Facebook, Twitter, LinkedIn, and others. Open the People app, summon the Charms bar by sliding your finger inward from the screen's right edge and then tap the Settings icon (shown in the margin).

   When the Settings pane appears, tap the word Accounts, and the Accounts pane appears, listing your Microsoft account. From the Accounts pane, tap the Add an Account link, and the People app lists the accounts you can add, just as the Mail app did back in Figure 9-1.

   Your importing experience will vary from account to account. For some accounts, you simply need to enter your username and password. Other accounts, such as Facebook, take you straight to Facebook's website, where you enter your information to authorize the action, as shown in Figure 9-2.

Figure 9-2:
Enter your
Facebook
e-mail
account and
password
to import
your friends'
names and
contact
information
into your
People app.

After you enter your account information, Windows finishes the job, filling your Mail app with e-mail, stocking the People app with your friends' contact information, and adding any appointments to your Calendar app.

- ✔ Your contact list updates automatically, constantly reflecting your relationships on Facebook, Twitter, or LinkedIn. If you manually add a contact to one of your online networks from any computer, that person's information automatically appears in your Surface's People app, as well.

- ✔ If somebody unfriends you from Facebook, or if you stop following somebody on Twitter, your People app silently erases them without notice.

- ✔ In addition to collecting contact information, the People app collects your friends' latest updates from *all* of your linked social networks. When you visit the People app's What's New section, you can read everyone's updates from every network without your having to visit them all.

- ✔ You can still visit the websites of Facebook and other networks to read your friends' updates. You can also download the Facebook app and visit your friends' updates through the app. The People app simply provides yet another way to keep track of your friends' lives.

Sending and Receiving E-Mail

The Mail app does a no-frills job of sending and receiving e-mail. It's free, pre-installed, includes a spell checker, and, if you follow the steps in the previous section, it's already filled with the e-mail addresses of your friends.

In fact, you don't even need to open the Mail app to see what's new. The Mail app includes a *live* tile, meaning it constantly updates with the latest information. When you glance at the Start screen, your Mail tile behaves like a mini-billboard, displaying the first few lines of your unread e-mails and their senders' names.

The following sections explain how to open the Mail app, send and receive e-mail, switch between folders and accounts, and send and receive files to friends or co-workers.

Adding other e-mail accounts to Mail

The Mail app sends and receives e-mail only from the accounts listed in the Accounts pane described early in this chapter, which includes e-mail from Outlook.com, Exchange (used by some businesses), Google's Gmail, America Online, and Yahoo!.

If you want to access mail from other accounts, you can launch Internet Explorer with a tap of its Start screen tile. Then visit your mail server's website to send and receive e-mail online. This trick bypasses the Mail app, but it's an easy solution.

Owners of a Surface RT or Surface 2 can also use the built-in version of Outlook on the desktop, which handles POP accounts.

But if you'd rather stick with the Mail app for its finger-friendly interface, follow these steps to add unsupported e-mail accounts to the Mail app:

1. **Open Internet Explorer, visit Outlook (www.outlook.com), and either log in with your Microsoft account or sign up for an Outlook.com e-mail address.**

2. **Open Settings area on Outlook.com and then add your unsupported e-mail addresses.**

   On Outlook.com, click the Settings icon (the little gear) and choose More Mail

Settings from the drop-down menu. On the More Mail Settings page, find the setting for adding other e-mail accounts. There, you need to enter your unsupported mail account's username and password as well as its type of mail servers, which usually contain the cryptic words POP3 and SMTP. Save your changes.

3. **In the Mail app, select Outlook as your e-mail program and enter your Outlook e-mail addresses name and password.**

   Then, Outlook.com automatically grabs e-mail from your unsupported POP accounts and routes them to your Outlook.com account in the Mail app, letting you read everything in one place.

You can also call your ISP and ask when it plans to support IMAP. (IMAP is pronounced just like it sounds.) The Mail app works fine with IMAP accounts, sparing you from jumping through this sidebar's admittedly uncomfortable hoops.

Also, Surface RT and Surface 2 owners can also use the Outlook desktop program for their e-mail. Being more powerful than the Mail app, Outlook can handle POP and SMTP accounts. I explain how to add e-mail accounts to Outlook in Chapter 13.

Switching between the Mail app's accounts, folders, and e-mail

A tap on the Mail app's Start screen tile brings the Mail app to the screen, shown in Figure 9-3. Even if the Mail app is already running in the background, a tap on its Start screen tile brings it front and center.

Currently viewed e-mail account

Number of unread messages

Currently viewed folder

Contents of currently viewed folder

Contents of currently viewed e-mail

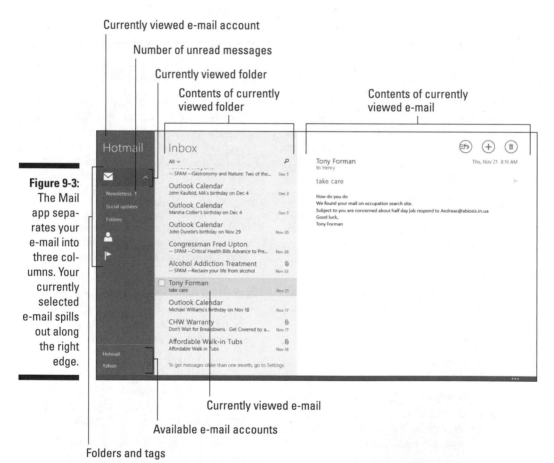

Figure 9-3:
The Mail app separates your e-mail into three columns. Your currently selected e-mail spills out along the right edge.

Currently viewed e-mail

Available e-mail accounts

Folders and tags

The Mail app splits the screen into three columns:

- **Left column:** The name of your currently viewed e-mail account appears in the top; that account's folders appear below its name. (You're currently viewing the highlighted folder.) At the column's bottom, you see names of any other e-mail accounts you've set up. To view mail from another account's mail, tap that account's name.

- ✔ **Middle column:** Tap a folder from the left column, and a list of that folder's e-mails appears in the middle column. There, you see the sender's name, the e-mail's arrival date, and the subject name.

- ✔ **Right column:** Tap an e-mail listed in the middle column, and its contents spill out in the right column.

To browse your mail, follow these two steps:

1. **From the left column, tap the account and then the folder you want to browse.**

   When you tap the folder, its contents appear in the middle column.

2. **From the middle column, tap the e-mail you want to read.**

   The message's contents spill out into the right column.

Can't read an e-mail's tiny letters? Then put two fingers on the screen to stretch or pinch it until it's the right size for your eyes.

Figure 9-3, for example, shows a Hotmail account in the left column. Beneath it, you see other available accounts, including one from Yahoo!. (If you set up only one account, you see only one account listed.)

The folders vary between e-mail accounts. If you've set up customized folders in Gmail, for example, those same customized folders appear in the Mail app. But every account always contains these basic folders:

- ✔ **Inbox:** When you open the Mail app or switch between accounts, you always see the contents of your *Inbox* — the holding tank for newly received messages. The Mail app only shows your last few weeks of messages; I show how to change that time frame in this chapter's sidebar, "Changing an account's settings."

- ✔ **Favorites:** Tap this area to see e-mail from people you've marked as Favorites in the People app. (I describe the People app in its own section, later in this chapter.)

- ✔ **Flagged:** To mark an e-mail for later attention, *flag* it: Slide your finger inward from the screen's top or bottom edge to fetch the App bar, and then tap the Flag icon. The Mail app stores flagged messages here for easy access.

Like all apps, the Mail app hides its menus. To reveal them, slide your finger inward from the screen's bottom or top edge. Slide up from the bottom, for example, and the App bar appears, with all the app's menus in tow. The App bar is *context-sensitive,* meaning it changes to show icons relevant to what you're currently viewing.

Changing an account's settings

Most e-mail accounts in the Mail app let you customize how they handle your mail. For example, most accounts contain hundreds if not thousands of e-mails. That's a *lot* of e-mail to sort through. To keep things simple and conserve storage space, the Mail app displays only a few weeks' worth of both sent and received e-mail.

To change that time frame — or to change the settings of any mail account — open the Mail app and follow these steps:

1. **Fetch the Charms bar by sliding your finger in from the screen's right edge and then tap the Settings icon.**

2. **When the Settings pane appears, tap Accounts. When the Accounts pane lists your e-mail accounts, tap the account you'd like to change.**

   The settings for your chosen account appear, ready for you to make your changes.

(To bring more of the Settings pane into view, slide your finger up or down the screen.)

3. **Tap in the area you'd like to change and then change the setting by tapping the adjacent toggle switch, tapping an item from a menu, or typing in words.**

   For example, to change the amount of downloaded mail, find the Download Email From drop-down menu. There, you can choose a time frame between three days and "any time," which downloads *all* of your mail. Your settings changes take place immediately; you don't need to tap a Save button.

To remove an account you no longer use, tap the Remove account button at the bottom of that account's Settings pane.

To close the Accounts pane, tap anywhere within the Mail app.

Composing and sending an e-mail

To write, spellcheck, and send an e-mail from your Surface's Mail app to a friend's Inbox, follow these steps:

1. **From the Start screen, tap the Mail app's tile and then tap the New icon in the program's top-right corner.**

   An empty New Message window appears, ready for you to fill with your words of glory. If you've set up several e-mail accounts in the Mail app, your e-mail will be sent from the account you last viewed.

   To send e-mail from a *different* e-mail account, delete that message by tapping the Delete icon (shaped like a trash can) in the screen's upper-right corner. Then switch to your desired account by tapping its name from the program's bottommost left corner. When your preferred account appears, tap the New icon to send an e-mail from that account instead.

2. **Add your friend's e-mail address into the To box.**

   Tap the word To next to the To box. The People app appears, letting you tap the name of everybody you want to receive the e-mail. Tap the Add button, and the Mail app automatically fills in everybody's e-mail address — a very handy thing on a tablet.

Or, you can tap inside the To box and type the recipient's name or e-mail address. With each letter you type, the Mail app scans the contacts listed in your People app, constantly placing potential matches below the To box. If the app happens to guess the right name, tap the name to place it in the To box.

3. **Tap inside the Subject box and type in a subject.**

Tap the words Add a Subject along the message's top; those words quickly vanish, letting you type your own subject, as shown at the top of Figure 9-4.

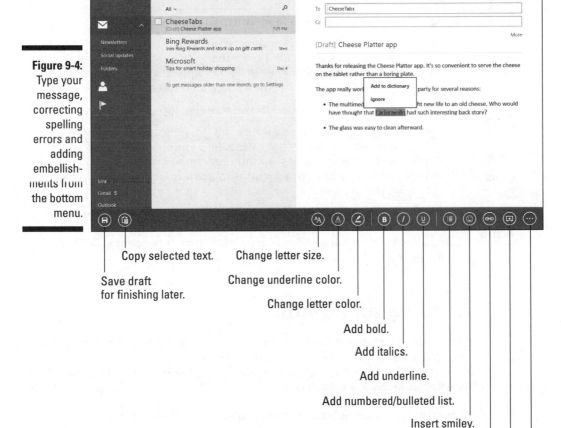

Figure 9-4: Type your message, correcting spelling errors and adding embellishments from the bottom menu.

Save draft for finishing later.

Copy selected text.

Change letter size.

Change underline color.

Change letter color.

Add bold.

Add italics.

Add underline.

Add numbered/bulleted list.

Insert smiley.

Insert hyperlink.

Edit in its own window.

Print/Sync with latest e-mails.

4. **Type your message into the large box beneath the Subject line.**

Head to Chapter 5 for typing tips for both the Surface's Type and Touch Cover keyboards, as well as the Surface's built-in keyboard. The Mail app watches as you type, automatically underlining words it doesn't recognize. To correct a misspelled word, tap the underlined word. A pop-up menu appears, as shown in Figure 9-4, letting you choose the correct spelling. (Choose Add to Dictionary to add a word that's unrecognized but correctly spelled.)

To embellish your prose, change the text's formatting by swiping your finger upward from the screen's bottom to fetch the App bar. Shown along the bottom of Figure 9-4, the App bar lets you change fonts, add italics, create numbered lists, and add other flourishes by tapping the appropriate icon.

5. **Attach any files or photos to your e-mail, if desired.**

I devote a section, "Sending and receiving files through e-mail," to this topic later in this chapter, but here's the gist: Tap the Attachments icon on the Mail app's App bar. The File Picker appears, letting you navigate to your file's location, tap the file's name, and tap the Attach button.

6. **Tap the Send button, located in the screen's top-right corner.**

The Mail app slides your e-mail through the Internet's blend of fiber-optics, radio waves, and copper wires into your friend's mailbox. Depending on the speed of your Internet connection, mail can arrive anywhere from within a few seconds to a few hours, with a minute or two being the average.

If you find yourself at a loss for words, slide your finger up from the screen's bottom edge and then tap the Save Draft button. The Mail app stashes your unfinished e-mail into your current account's Drafts folder for later polishing.

Reading an e-mail

Every time your Surface finds itself connected with the Internet, it automatically grabs any new e-mails it can find. Proud of its background work, the Mail app's Start screen tile updates itself, listing the sender, subject, and first line of your latest few e-mails.

To respond to a particularly enticing e-mail, follow these steps:

1. **Tap the Start screen's Mail tile.**

The Mail app appears, displaying the newest e-mail in your last-viewed account's Inbox, shown earlier in Figure 9-3. Below that, older e-mails appear, listed chronologically.

2. **Open a message by tapping its name.**

   The message's contents fill the window's right edge.

3. **Tap an option from the buttons along the e-mail's top edge:**

   - **Do nothing:** If the message doesn't warrant a response, move on to something more interesting by tapping a different message from the Mail app's middle column.

   - **Respond:** To reply to a message, tap the Respond button in the screen's top-right corner. When the menu drops down, tap Reply. A new e-mail appears, pre-addressed with the recipient's name and subject and containing the original message for you both to reference.

   - **Reply All:** When an e-mail arrives that's been addressed to several people, tap the Respond button but choose Reply All from the drop-down menu. That sends your response to *everybody* who received the original e-mail.

   - **Forward:** Choose Forward from the Respond button's drop-down menu to send a copy of your friend's must-see cute cat photo to your own friends.

   - **Delete:** To delete a message, tap the Delete icon. The message, having no place left to hide, vanishes.

You can print a message the same way you print from any other app: Open the message, fetch the Charms bar, tap the Devices icon, tap your printer from the list of devices, and tap the Print button.

Selecting e-mails and moving them to a folder

The Mail app seems incredibly frustrating when it comes to this simple task: How do you select several e-mails and move them to a different folder? However, when you know the trick, it's surprisingly easy: Select one e-mail by tapping on it. Then, tap the little box that appears along the mail's right edge. When you tap the box, a check mark appears inside, showing that the e-mail is selected. Plus, empty check boxes appear next to all of your other e-mails.

After the boxes appear, you can select more e-mails by tapping their boxes.

Select as many e-mails in a column as you want. When you select one e-mail, the Mail app's menu appears automatically along the bottom. Tap the Move icon, select a destination folder, and you're through.

You can even add a folder to the Mail app. Just slide your finger down from the top to fetch the App bar, tap Manage Folders from the bottom menu, and choose Create Folder or Create Subfolder from the pop-up menu.

Even though the Mail app gathers your e-mail, you can still view your e-mail from your mail service's website in Internet Explorer. Your same e-mails still appear in Gmail (`www.google.com/gmail`), for example, or Hotmail (`www.hotmail.com`).

To avoid hogging space on your Surface, many e-mail accounts display only your latest few weeks' worth of messages in the Mail app. After that deadline, the files scroll off your Surface's Mail app.

Sending and receiving files through e-mail

Files, referred to as *attachments* by computer linguists, can be tucked inside an e-mail message. You can send or receive nearly any file, but with a few stipulations:

✔ Most *mail servers* — the computers that process mail — can't handle files totaling more than 25MB. So, you can usually send a song or two, a handful of digital photos, and most documents. That's usually *not* enough to send videos, however.

✔ If you send a Microsoft Word file and the recipients don't have Microsoft Word, they won't be able to open or edit your file. To avoid confusion, let the recipient know what program you used.

With those two stipulations out of the way, plunge onward into the following sections, which explain how to open, save, and send attachments.

Viewing or saving a received attachment

When somebody attaches a file or two to your incoming e-mail, the Mail app lets you know with two signals:

✔ Messages bearing attachments include a tiny paperclip icon next to their subjects. (The paperclip appears in the Mail app's second column.)

✔ When you open an e-mail with an attachment, an icon appears, showing what's been attached. For example, an attached photo will appear as a thumbnail-sized preview icon; a PDF file will appear with the icon for the *Reader* app, which is your Surface's app for displaying PDF files.

To open or save the file or files attached to the e-mail you're reading, follow these steps:

1. Tap the icon representing the attached file.

If you just want to view the attached file (or play an attached song), tap the file's icon. If your Surface has an app or a program capable of opening the file, the file opens in a new window to the right of the Mail app, letting you see or listen to the attachment.

If your Surface can't open the attachment, it displays the message, "We Can't Open This File." If you see that message, write back to the sender, saying you can't open the file.

After you've seen or heard the file, you may be done and ready for different adventures. But if you want to save the file for later access on your Surface, give the attached file a more permanent home by moving to Step 2.

2. **Tap and hold the attached file's icon and tap Save or Download from the drop-down menu.**

   Windows's File Picker appears, shown in Figure 9-5. Covered in Chapter 4, the File Picker serves as the Start screen's equivalent of the desktop's File Explorer: It lets you shuttle files from one place to another.

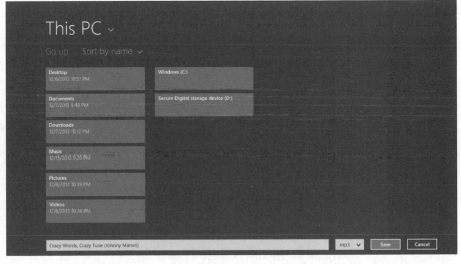

Figure 9-5: To save a file sent through e-mail, tap This PC, navigate to a location to save the file, and then tap the Save button.

3. **Choose a folder to receive the saved file.**

   Tap the word This PC in the File Picker's top-left corner, and a drop-down menu of your Surface's available storage areas appears. Depending on your Surface's connections, you may see any or all of these items: OneDrive, This PC, Libraries, Homegroup, and Network. Tap the name of the place you'd like to save the attached file.

   To store the file on one of your Surface's libraries, for example, choose Libraries or This PC from the drop-down menu. When the File Picker lists your Surface's available libraries, tap the name of the library where you'd like to store the file: Documents, Pictures, Music, or Videos.

   Don't know where to stash an attached file? Choose the Documents folder or library, which serves as a catch-all for anything that's not a photo, song, or movie.

4. **Tap the Save button in the File Picker's lower-right corner.**

   After you've chosen the file's destination, the File Picker places a copy of the e-mailed file in that location.

   Windows 8.1's built-in virus checker, Windows Defender, automatically scans your incoming e-mail for viruses, worms, and other malware.

- ✔ Even after you save the file to a folder, it remains stored in your e-mail. If you somehow lose your saved file, revisit the original e-mail and repeat these steps to save a fresh copy.

- ✔ If you need an attachment you received long ago, it's probably not lost forever, even if it's scrolled off the Mail app. Try visiting your e-mail's website. Some sites such as Outlook.com and Gmail let you access *all* your e-mails, no matter how old they are.

Sending a file as an attachment

Sending a file through the Mail app works just the opposite of saving an attached file, covered in the previous section. Instead of finding a place to save an e-mailed file, you're finding a file on your Surface and saving it inside an e-mail.

To send a file through the Mail app, follow these steps:

1. **Open the Mail app and tap the New icon (shown in the margin), as described earlier in this chapter's "Composing and sending an e-mail" section.**

   Choose the recipient and write your message.

2. **Tap the Attachments icon.**

   Tap the Attachments icon (shown in the margin), and the File Picker appears, shown earlier in Figure 9-5.

3. **Navigate to the file you'd like to send.**

   Tap the word This PC to see a drop-down menu listing popular storage areas: OneDrive, This PC, Homegroup, Libraries, and Network. To send a file stored on your Surface, tap This PC or Libraries.

   Tap any storage area's name to see a list of the files stored inside. Don't see the files you want? Tap the File Picker's Go Up link to retreat from that spot and try again with a different location.

   Keep tapping until you navigate to your file's location, usually stored in your Documents, Pictures, Music, or Videos folder.

4. **Tap the name of each file you want to send and then tap the Attach button.**

   A tap selects a file; tap a file again to deselect it. As you tap files, their color changes to show that they're selected.

I can't find an e-mail!

Instead of envelopes piling up on a table, e-mail now piles up in your Inbox. And, if you've set up several e-mail accounts, mail can be hiding in several different Inboxes. You can relocate a wayward e-mail in the Mail app, but it's not easy.

From within Windows Mail, tap the account holding the e-mail you want to search for. Then tap the Magnifying Glass icon near the upper-right corner of the Mail app's *middle* pane — the pane displaying the subject line of each message.

When the Search pane appears, type a word you recall seeing in your lost e-mail — even the person's name will do — and then press Enter; the Mail app fetches a list of e-mail containing that specific word.

At the time of this writing, the Mail app doesn't provide a way to search through all your e-mail accounts simultaneously. To search through *all* of your e-mail accounts, you must use the Search command on each individual account.

A tap of the Attach button returns to the Mail app and attaches the file or files to your e-mail.

5. **In the Mail app, tap the Send button.**

   The Mail app sends your mail and its attached file or files to the recipient. Depending on the size of your attached files, this may take from several seconds to several minutes. The Mail app does its work in the background, so feel free to switch to another app, browse the web, or grab another bagel at your free Wi-Fi spot.

Most e-mail providers won't send large attachments. You can usually send documents without a problem, as well as a handful of photos. But you won't be able to send anything bigger than small movie clips.

Managing Your Contacts in the People App

I explain in this chapter's first section how to link the People app with your online social networks. Your People app then stocks itself with your favorite people from Facebook, Twitter, LinkedIn, and other networks.

To see them, open the People app with a tap on its Start screen tile. The People app appears, shown in Figure 9-6, listing every friend grabbed from your online social networks. And, in keeping with the latest computing trend, People alphabetizes your contacts by their first names. Your friend Adam Zachman *finally* appears first.

Figure 9-6: Tapping different places on the People app lets you keep up with your contacts, including those pulled in from your social media accounts.

Your column   Your favorite contacts   All of your contacts

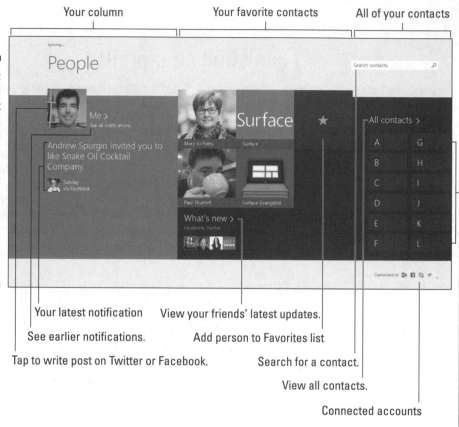

Your latest notification

See earlier notifications.

Tap to write post on Twitter or Facebook.

View your friends' latest updates.

Add person to Favorites list

Search for a contact.

View all contacts.

Connected accounts

Jump to contacts that begin with that letter.

The People app updates itself automatically, adding and dropping people as they enter or leave your social networks. It also lets you mark people as Favorites so their tiles appear front and center for easy access.

If you create an extraordinary cat photo, you can post it directly onto Twitter or Facebook by tapping your own entry in the People app and then filling out your personalized What's New section.

The People app's reliance on social networking comes with a downside, though. Friends who don't share their lives through a social network stay out of reach of the People app. Also, networks such as Facebook contain huge switchboxes full of privacy controls. Some of your friends may have flipped a Facebook switch that keeps their information sequestered in Facebook's walled garden, safely hidden from the People app.

The point? You eventually need to remove your gloves and manually add or edit entries in the People app. This section explains the details of a job that can't be sloughed off to the People app's robotic trawler.

To explore the People app, try these tips first:

✔ The People app's first column shows your profile photo and your notifications. The second column shows people you've marked as Favorites, making them easier to access with a tap on their profile photos. The third column displays only letters; tap a letter to jump to the contacts beginning with that letter.

✔ To post your Facebook status, tap your profile photo in the People app's upper-left corner. Then type your message in the What's On Your Mind box. (To send the message to Twitter, tap the Facebook link and choose Twitter from the drop-down menu.)

✔ To see everybody's latest updates from Facebook and Twitter, tap the What's New link in the bottom of the second column.

✔ Tapping your way through the People app's What's New section can lead you to friends, their adventures, and even the adventures of your friends' friends. If you're feeling lost in a sea of people, slide your finger up from the screen's bottom edge and tap the Home button. That takes you back to the front page.

Adding contacts to the People app

When somebody doesn't appear in your People app, you can add her in either of two ways:

✔ Using any computer, add the missing person to the contacts list of one of your online accounts, like Gmail (www.google.com/gmail) or Outlook (www.outlook.com). Befriending people on Facebook adds them to the People app, too, as does following them on Twitter. After a person appears in a social network or one of your linked online contact lists, the People app automatically pulls that person's shared details into your Surface.

✔ Manually type your contact's information into the People app. This isn't a one-way street, either; the People app adds your hand-typed information to the online account of your choice, too.

To type a new contact into the People app, follow these steps:

1. **Tap the Start screen's People tile to load the People app.**

2. **When the People app appears, make sure you're on the home page: Slide your finger up from the screen's bottom edge and tap the Home icon.**

3. **Slide your finger up slightly from the screen's bottom edge to fetch the App bar. Then tap the New icon.**

   Like many apps, the People app includes an App bar along both the top and bottom edges; the New icon lives alone on the bottom menu. A tap of the New icon reveals a blank New Contact form, as shown in Figure 9-7, ready for you to type your contact's details.

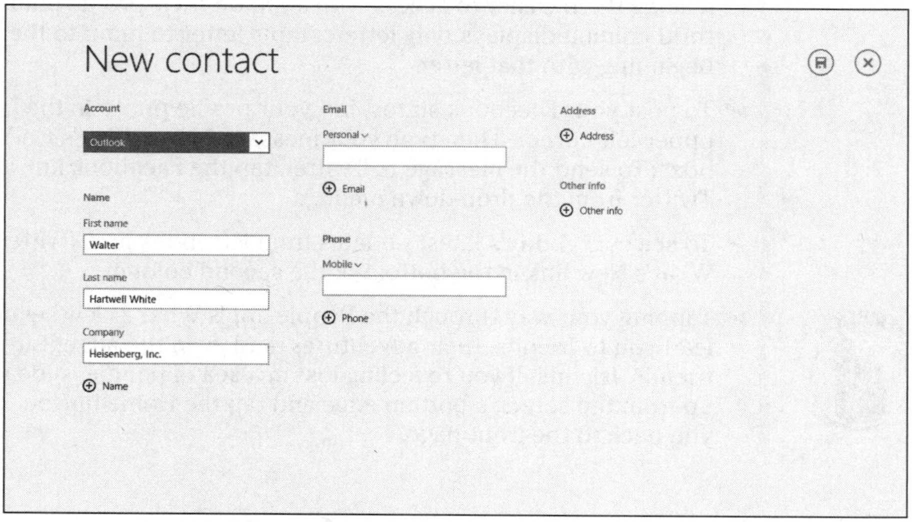

Figure 9-7:
Add your
new con-
tact's name
and any
other details
you have
on hand.
Then tap the
Save button
to add the
person to
your People
app.

New contact

Account	Email	Address
Outlook	Personal ⌄	⊕ Address
		Other info
Name	⊕ Email	⊕ Other info
First name		
Walter	**Phone**	
Last name	Mobile ⌄	
Hartwell White		
	⊕ Phone	
Company		
Heisenberg, Inc.		
⊕ Name		

4. **Fill out the New Contact form.**

   Type your contact's details, including name, address, e-mail, and phone. To add other information, tap the Other Info button. There, you can add tidbits such as a job title, website, significant other, or notes that don't fit anywhere else.

   If you've added more than one online account to your People app, you need to choose which account should receive the new contact's details. To choose the account, tap on the Account field in the top left corner. There, you can choose between Outlook.com or Live.com, among others. To add the contact to your Gmail contacts, you must add the information manually online at Google's Mail website (www.google.com/gmail).

5. **Tap the Save button.**

   The People app saves your new contact, both on your Surface and on the online account you chose in Step 3. Spot a typo? In the next section, I explain how to edit an existing contact.

Deleting or editing contacts

As our social and professional relationships change, the People app automatically takes care of the paperwork. When somebody unfriends you on Facebook, they simply drift off your People app without notice. Similarly, if you stop following somebody on Twitter, the People app trims them off your list.

But if you need to edit or delete a contact you've added manually, either on your Surface or on your Google or Microsoft accounts, it's fairly easy to do by following these steps:

1. **Tap the People tile on the Start screen.**

   The People app appears, as shown earlier in Figure 9-6.

2. **Tap the contact that needs changing.**

   Tap the first letter of their name, if necessary, to jump to your contacts beginning with that letter. When you tap the contact's profile photo, her contact page appears full-screen.

3. **Slide your finger up slightly from the screen's bottom edge to fetch the App bar.**

   The App bar appears as an icon-filled strip along the screen's bottom.

4. **To delete a contact, tap the Delete button. To update a contact's information, tap the Edit button and make your changes. Then tap the Save button to save your changes.**

   The Delete icon appears only for Contacts added to Live or Outlook accounts. Don't see a Delete icon? Then you need to drop by the social network that added the person, and delete her from there. The People app will update shortly afterward, wiping that person off your list.

   Tapping the Edit button (shown in the margin) returns you to the screen shown earlier in Figure 9-7. There, you can update or add information. Finished? Tap the Save button to save your changes.

You can send e-mail from within the People app by tapping a person's name. When her contact information appears, tap the Send E-Mail button. The Mail app appears, bearing a pre-addressed New Message window, ready for you to type your message and tap Send. (This trick works only if you have that contact's e-mail address.)

If the People app imported contacts from your Facebook or Twitter accounts, you can't delete any of their imported contact information. But you can *add* information to their contacts page, a handy trick for adding personal details that your friend hasn't posted on Facebook. Details you add don't go to Facebook, though. They remain on your Surface, as well as on the contact list that syncs with your Microsoft account.

Managing Appointments in Calendar

If you manage your appointments through Outlook.com, you're in luck: The Windows 8.1 Calendar app harvests that information automatically, just as it does with the People app. The Calendar app also picks up any birthdays it finds on Facebook.

Then it neatly packages your past, present, and future activity into the Calendar app, shown in Figure 9-8. (The app also cycles through your latest appointments on its Start screen tile.)

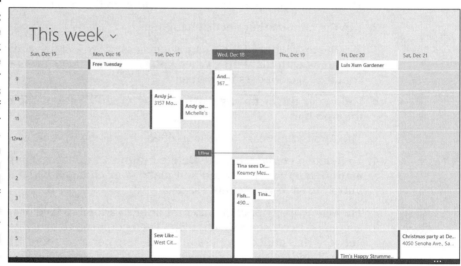

Figure 9-8: Shown here in Week view, the Calendar app stocks itself with your appointments, both those you entered yourself and those from your online social networks.

Don't keep your appointments online? Then you need to add them by hand. And even if your appointments *are* online, you occasionally need to edit old entries, add new ones, or delete ones that conflict with new engagements. This section explains how to keep your appointments up to date.

To add an appointment to your Calendar app, follow these steps:

1. **Tap the Calendar tile on the Start screen.**

   The Calendar appears, as shown earlier in Figure 9-8.

2. **Open the Apps bar and tap the New icon.**

   Slide your finger up from the screen's bottom edge to reveal the App bar and its icons, including the New icon for creating new appointments.

3. **Fill out the Details form.**

Shown in Figure 9-9, most of the choices are pretty easy to figure out: Enter the date, time, duration, location, and a *message* — notes about what to bring to the potluck.

The Calendar app sends your appointment to your online calendar, as well, if you have one. To see your options, tap the downward-pointing arrow next to Calendar in the top right. A menu appears, letting you choose which online calendar should receive the appointment.

Unfortunately, you won't see online calendars from Google or Apple; you're stuck with Microsoft's Live and Outlook.com calendars, as well as calendars on Exchange, a system used by some businesses.

Changed your mind about an appointment? Tap the back arrow in the screen's top-left corner and then choose Discard Changes from the drop-down menu.

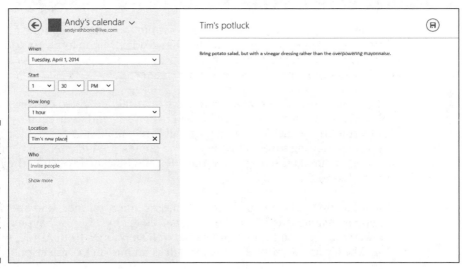

Figure 9-9: Add your appointment's date, start time, duration, and other details.

4. **Tap the Save button.**

The Calendar app adds your new appointment to your Surface's Calendar, as well as to the calendar of the online account you chose in Step 3.

When browsing the Calendar app, these tips help you find your way around:

✔ When in use, the Calendar opens to show the view it last displayed, be it day, week, or month. To switch to other views, slide your finger up from the screen's bottom edge to fetch the App bar. Then, tap one of the buttons: Day, Week, or Month.

✔ To delete an appointment, open it from the Calendar. Then tap the Delete button (shown in the margin) in the appointment's upper-right corner.

  ✔ To edit an appointment, open it with a tap on its entry in the Calendar app. Make your changes and then save your edits with a tap on the Save icon.

  ✔ When browsing the Calendar app, flip through the appointments by flipping your finger across the calendar as if you were paging through a book. Slide your finger to the left to move forward in time; slide it to the right to move backward.

  ✔ To jump immediately to the current date, slide your finger up from the bottom to fetch the App bar and then tap the Today button.

Talking with Friends through Skype

Skype began life in 2003 as a way for people to make free phone calls over the Internet, talking from one PC to another. Today, Skype lets you do more than talk: You can send instant messages and make free *video* calls — talking face to face — from one computer screen to another.

Of course, the computers need to have an attached video camera, microphone, and speaker before their owners can see and hear each other. Conveniently, your Surface includes all three, making it perfect for chatting or video-chatting through Skype. Skype comes pre-installed on every Surface model, including the original Surface RT and Surface Pro when they're upgraded to Windows 8.1.

Most laptops today include video cameras, microphones, and speakers, and Skype is available as a free download at www.skype.com. Skype runs just as well on iPads and other tablets, as well as phones from Apple, Android, Blackberry and Windows. It also requires an Internet connection.

This section describes how to set up Skype the first time, as well as how to use it to send messages to friends, call other friends on their computers and landlines, and, if you're feeling presentable, hold a video chat.

When owners of the original Surface and Surface Pro models upgrade to Windows 8.1, Skype appears, replacing the old Messenger app.

Setting up Skype for the first time

To run Skype for the first time on your Surface, follow these steps:

1. **Open the Start screen and tap the Skype tile or icon.**

   Don't see the Skype tile on your Start screen? Then slide your finger upward from the screen's middle to reveal the All Apps area. There, the Skype icon appears listed alphabetically, ready to launch with a tap of your finger.

2. **If asked, tap the Allow button to give Skype permission to use your webcam and microphone.**

   Apps always ask permission the first time they need to use your Surface's webcam, microphone, or location data. After you grant permission, the apps stop bothering you.

   If you download an app that shouldn't need access to your webcam or microphone, click the Block button instead. You may have downloaded a rogue app that's trying to do something malicious.

3. **Sign in with your Microsoft account if asked.**

   Skype, along with many other bundled apps, requires you to sign in with a Microsoft account.

4. **Tap the I'm New to Skype link, agree to the terms, and click Next. Or, if you already have a Skype account, tap the I Have a Skype Account link and move to Step 5.**

5. **Skype appears, shown in Figure 9-10, listing Skype-equipped names from your People app, as well as an account for testing your equipment.**

   If you already have a Skype account, Microsoft gives you the chance to merge it with your Microsoft account, bringing your existing Skype address book along with it. If you've added friends previously through the Windows 8 Messaging app, they appear here, as well.

   Even if you haven't added any Skype contacts, you'll see one listed: a test account named *Echo \ Sound Test Service*. Take note of the green dot next to its name. That green dot means that the account is online and available to be called. (When you add friends to Skype, the same green dot will appear next to the names of friends when they're online.)

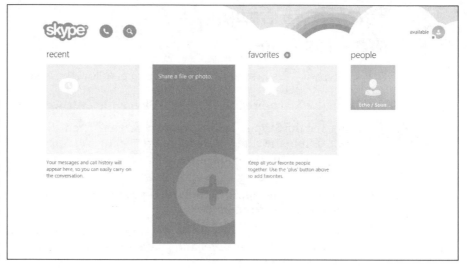

Figure 9-10:
Skype lets
you commu-
nicate with
your friends
using text,
conversa-
tion, or
video chats.

6. **Test your settings by tapping the Echo \ Sound Test Service account.**

   When you tap the Echo \ Sound Test Service account, the Skype Test
   screen appears, and a voice asks you to leave a message at the beep.
   Leave a test message in your normal speaking voice. After a moment, you
   hear another beep, followed by your recorded voice playing back to you.

   If you hear yourself clearly when your voice plays back, everything
   is fine. If you can't, something is wrong. Try testing the settings, as
   described in the rest of this section.

To test your Surface's Skype settings, fetch the Charms bar by sliding your
finger in from the screen's right edge. Tap the Charms bar's Settings icon, and
when the Settings Pane appears, tap Options. When the screen in Figure 9-11
appears, make sure these settings are correct:

   ✔ In the Audio section, choose Use Default Device from the Microphone
   drop-down menu. As you speak, watch the little bars next to the option
   rise and fall according to your voice level.

   ✔ Also in the Audio section, choose Use Default Device from the Speakers
   drop-down menu. To test the speakers, tap the little blue Play icon.
   You should hear a tone. If you don't hear a tone, try turning up your
   Surface's speakers using the Volume toggle on its upper-left corner.
   (I show you where to find the Volume toggle in Chapter 2.)

   ✔ In the Video section, make sure you can see your face in the test window.
   If you don't see it, tap the Camera drop-down menu and select the front-
   facing camera.

   ✔ If you still have trouble seeing or hearing yourself with Skype's test
   account, visit the Skype support site at www.skype.com.

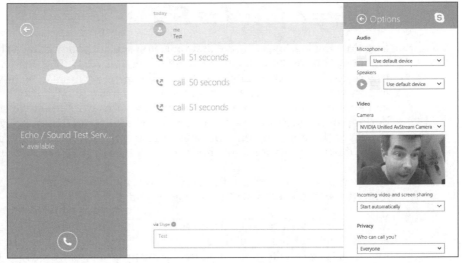

Figure 9-11:
The Options pane in Skype's settings panel lets you test your microphone, speakers, and camera.

What is Skype WiFi?

No doubt about it, Microsoft creates confusion with its product names. When one of its products takes off, Microsoft stamps that product's name on its other, less-successful, products. For example, Microsoft's Outlook, the e-mail program in its Office suite, became a huge success. So, Microsoft created *Outlook.com,* an online e-mail service that has nothing to do with the original Outlook program.

Microsoft's Xbox turned into a popular video game console. So, Microsoft renamed its old-and-struggling online music and movie stores with the new terms *Xbox Music* and *Xbox Video.*

Similarly, many people know Skype as a way to make computerized phone calls. So, Microsoft created *Skype WiFi,* a product that has nothing to do with Skype.

Instead, Skype WiFi is a *payment system.* When you pay up-front for Skype time, Microsoft lets you use that credit to pay for some third-party WiFi hotspots. However, not all Wi-Fi hotspots accept Skype WiFi payments, and the list of those that do constantly changes. Microsoft offers an online map at http://wifi.skype.com/maps.

If you ever try to log on to a Wi-Fi hotspot and see the words Pay with Skype WiFi, that simply means you can take some of the up-front money you've paid for Skype and hand it to the company running that particular Wi-Fi hotspot. There's one perk: Paying with Skype WiFi credits means you only pay for the *minutes* you use rather than being billed at longer durations.

Other than that, the two Skype products have nothing in common.

Adding a friend to Skype

If you're opening Skype for the first time, you see only one contact: the testing robot you encountered in the previous section. And, unfortunately, adding friends to Skype is one of its weak links: The Skype program currently can't import your Facebook or Messenger contacts. So, if you have a lot of messaging contacts and a Surface Pro or Surface Pro 2, try this workaround: Install Skype's desktop program from www.skype.com. More powerful than the Skype app, the Skype desktop program *can* import those contacts. And when it does, the Skype desktop program stuffs those contacts into the Skype app, as well.

Because adding contacts to the Skype app is awkward work, you have to jump through these hoops to add your friends.

Note: Before trying to add a friend to Skype, make sure she has a Skype account, and ask for the name she uses on Skype. That makes it easier to find her in Skype's directory and add her to the program.

1. **Open the Start screen and tap the Skype tile or icon.**

   Don't see the Skype tile on your Start screen? Then slide your finger upward from the screen's middle to reveal the All Apps area. There, the Skype icon appears listed alphabetically, ready to launch with a tap of your finger.

2. **In Skype, open the App bar and summon Skype's directory by tapping the Add Contact icon.**

   Slide your finger down from the screen's top edge to fetch the App bar, and tap the Add Contact icon.

3. **Search for your contact by her Skype name, real name, or e-mail address and then tap the Search icon.**

   If you don't find any matches, tap the Directory button to search Skype's global directory of Skype accounts.

4. **When the list of matching people appears, tap the name of the person you want to add.**

   The person's messaging window opens.

5. **Tap the Add to Contacts button, write a brief message, and tap the Send button.**

   Your brief introductory message lets your friend know that you're not a random creep indulging in random creepiness.

Then, you wait patiently until your friends approve your requests to be added to your Skype contacts. When they approve, they appear in your Skype's opening page with an icon letting you know whether they're online and available to accept voice or video chats.

Managing your contacts takes a little work, helped through these tips:

✔ If you open Skype to find a cherished friend sending you a contact request, tap the Accept button. If they're no longer a friend — or they're a random creep (yes, it happens) — tap the Decline button.

✔ If Skype's directory doesn't find your friends, e-mail them to ask for their "Skype Name." That makes them easier to find in the directory. Or, have them send *you* a contact request; accepting it places you both on each other's Skype lists.

 ✔ Each friend you add to Skype appears on the opening screen, ready to be called with a tap of his name. If your list of contacts grows unwieldy, add your favorite friends as, um, Favorites: Tap a favorite friend's name, open the App bar by sliding your finger up from the screen's bottom, and tap the Favorite icon. (Repeat the process to remove them should they fall from favored status.)

 ✔ If somebody falls to even lower-than-favored status, remove her *completely:* Open the Skype App bar and tap the Remove icon. When removed, the newly humbled person must repeat the same Request and Accept steps that originally placed her on your Skype list.

Calling a friend

The Skype app lets you talk with friends for free, provided you're communicating entirely through the Internet. That lets you communicate three ways: sending text messages, chatting by voice, or videochatting.

But no matter how you want to yak it up, talking to a friend through the Skype app starts when you follow these steps:

1. **Tap the name of the person you want to reach.**

   Open the Skype app, and you see your list of contacts added in the previous section. Contacts with a green dot next to their names are online and accepting calls. Tap the person's name, and his Conversation window appears.

2. **Choose how you'd like to contact the person.**

   Skype offers three ways, each designated by a different icon.

   • **Message:** To send the person a message, just start typing it in the Message box along the screen's bottom. If the recipient receives the message and responds, their response appears in the Conversation window. A simple "Are you there?" message often works best if you're not sure a friend is available.

Receiving a Skype call

Receiving a Skype call is easier than making one because you don't need to do any of the work. When somebody contacts you through Skype, a tile appears in the top-right corner of your currently viewed screen.

Not using your Surface at the time? You'll see a notification appear as soon as you sign in to your Surface. And, when you open Skype, you'll also see a list of anybody who tried to contact you while you were away.

If somebody sends you a message through Skype, the tile displays the message. Tap it to respond; Skype automatically appears for you to begin communicating. If the tile disappears before you can tap it, open Skype; you see the message waiting in the screen's left column. Tap the message to reciprocate, this time sending them a message.

If somebody sends you a voice or video call request, a tile also appears in your screen's top-right corner. This time, though, the tile offers three choices: Tap the tile's Video icon to start a video chat; tap the Voice icon to start a voice conversation; or, if it's an inopportune time, tap the Decline icon. If you Decline, the request will be waiting for you in the left column the next time you open the Skype app.

- **Video chat:** Tap the Video Chat icon to switch to a video stream, where you can see each other as you speak.

- **Voice call:** Tap the Call Now icon to begin talking, rather than typing, to each other.

3. **Wait for the person to respond.**

   If the person responds, Skype either displays his responding message, plays his voice, or fills the screen with his smiling face. If the person doesn't respond, nothing happens. But take heart that your message will remain in his Skype Recent column, so he can return your call with a tap of your name.

To end a call, first say goodbye, either by typing it out in a chat session or saying the words when talking or video conferencing. Then slide your finger down from the screen's top edge and tap Skype's Home button. Skype returns to its opening screen, ready for you to make a new call or to accept an incoming call or message. (Alternatively, you can close the app by sliding your finger all the way down the screen, from top to bottom.)

Calling a landline

The Skype app lets you make free voice calls from your Surface to another Surface, PC, or almost any other type of computer gadget. But if you want to call a *real* telephone number — a landline or cell phone — you need to pay with *real* money. That's where Skype Credits come in. You buy them in advance and then use them on a per-minute basis as you talk to somebody on their landline.

The first time you try to dial a real phone number, Microsoft offers you a chance to buy Skype Credits. But before paying up, take advantage of the free one-year Skype subscription that came with your Surface 2 or Surface Pro 2. (I describe how to do that in Chapter 3.)

To dial a real phone number with Skype, follow these steps:

1. **Start Skype with a tap on its Start screen tile.**

2. **Tap the New Call icon in the screen's upper-left corner; when the numeric keypad appears, tap in the number you want to call.**

   If you're calling somebody in a country other than your own, first choose that country from the drop-down list above the keypad.

After you dial the number, the experience is much like a "real" phone. You hear the sound of the other phone ringing, and then you hear either the happy voice of your friend or the robotic voice of her answering machine.

Part III
Play

Visit www.dummies.com/extras/surface for a step-by-step tutorial on how to play songs from a flash drive inserted into your Surface's USB port.

In this part . . .

- ✔ Discover the fun of using your Surface's built-in apps for viewing photos and movies.

- ✔ Enjoy listening to your own music.

- ✔ Find out how to purchase music or videos through Microsoft's built-in Xbox music store.

- ✔ Download new apps from the Windows Store.

Chapter 10

Photos and Movies

. . . .

. . . .

*E*very Surface tablet includes two cameras: one on its front side and the other on its back. However, your Surface doesn't make for a very satisfying camera. There's no viewfinder, and screen reflections make it hard to aim at your subject. Forget about taking flash photos or zooming in. And face it, everybody looks pretty dorky when taking a picture with a tablet. Your ever-present smartphone probably takes better-quality photos.

No, your Surface shines when *displaying* photos and videos, and this chapter walks you through doing both. (I describe how to use your Surface's built-in cameras for holding video chats with friends in Skype in Chapter 9.)

Note: Need to import photos from your digital camera or cell phone? I explain how in Chapter 6.

Snapping Photos or Videos

Your Surface displays photos much better than it can capture them. Most Surface models include a miserly 1.2-megapixel cameras. Only the Surface 2 ups the game slightly to a 5-megapixel rear camera. By comparison, the Samsung Galaxy S4 smartphone offers a whopping 13-megapixel rear camera.

But if you're struck with a Kodak moment and your Surface is the only camera you have handy, follow these steps to snap a quick photo or movie:

1. From the Start menu, tap the Camera app's tile.

The Camera app appears, shown in Figure 10-1, immediately filling the screen with what it sees before its lens. (Your Surface remembers whether you last shot with the *front* or *rear* camera, and it uses that camera accordingly.)

Note how a light begins glowing next to the lens currently in use, letting you and your subject know what's being filmed.

Folding back your Surface's Touch or Type Cover blocks the bottom half of the rear camera's lens. Remove the keyboard cover before snapping a photo.

Figure 10-1:
Touch any part of the screen to snap the photo.

2. Change the camera's controls, if desired.

The Camera app always displays the first three controls in the following list; you see the other four only when you open the App bar by sliding your finger up from the screen's bottom edge:

- **Take video:** Tap this to begin shooting video rather than snapping a still photo.

- **Take photo:** Tap this to snap a photo. (Or, if you're already in Photo mode rather than Video mode, you can take a photo by tapping anywhere on the screen.)

- **Take panorama:** An oddity, this feature stitches together a 360-degree panoramic photo of your surroundings — front, sides, rear, up, and down — as you slowly move your Surface in all directions.

- **Camera Roll:** Found on the App bar, this lets you view previously snapped photos.

- **Change Camera:** Tap this App bar icon to toggle between your Surface's front- and rear-facing cameras.

- **Timer:** Tap this App bar icon to toggle between a three- or ten-second delay. (That delay gives you time to jump in front of the lens and smile.) Tap the icon a third time to turn off the shutter delay.

- **Exposure:** This App bar icon brings a sliding bar to the screen to manually adjust the light levels.

3. **To snap a photo or begin shooting a movie, touch the screen.**

   When you're shooting a photo, the Camera app emits a mechanical shutter click sound and then quickly saves the snapshot. Your newly saved snapshot quickly scoots out of sight to the screen's left edge, letting you snap another photo.

   When you're shooting videos, a timer appears in the screen's lower-left corner to show your movie's current length. To stop shooting the movie, tap the Stop Video icon along the screen's right edge.

Your photos and videos both live in your Picture library's Camera Roll folder, where they can be viewed with the Photos app, described in the next two sections.

These tips help you explore the Camera app for the first time:

- ✔ To view your newly shot photo or movie, slide your finger across the screen from left to right to drag your last-shot photo (or the first frame of your movie) back into view. To return to shooting, slide your finger in the other direction, and the live view reappears.

- ✔ Need to take a picture in a hurry? Turn on your Surface, and at the Lock screen, slide your finger *downward* on the screen rather than upward. If you're already signed in, the Camera app quickly appears, letting you snap your photo without stopping to unlock the screen and type your password.

- ✔ When shooting in Panorama mode, pretend your Surface is mounted on a tripod. As you hold it, keep it level and then slowly rotate and tilt it, moving so it eventually points in all directions. If the Camera app says you've moved too far or too fast, slow down, and point the Surface back to the previous location.

Why are my Surface's photos stored on OneDrive?

In the past, your photos always stayed inside your camera until you removed them. For many years, that same logic held true when you took pictures with your cell phone or even with your computer's webcam.

Now, your Surface and some smartphones change that basic rule of photography. Unless you chose otherwise when first setting up your user account on your Surface, the photos you snap on your Surface are automatically copied to OneDrive. This copying affects you several ways:

- The process takes place in the background so transparently that you probably won't notice.

- If your Surface isn't connected to the Internet when you snap a photo, your Surface uploads the photo the next time you connect with the Internet.

- Your Surface sends *low-resolution* photos to OneDrive. That means they're fine for viewing onscreen, but not good enough to make the best prints.

- Your original, full-quality photos remain on your Surface, where you can view them and show them to friends, even without an Internet connection. (If you want to print them, print your *Surface's* photos rather their lower-resolution versions on OneDrive.)

- You can view or share your photos on OneDrive from *any* Internet-connected device, even when your Surface is nowhere in sight. Because they're low-resolution, they're also easy to download and view quickly on smartphones.

- You can send your friends a link to your OneDrive photos, making it easy for them to view them.

- Keeping copies on OneDrive is generally a good thing. It gives you an automatic backup in case you lose the originals. Also, your OneDrive photos can be viewed from any of your gadgets, including your phone, which makes your photos easier to show to friends.

If you want to keep your photos *away* from OneDrive, follow these steps:

1. **From any screen, fetch the Charms bar by sliding your finger in from the screen's right edge. Then tap the Settings icon.**

2. **Tap the PC Settings link at the bottom of the Settings pane.**

3. **When the PC Settings screen appears, tap the OneDrive link from the right column.**

4. **When the OneDrive settings screen appears, tap the Camera Roll link in the left column.**

5. **Tap the Don't Upload Photos button to keep your photos from appearing on OneDrive. Your changes take place immediately.**

An adjacent button lets you choose to Upload Photos at Best Quality, which keeps a copy of your original photos both on your Surface and OneDrive. Choose this option *only* if you plan to make prints from your OneDrive photos. Otherwise, stick with the low-resolution photos so you can show them off on your phone without worrying about using up your data plan.

To send a copy of your videos to OneDrive, as well, tap the adjacent toggle named Automatically Upload Videos to OneDrive.

Viewing Photos

As soon as you add a few photos to your Surface, the Photos app begins displaying them even without being told. That's because the Photos tile on the Start screen is a *live* tile: When you open the Start screen, the Photos tile automatically cycles through your photos in a mini-slideshow.

Note: Desktop fans can view their photos by opening the Start screen's Desktop app, opening File Manager, tapping This PC in File Manager's left pane, and tapping the Pictures folder.

To view your photos as more than thumbnail-sized previews, open the Photos app with a tap of its Start screen tile, and the results appear, as shown in Figure 10-2.

When first opened, the Photos app displays your Surface's folders along the left edge, and your photos along the right.

Toggle between Thumbnail view (shown) and Details view.

Toggle between viewing photos on OneDrive or your Pictures library.

Tap a photo to view it.

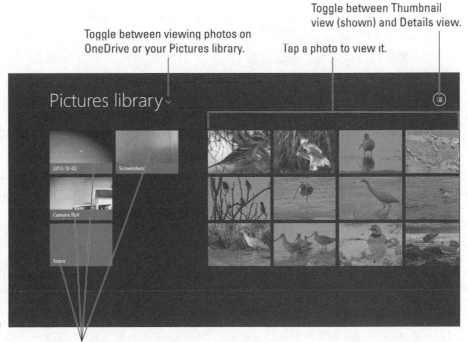

Figure 10-2: The Photos app shows photos stored on your Surface, as well as on OneDrive, Microsoft's online storage service.

Tap a folder to view its contents.

The Photos app shows a tile for each folder, and each folder usually shows a preview of a photo stored inside. Oddly enough, the folder's name helps explain the photos' source:

- **Date:** Folders named after a particular date usually contain photos imported from a point-and-shoot camera on that particular day. (I describe how to copy photos from your camera into your Surface in Chapter 6.)

- **Camera Roll:** Photos and videos taken with your Surface's built-in cameras always end up in the Camera Roll folder. A photo named WIN_2014122_215505 means it was taken in 2014 on January 22 at 9:55 pm and 5 seconds.

- **Screenshots:** Look in here to see *screenshots,* which are images you've copied from your Surface's screen. (To take a screenshot, press the Volume Down toggle switch while pressing the Windows key below your Surface's screen.)

- **Scans:** If you connect a scanner to your Surface, the Scanner app stores your scans in this folder.

Follow these steps to view the photos, scans, or screenshots stored in your Surface's Pictures folder or OneDrive:

1. **Open the Photos app.**

   If the Photos app doesn't resemble the icon in the margin, then its tile is probably displaying one of your photos. When opened, the Photos app shows folders and photos stored in your Surface's Pictures folder.

2. **Navigate to the folder you'd like to open.**

   Tap a folder, and it opens to display its contents.

   To back out of any folder, tap the backward-pointing arrow in the upper-left corner. Keep tapping the arrow, and you'll eventually return to the Photos app opening menu, shown earlier in Figure 10-2.

   To browse photos stored on your OneDrive account, tap the words Pictures Library in the screen's upper-left corner, and choose OneDrive from the drop-down menu. (To return to the Pictures library, reverse the steps: Tap the word OneDrive, but choose Pictures Library from the drop-down menu.)

3. **Tap a photo to view it full screen.**

   When you tap a photo, it fills the screen. Pinch or stretch the photo between your fingers to zoom in or out. To see its menus, shown in Figure 10-3, slide your finger up from the screen's bottom edge.

   To back out of a photo, tap it; then tap the Back arrow icon that appears in its upper-right corner.

Figure 10-3:
The Photos app lets you zoom in and out of photos with your fingertips and watch slide shows.

The Photos app's App bar displays different buttons depending on what you're viewing. For example, the App bar offers these buttons when you're viewing a single fullscreen photo or movie:

- **Delete:** Delete your currently viewed photo or movie and then view the next one.

- **Open With:** Tap this, and a pop-up menu lets you choose which program should open the photo for viewing or editing. It's a handy way to tell a desktop program to open your photo, for example.

- **Set As:** Tap this to fetch a pop-up menu; there, you can turn your currently viewed photo into the background for your Surface's Lock screen or a current background for the Photos app's tile.

- **Slide Show:** A handy way to show off photos, tapping this button · launches a slideshow of every photo or movie in the currently viewed folder. To stop the show, tap anywhere on the screen.

- **Rotate:** This rotates the picture but only *clockwise* (to the right). So, tap it *twice* to correct an upside-down photo. Tap it three times to rotate the photo to the *left*.

- **Crop:** Tap this when viewing a photo, and a rectangle overlays itself across your photo. Drag the entire rectangle or just its corners to frame a different portion of the photo. Tap the Apply button to crop, and the app saves your crop as a new picture with a different name, preserving the original photo.

When you tap the Crop button, an optional Aspect Ratio button appears. Tap it to see a pop-up menu with options for cropping your photo to match common print sizes such as 4x3, 5x7, 8x10, square, and others. (The menu's Lock Screen option lets you crop the best portion of your photo to fit perfectly on your Surface's Lock screen.)

✔ **Edit:** Tap this to enter Editing mode, where you can change the photo's lighting, color, or add special effects. (For quick results, tap the AutoFix button and then tweak the edits at that point.)

✔ **Trim:** Tap this when viewing a movie, and a circle appears at each end of the video's timeline, shown along the screen's bottom. Drag the circles along the timeline to mark the video's new starting and stopping points. Then tap OK to save your newly trimmed video.

When you first open or return to the Photos app, the App bar changes yet again to offer these helpful buttons:

✔ **Select All:** This selects all of the currently shown folders and photos for later action, including Delete, Share, or Print. (If tapped by mistake, tap the App bar's Clear Selection button to return the selected items to normal.)

✔ **New Folder:** Tap this to create a new folder, handy for categorizing photos according to subject.

✔ **Import:** Tap the Import button to import photos from an attached camera or your memory card, as I describe in Chapter 6.

The Photos app shows only photos stored on your Surface or OneDrive. It's not smart enough to show photos stored on network locations. To see those, open the Desktop app and open File Explorer, covered in Chapter 12. There, you can navigate to any location available to your Surface. Tap a photo, and the Photos app reappears, ready to show off the photos in that location.

Sharing or Printing Photos

Photos and videos aren't much fun when they sit alone on your Surface. No, your cat photos are more fun when your friends can see your beloved feline, as well. The Photos app lets you share or print photos and videos by following these steps:

1. **Open the folder containing your photos or videos and then select the videos or photos you want to share or print.**

   To select individual photos, videos, and folders, slide your finger downward on their tiles. As you select them with a short downward swipe, the tiles sprout check marks in their upper-right corners.

   Or, to select *all* the folders and photos currently displayed in the Photos app, tap the Select All icon from the App bar.

2. **Visit the Charms bar and choose Share or Devices.**

Swipe your finger inward from the screen's right edge to fetch the Charms bar and then tap either Share (for sharing with friends) or Devices (for printing your images).

- **Share:** The Share pane opens, listing every app able to share your photo or video. A tap of the Mail app, for example, opens the Mail pane, where you enter the recipient's e-mail address and tap the Send button. (I cover mailing attached files in Chapter 9.) If your social network doesn't yet have an app, visit the site through Internet Explorer to share the photo.

- **Devices:** When the Devices pane appears, tap Print to see your installed printers. Tap your printer's name, and the Printer window appears, offering you a preview of the printed page. (I explain how to print, as well as how to connect a printer to your Surface, in Chapter 6.)

Watching Movies

More a shopping mall than an app, Microsoft designed the Video app to pull you into its two storefronts: The movies section entices you to buy or rent movies, and the television section adds the hook for TV shows, both past and present.

Be sure to use the Video app only when you're logged in with a Microsoft account, and your wallet will always be available. You also need a strong Wi-Fi connection for downloading or streaming videos.

Watching your *own* movies

For some reason, the Video app doesn't list movies you've shot with your Surface's built-in Camera app. To play those movies in the Video app, slide your finger up from the Video app screen's bottom edge to reveal the App bar. Tap the Open File icon and then use the File Picker, covered in Chapter 4, to navigate to the videos in your Pictures library's Camera Roll folder.

The Surface works with videos encoded in WMV (Windows Media Video) or H.264/MP4 movie formats. The Video app doesn't support other video formats, like TV shows recorded by Windows Media Center or TiVo. If your movies are encoded in another format, you need a conversion program to copy them into MP4 format.

Or, if you own a Surface Pro or Surface Pro 2, you can upgrade your Desktop app to Windows Media Center. It's a $10 upgrade that lets you watch any show recorded with Windows Media Center; I explain how to upgrade in the sidebar in Chapter 12.

To open the Video app and browse its wares, follow these steps:

1. **From the Start screen, tap the Video tile.**

   The Video app appears, shown in Figure 10-4. The Video app immediately confuses things by changing its name to *Xbox Video*. That's because the Video app lets you play videos to your Xbox game console, if you have one, so you can watch your movies on the big screen.

Figure 10-4: The Video app lets you watch your own videos, as well as rent or buy movies and TV shows.

2. **Browse to the type of video you want to watch.**

   The Video app sprawls horizontally across your screen. If offers four main sections, most of which hide beyond the screen's left and right edges:

   • **Home:** When first opened, Xbox Video shows this screen that lists currently popular shows and movies.

   • **Personal Videos:** Scroll to the left of the opening Home screen to see the hidden area that shows any videos living in your Surface's Videos library. (That area also contains videos you've purchased or downloaded from the Video app.)

   • **My TV/My Movies:** Next to your Personal Videos section, the app lists TV shows or movies you've purchased previously from Xbox Video.

   • **Recommendations:** If you've purchased or rented other movies, Xbox Video lists similar movies here.

- **New Movies/Featured Movies:** Head here for the latest releases so you can catch up on movies you've missed on the big screen.

- **New TV Shows/Featured TV Shows:** Similar to the previous category, this lets you watch the TV shows everybody was talking about at the water cooler last week.

3. **Tap a video's tile to see more about it.**

   As you browse the categories, tap any tile to browse trailers and to buy or rent movies and TV shows. (Some shows offer a free episode, usually a season opener.)

   Other buttons let you buy the video, see more about it, watch its trailer, or in the case of TV shows, buy a discounted season package or individual episodes.

   Most shows come in both high-definition video (more expensive) and standard-definition video (usually discounted by about 30 percent).

4. **Watch a video.**

   Tap a movie or TV show tile from the storefronts to rent, buy, or download the video to your My Videos section. The app charges the credit card associated with your Microsoft account, or prompts you to set one up.

   As you watch a video, slide your finger up from the screen's bottom to expose buttons for pausing, playing, and skipping forward/backward. The Play To button lets you play the video through your Xbox game console if you have one.

Before diving into the Video app with your credit card, keep these tips in mind:

- ✔ When starting with the Video app, view free things at first to familiarize yourself with the app's mechanics. The Video app often offers free TV pilots, free movie trailers, and behind-the-scenes promo videos.

- ✔ Can't find a particular item? Tap the Search box in the app's upper-right corner, type a keyword, and press Enter. The Video app lists all matching videos.

- ✔ Rental items and some specials are time-dated, meaning they'll disappear from your Videos library after a certain date. Read the fine print so you know exactly what you're buying and how long you have to watch it.

- ✔ If you'll be traveling, look for items with a Download option. After these items are downloaded, you can watch them when you're out of range of a Wi-Fi connection. (Again, read the fine print because even some downloaded videos will expire after a certain time.)

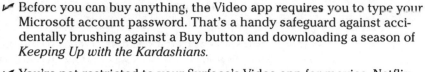

✔ Before you can buy anything, the Video app requires you to type your Microsoft account password. That's a handy safeguard against accidentally brushing against a Buy button and downloading a season of *Keeping Up with the Kardashians.*

✔ You're not restricted to your Surface's Video app for movies. Netflix offers a free app for watching streaming movies, and you can watch Amazon's instant videos, as well. (Amazon hasn't released an instant video app at the time of this writing, but you can still watch Amazon's videos through your web browser.)

Chapter 11

Listening to Music

. . . .

. . . .

Some people spend more time organizing their music than listening to it. They store each album in its own folder and meticulously rename each song's title to include the album name and recording year.

Your Surface, however, isn't built for micromanaging your songs. No, like any tablet, your Surface works best for *playing* music, and the Music app tries to simplify that task by letting you listen to music in any of three ways: You can play music that's already on your Surface, listen to music on Microsoft's streaming music service, and buy new songs and albums through Microsoft's music store.

This chapter covers all three ways to move music from your Surface into your ears.

Understanding the Music App

When you first open the Music app, shown in Figure 11-1, the opening screen's left side highlights the app's three main features:

✓ **Collection:** Tap here to view and play music already stored on your Surface.

✓ **Radio:** Tap this to listen to music from Microsoft's free or paid streaming music services.

✓ **Explore:** Tap Explore to browse the bins at Microsoft's online shop for buying songs or albums.

Buy music.

Listen to streaming music.

See your own music.

Search for music in your collection
in Microsoft's catalog.

Close column for fullscreen view.

Sign in with Microsoft account, if asked.

Figure 11-1:
The Music
app lets you
play music
stored
on your
Surface,
listen to
stream-
ing music,
and buy
music from
Microsoft's
music store.

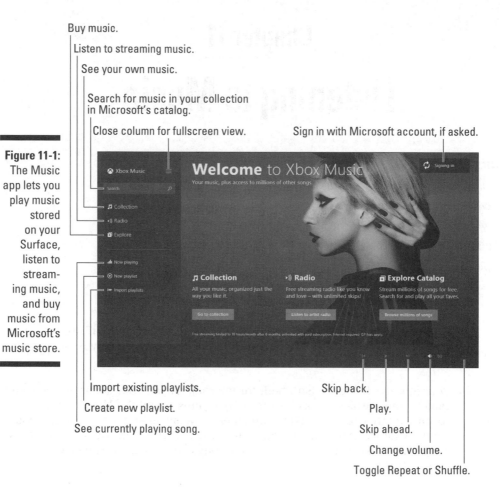

Import existing playlists.

Create new playlist.

See currently playing song.

Skip back.

Play.

Skip ahead.

Change volume.

Toggle Repeat or Shuffle.

The Music app's opening screen will change when you begin listening to
music, but the column along the app's right edge always provides access to
those three core areas.

The rest of this chapter explains how to get the most out of each category.

 If the Music app's right column shrinks, tap the three green lines near its top,
shown earlier in Figure 11-1. That icon serves as a toggle to open or collapse
the column, leaving more space to view your music.

Don't mess with my metadata

Music players, including the Music app, rarely look at your songs' *filenames*. Instead, players read each file's *metadata* — information stored inside the files that contains the name of the song, artist, album, recording date, genre, and other information.

When the Music app begins adding your music, the app visits the Internet to identify your song and examine its metadata. The app fills in empty spots, corrects misspellings, adds cover art, and performs other mostly hidden touches.

Most people enjoy the Music app's background work. Others, particularly those who spend a lot of time manually editing their songs' metadata, view it as meddling. In fact, sometimes the Music app makes mistakes.

If you don't want the Music app to mess with your songs' metadata, tell it to stop by following these steps *before* you import your music:

1. **Open the Music app, fetch the Charms bar, tap the Settings icon, and tap Preferences from the Settings pane.**

2. **In the Preferences pane's Media Info section, tap the toggle called Automatically Retrieve and Update Album Art and Metadata.**

That keeps Microsoft from comparing your music to its vast database and changing your songs' metadata to match its own.

The Music app doesn't provide any way to edit metadata, but you can edit it from the Desktop app's File Explorer: Right-click the file you want to edit, choose Properties from the pop up menu, and click the Details tab.

Listing to Your Own Music

The Music app would make a poor student because it rarely finishes a task to completion. For example, when first loaded, the app searches your Surface's Music folder to add your music. However, it doesn't bother to search any memory cards or drives attached to your Surface.

Even when told to play your own music, the app lapses into a salesman role, trying to convince you to buy songs or subscribe to Microsoft's pay services.

The following sections explain how to quiet the Music app's built-in salesman and instead concentrate on playing music already on your Surface.

Adding your own music to the Music app

To start listening to your own music, tap the Collection button from the Music app's right edge, shown earlier in Figure 11-1. The Music app takes a quick dive into the Music library on your Surface, and displays the results, shown in Figure 11-2.

Figure 11-2:
Unless told otherwise, the Music app searches only your Surface's Music library for your music.

If you store all of your music in your Surface's Music library, you're fine: All of your music will appear in your Collection folder.

Chances are good, though, that you may keep your music in other locations. For example, to conserve your Surface's meager storage space, you may store music on a memory card tucked into your Surface's memory card slot. (I explain how to expand your Surface's storage with memory cards in Chapter 6.)

You may also store music in other places, such as OneDrive, a flash drive, or perhaps on a home network.

The Music app won't find *any* of that music until you tell it exactly where to look by following these steps:

1. **Open the Music app and tell it where to look for your music files.**

   If the opening screen says, "If you're not seeing your music, tap to change where we look," then tap that message. The screen shown in Figure 11-3 appears.

   If the Music app's opening screen *doesn't* offer to find your music, add your songs this way: Open the Charms bar by sliding your finger in from the screen's right edge. Then tap the Settings icon, tap Preferences from the Settings Pane, and tap the Preferences link called Choose Where We Look for Music on This PC.

   No matter which of the two routes you take, the Music app screen looks like Figure 11-3, where it lists the folders currently monitored by the Music app.

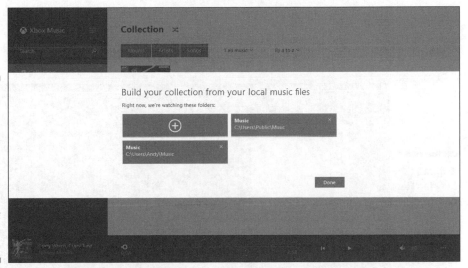

Figure 11-3:
The Music app lists the two folders it searches for music; tap the plus sign icon to add other places to the list.

2. **Tap the plus sign icon to bring the File Picker to the screen. Then use the File Picker to navigate to a folder holding your music. Finally, tap the Add This Folder to Music button. Repeat to add other folders.**

The File Picker lists your currently viewed storage area in the screen's top-left corner; tap that area to see a drop-down menu listing all of your Surface's storage areas, as shown in Figure 11-4.

For example, to add a folder called *Music* on OneDrive, tap the currently listed storage area listed in the File Picker's upper-left corner. When the drop-down menu appears, as shown earlier in Figure 11-4, choose OneDrive. When the File Picker lists your folders on OneDrive, tap the Music tile. Then tap the Add This Folder to Music button from the screen's bottom-right corner.

Or, to add a Music folder on your Surface's memory card, tap the currently listed storage area in the File Picker's top-left corner and then choose This PC from the drop-down menu. Then tap the Secure Digital Storage Device (D:), which is Microsoft's odd name for your memory card. Tap your memory card's Music folder, then tap the Add This Folder to Music button.

As you add folders, they appear listed in a row beneath the File Picker, ready to be added.

Tap here to see the drop-down menu.

Tap a storage area to view its contents.

Tap a folder to view its contents.

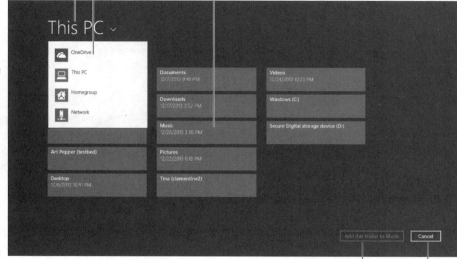

Figure 11-4:
Tap File
Picker's
current stor-
age area
and choose
your desired
storage
area from
the drop-
down menu.

Tap to add currently displayed
files and folders to Music app.

Tap to cancel and return to Music app.

3. **Tap the OK button to add the selected folders to the Music app, and then click the Done button to close the window shown earlier in Figure 11-4.**

   Tap the OK button in the File Picker's lower-right corner to add your chosen folder or folders to the Music app.

   The screen shown earlier in Figure 11-3 reappears, displaying your newly added folder or folders. Tap Done to close the screen and return to the Music app.

When you return to the Music app, it lists your newly added music.

✔ To remove a folder from the Music app's catalog, follow the preceding Step 1. When Figure 11-3 appears (shown earlier), tap the X in the upper-right corner of the folder you want to remove. (That doesn't delete the folder; it just tells the Music app to ignore it.)

✔ If you're a Windows desktop person, take note that the Music app catalogs all the music stored in your Desktop app's Music library. So, a simple way to add songs to the Music App is to place those folders in your Music library, a task I cover in Chapter 12.

✔ The Music app may display unexpectedly different artwork for your music. That's because the app grabs the artwork from the Internet along with other bits of metadata. I explain more about the Music app's reliance on metadata in the sidebar, "Don't mess with my metadata."

Playing your music in the Music app

After you've stocked the Music app with your own music, as I describe in the previous section, the app plays it fairly predictably.

When looking at your collection, shown in Figure 11-5, you can choose to display your music by Albums, Artists, or Songs by tapping those three labeled buttons along the app's top edge.

To move up or down the list of displayed music, slide your finger up or down the list. When you spot the album, artist, or song you want to hear, follow these steps:

1. **Tap the album artist or song you want to hear.**

   The Music app works a little differently depending on what you've tapped:

   • **Album:** The Music app displays a list of songs on the album.

   • **Artist:** The app displays a list of albums you own from that artist, followed by a list of that artist's albums and popular songs you can buy.

   • **Name:** Every song in your collection appears, sorted by the order you choose from the drop-down list at the top, shown in Figure 11-5.

    To back out of a list, tap the Back arrow in the screen's upper-left corner.

2. **Tap the Play button to listen to your selected music. Control the music's playback by tapping the buttons on the strip along the app's bottom.**

   The Music app always shows familiar control buttons along the bottom edge. Shown earlier in Figure 11-5, they let you skip forward or back, stop, and play your currently selected song.

Display music by album (shown).

Display music by artist.

Play every song randomly.

Display individual songs.

Toggle between music stored on your Surface, the cloud, or both.

Toggle to shrink column.

Sort displayed music by date added, alphabet, release year, genre, or artist.

Figure 11-5:
The Music app offers to display your music by album, artist, or song, and sorted by date added, alphabet, genre, artist, or album.

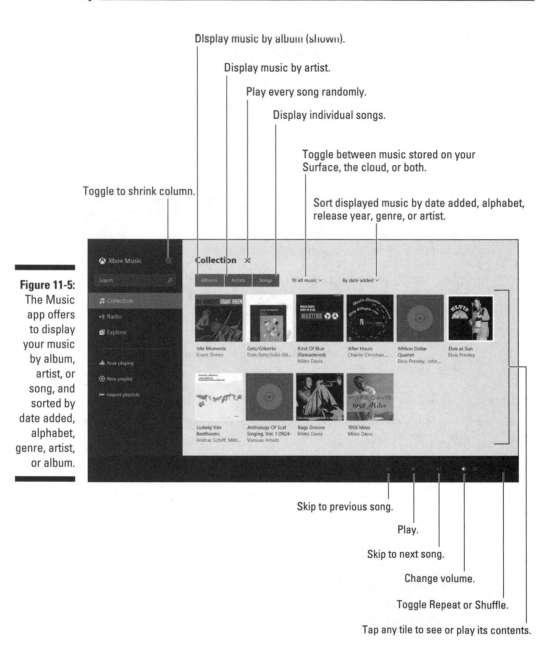

Skip to previous song.

Play.

Skip to next song.

Change volume.

Toggle Repeat or Shuffle.

Tap any tile to see or play its contents.

If you continue to explore the Music app, your music continues to play in the background. The Music app displays different buttons on different screens. Here's what happens when you tap any of these buttons:

- **Back Arrow:** Tap this to back out of your current screen and return to the previous one.

- **Play:** Play the currently viewed songs or album.

- **Pin to Start:** Pin a tile for this album to the Start screen for quick one-tap access.

- **Add to playlist:** A playlist is simply a list of currently playing songs. When you play an album, you're creating a playlist of that album's songs. Tap this icon to add a selected song or album to either the list of currently playing songs or a new playlist. Or, if you have an Xbox Music Pass, copy your music to the cloud by matching it with a song from Microsoft's song catalog, as described in the "Matching music" sidebar.

- **Explore artist:** When viewing an album, tap this to see more information about the artist, including other popular albums.

- **Start Radio:** Shown next to an artist's name when viewing by Artist, this begins playing a radio station with songs by that artist or similar to the artist's style. (I cover the Music app's Radio feature in the next section.)

- **More:** Found on crowded button lists, this launches a pop-up menu to show any buttons that didn't fit in a neat row.

Your Surface's Touch and Type Cover keyboards have dedicated music playback keys along the top row. There, you can toggle between Play and Pause, as well as toggle the Mute button/Volume bar.

The Music app works in a fairly straightforward way, but Microsoft constantly tosses in extra buttons, eager for you to buy new music or subscribe to its music services.

If you're looking for a no-frills player that concentrates solely on managing your own music, drop by the Windows Store and try a few of the alternative music players. (I like Media Monkey.)

While working your way through the Music app, try these tips to discover some of the app's less-obvious features:

- To make the Music app begin playing your entire library in Shuffle mode, tap the Shuffle icon next to the word Collection.

- To select a particular song or album from a list, hold your finger down on it and then slide your finger slightly to the left. Repeat with other items to select them, as well. Slide your finger in the reverse direction to deselect an item.

Matching music

As you peruse the Music app's menus, you may spot an offer to "match music" or "create a cloud collection." That odd phrasing boils down to these mechanics:

Matching means that you grant Microsoft permission to compare the music on your Surface with the music in Microsoft's *own* music catalog. For example, if you own Michael Jackson's *Thriller* album, Microsoft will also find that album in its catalog.

Because you and Microsoft both own the album, Microsoft then lets you stream its cloud version to *any* Windows device with an Xbox

Music app: your Surface, your Windows 8 or 8.1 PC, your Xbox game console, and even your Windows Phone.

By matching your music with Microsoft's collection, you no longer have to keep copies of all your music on all of your gadgets. Instead, you play Microsoft's *cloud* version of your matched tunes, streaming the songs to whichever device you want.

The catch? You need to buy an *Xbox Music Pass*, which I describe in this chapter's "Listening to the Radio" section.

 ✔ To play music on a newly inserted flash drive, fetch the App bar by sliding your finger up from the screen's bottom edge. Then tap the Open File icon. The File Picker appears, letting you navigate to your flash drive and play its music.

✔ If you're more accustomed to the Windows desktop, feel free to play your music from your desktop's Music library. Double-tap any selected song or songs, and the Music app opens to play them.

 ✔ The Surface RT and Surface 2 don't include the desktop's Media Player. However, Media Player lives on in the Surface Pro and Surface Pro 2, offering an alternative way to manage and play your music.

 ✔ The Music app plays only MP3 and WMA files, including WMA lossless. It won't play other lossless formats such as `.flac`, `.ogg`, or `.ape`.

Listening to the Radio

I describe how to fill your Music app with music earlier in this chapter. But even an empty Surface can dish out just about any song you want to hear. Those songs come from an *Xbox Music Pass,* a service Microsoft entices you with when you open the Music app.

The Music app refers to the Xbox Music Pass as *Radio* because it's a similar concept: Music you don't own comes streaming into your Surface, just as if your Surface were a radio. It's free for a limited time, supported by built-in ads. When your trial period expires, Microsoft limits your listening time to ten hours of ad-supported music per month unless you pay up. (I explain the details later in this section.)

If you have no interest in Microsoft's Xbox Music Pass, stick with the previous section, where you can simply play your own tunes.

But if you're curious as to Microsoft's way of letting you listen to more than 30 million songs for free, follow these steps to turn on the Radio and sample the Xbox Music Pass. (I explain the fine print at this section's end.)

You need an Internet connection to hear the Music app's Radio. When you're out of range of a Wi-Fi connection, the music stops streaming.

1. **Load the Music app with a tap of its tile on the Start screen.**

    The Music app loads, shown earlier in Figure 11-5, showing its three categories along the left edge: Collection, Radio, and Explore.

2. **Tap the Radio category from the Music app's left column and tap the Start a Station button.**

    A window appears, shown in Figure 11-6, prompting you to enter an artist's name.

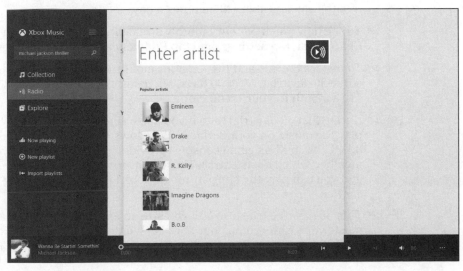

Figure 11-6:
Type an artist's name and press Enter to hear a radio station based around that artist's music.

3. Type a musical artist's name into the Enter Artist box and then press Enter.

When you type the artist's name and press Enter, the Music app begins playing a song either by that artist or by an artist with a similar style.

To see the list of songs that the Radio will play, tap the Now Playing link from the app's left column; the list usually contains about twelve songs.

The Music app's usual playback controls work with the Radio, letting you pause or skip between tracks.

You're now free to listen to millions of songs by thousands of artists simply by tapping the Radio category and typing the artist's name.

 You can also launch the Radio while browsing your own music collection by artist. Click the Radio button next to the artist's name, and the Radio begins playing songs based on that artist — for free.

Now, a moment for the fine print:

- If you haven't signed in with a Microsoft Account, the Radio feature eventually stops. At this point, you need to sign in with a Microsoft account to continue playing the Radio.

- When you listen to the Radio with a Microsoft account, Microsoft plays ads in between the songs. Sometimes you just hear a voiceover, at other times, the Music app plays a fullscreen video ad. And after six months, Microsoft limits your ad-supported-but-free streaming to ten hours each month, which is about 20 minutes a day.

- To see how much of your monthly streaming limit is left, fetch the Charms bar, tap Settings, and tap Preferences from the Settings pane.

- To bypass the ads and the ten-hour monthly limit, you must sign up for a free 30-day trial. After 30 days, Microsoft begins automatically charging $10 a month to your credit card.

- During that 30-day trial (and if you subscribe to the service), you can play the music on your Surface, a Windows Phone, a Windows 8 or 8.1 PC, or an Xbox game console (provided you're an Xbox Live Gold member, which costs extra). Those platforms all run Xbox Live Music, and you can play the songs through Xbox Live only by signing into the service.

- That 30-day free trial also lets you stream any of your own "matching" music you've stored on your Surface, Windows Phone, a Windows 8 or 8.1 PC, or an Xbox game console. (I describe matching in the "Matching music" sidebar.)

✔ If your subscription lapses, you can no longer play your music, including music you've downloaded — *unless* you've bought the music, that is, which costs extra. After they're purchased, however, those individual songs are yours to copy to CD or play on other PCs and music players.

✔ Xbox Music Pass isn't cheap, and it's filled with fine print. But if you pony up $10 a month for the service, it's very convenient — until you stop paying, that is. Then your unlimited music disappears, and you're back to ten hours a month of ad-supported music.

Exploring and Buying Music

The Music app's Explore area lets you browse through the music bins for music to add to your own collection. Much like shopping for music on Amazon or iTunes, the Explore section lets you hear 30-second snippets of music to make sure you're buying the right songs.

To start browsing and shopping, follow these steps:

1. **Open the Music app from the Start screen and tap Explore from the app's left column.**

   The Music app's Explore section opens, as shown in Figure 11-7.

   The opening screen lets you browse selections devoted to new albums, top songs, and top albums.

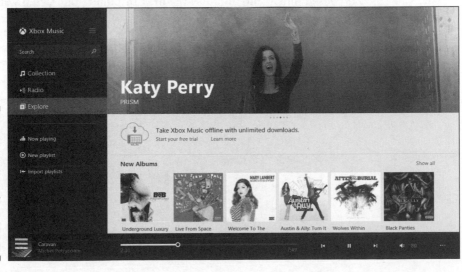

Figure 11-7: The Explore app lets you browse music by New Albums, Top Songs, and Top Albums.

2. **Tap one of the selections to browse its wares.**

   Tap the New Albums category, for example, and the store lets you sort the new albums by category — Jazz, for example — as well as subcategories within that genre.

   Spot an album or song you need? Jump to Step 4. If you're still looking for a song, move to the next step.

3. **Search for a particular song or artist.**

   The Search box atop the left column searches whatever category you've chosen, be it your own Collection, Radio, or Explore. Because you're in the Explore category, type an artist's name or song into the Search box and press Enter to see the matches.

4. **When you're looking at an item you want to purchase, tap the Buy button.**

   If you want to buy an entire album, click the Buy Album link to download MP3 files of every song on the album.

   Want just one song from the album? Then select that song by sliding your finger horizontally across the song's name. The app highlights the song, and the App bar along the bottom sprouts a Buy Song button.

5. **Pay for the item with the credit card associated with your Microsoft account.**

   If you don't have a credit card linked with your Microsoft account, the program walks you through the process. After you complete the purchase, the app downloads the music into your collection.

   Purchased music and albums stay in your collection even if you stop your Xbox Live Pass subscription.

Part IV
Work

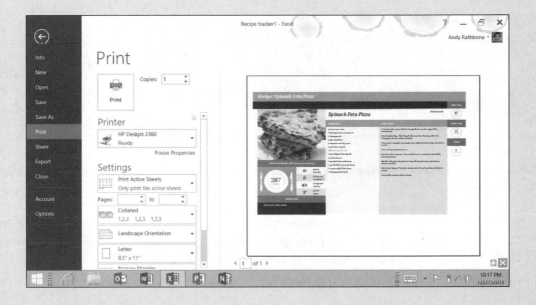

Visit www.dummies.com/extras/surface to find out how to delete old File History backups to free up extra storage space.

In this part . . .

- ✔ Take a good look at how the Windows desktops differ on the RT and Pro versions of the Surface.

- ✔ Understand the basics of Microsoft Word, Excel, PowerPoint, and OneNote. (Those programs come built into the Surface RT and Surface 2 and can be purchased at extra cost for the Surface Pro and Surface Pro 2.)

- ✔ Find out where to go to customize and tweak your Surface's settings.

Chapter 12

Visiting the Windows Desktop

*T*he Start screen and its apps ecosystem specialize in serving up information while you're on the run. You can find appointments, scan the headlines, check the e-mail, browse the web, listen to music, and still step onto the subway before the doors close. When you sit down, your Surface doubles as an e-book reader, letting you browse books, magazines, and newspapers.

What's missing from the Desktop of the Surface RT and Surface 2?

The Surface RT and Surface 2 offer loads of battery life and a reduced price compared with their Pro counterparts, but they also come with reduced power: Their Desktop app isn't powerful enough to run traditional desktop programs. You can't install any new desktop programs onto the Surface RT and Surface Pro.

The Desktop app still works on those Surface models, however. And when you open the Desktop app, you find Microsoft Office's heavyweights — Microsoft Outlook, Word, PowerPoint, Excel, and OneNote.

Also, these desktop staples are missing from Surface RT and Surface 2: WordPad, Windows Media Player, Windows Media Center, Sticky Notes, and Windows Journal.

On the positive side, the desktop on the Surface RT and Surface 2 tablets still includes File Explorer for managing files, as well as Paint, Notepad, Calculator, and a few other classic Windows programs.

But when you need to *create*, your Surface can mimic a desktop PC. It lets you manage files, create documents, and crunch numbers into neatly formed columns.

The Desktop app works much like the desktop found in previous Windows versions, so I don't spend time on the basics. Instead, I walk you through the most common desktop task a Surface owner needs: transferring files onto your Surface so you can access them while on the go.

Changes in Windows 8.1 Update 1

Early in 2014, Microsoft released Windows 8.1 Update 1, which automatically installs itself on your Surface through Windows Update. Unofficially referred to as the *Spring Update,* the updates mostly help you navigate Windows 8.1 more easily with a mouse. If you control your Surface with your fingertips, you won't notice many changes.

Nevertheless, the Spring Update brings these changes:

✔ **OneDrive:** Microsoft changed SkyDrive's name to OneDrive. That's the only thing about the cloud service that changes, though; OneDrive behaves just like SkyDrive. The SkyDrive Start screen app changed its name to OneDrive, and the name OneDrive (instead of the name SkyDrive) now appears in the navigation pane along every folder's left edge.

✔ **Search and Power icons:** Two new icons, Search and Power, appear in the Start screen's upper-right corner, next to your user account name. For quick searches, click (or tap) the magnifying glass icon for one-click access to the Charms bar's Search icon. Click or tap the Power icon to fetch a drop-down menu, where you can choose to put your Surface to sleep, turn it off, or restart it.

✔ **Apps on the taskbar:** The desktop's taskbar — the strip along the desktop's bottom edge — shows icons for currently running Start screen apps. You can also pin Start screen apps to the taskbar so that you can launch them without visiting the Start screen.

✔ **Taskbar on the Start screen:** When you switch from the desktop to the Start screen, the desktop's taskbar temporarily appears along the Start screen's bottom edge. (Move the mouse pointer away from the taskbar, and the taskbar disappears.)

✔ **App's top menu:** Point your mouse pointer at the top of a Start screen app, and a title bar appears, listing the app's name. Close the app by clicking the X in the title bar's right corner. Click the app's icon in the title bar's left corner, and a drop-down menu appears, letting you snap the app to the screen's right or left side, or close it.

✔ **Right-click Start screen menus:** Instead of fetching the Start screen's hidden App bar menu to make changes, you can simply right-click the app you want to tweak. A pop-up menu appears, letting you unpin the app from the Start screen, pin it to the taskbar, uninstall it completely, or change the app's tile size.

Most Surface owners won't notice these changes, because they're designed mostly to placate desktop owners. But if you spend a lot of time with the trackpad on your keyboard cover, or if you connect a mouse to your Surface, you may find some of these changes useful.

Making the Desktop Finger-Friendly

Although the Desktop app looks like a normal Windows desktop, don't forget it's just an app. And, as with all other apps, you still have the Charms bar at your disposal, making it easy to jump between apps.

The Charms bar is the only portion of the desktop that's finger-friendly, though. The desktop remains rooted in the mouse-pointer-controlled menus of yesteryear.

You can make things easier by telling Windows to make everything on the desktop *larger*. After you flip that switch, everything on your desktop expands.

Following these steps packs less information onto the screen. But you'll at least be able to take advantage of the information you see. And these steps are reversible, letting you return to mouse-sized controls if needed.

To enlarge everything on the desktop so it's easier to touch, follow these steps:

1. **Launch the Desktop app from the Start screen.**

   The traditional Windows desktop fills the screen.

2. **Summon the Charms bar by sliding your finger inward from the screen's right edge and then tapping the Settings icon.**

3. **From the top of the Settings pane, tap Control Panel.**

   The desktop's Control Panel appears.

4. **On the Control Panel window, tap the Hardware and Sound category and then tap the Display link.**

   The Display window appears, as shown in Figure 12-1.

5. **In the Change the Size of All Items area, tap the setting Medium - 125% and then tap the Apply button.**

6. **When Windows asks you to sign out of your computer and apply your changes, tap the Sign Out Now button.**

   If you haven't saved any work, save it before clicking the Sign Out Now button. If you don't, your hard work disappears.

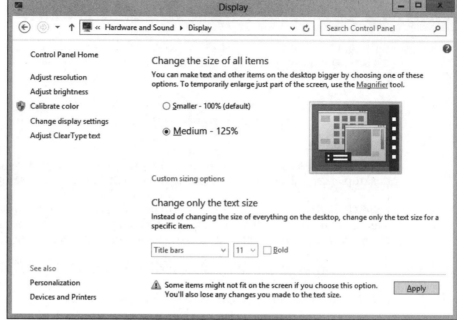

Figure 12-1:
Figure 12-1:
Choose
Medium -
125% to
make the
desktop
controls
easier to
touch with a
finger.

When you sign back into your Surface, your desktop will be larger and easier to control by touch alone.

- ✔ The larger size affects *only* the desktop. Your Start screen and apps remain unaffected.

Tapping an item from a drop-down menu

When you try to tap on an item from a desktop window's drop-down menu, you'll rarely hit the desired option with your finger on the first try. And when you miss, the menu often disappears. Drat!

So, when you encounter a drop-down menu — or any scrolling menu for that matter — aim and tap your finger anywhere on the list, but *don't* lift your finger.

Instead, slide your finger up or down the list. As your finger moves, Windows highlights different choices. When Windows highlights the choice you were originally aiming for, *lift* your finger.

This little trick ensures that you make the correct choice, saving you from tapping repeatedly until you eventually land on your desired option.

✔ If a crucial portion of a desktop window drops off the screen's bottom, turn your Surface sideways; the desktop automatically rotates, leaving you more space along the desktop's bottom edge. (I explain how to maneuver windows with your fingers in this chapter's "Mastering Basic Window Mechanics" section.)

✔ If you have a stylus for your Surface, don't underestimate its power on the desktop. It works very well as a makeshift mouse, letting you select files and tap buttons, as well as enter and edit text, as I describe in Chapter 5.

Mastering Basic Window Mechanics

The key to maneuvering windows on the desktop with your finger is to think of your finger as a mouse pointer. Then follow these rules:

✔ To move a window around on the screen, use your finger to drag the window's *title bar* — that thick strip along its top edge. When you drag the window to its desired position, lift your finger, and the window stays in place.

✔ To make a window consume exactly half the screen, drag it with your finger all the way to the screen's right or left edge. As your finger reaches the edge, the window begins to resizes itself; lift your finger, and the window consumes exactly half of the screen. This helps you position two windows side by side, handy when copying files from a flash drive to your Surface.

✔ To close a window, tap the X in its upper-right corner.

✔ To minimize a window, tap the little line icon near the window's upper-right corner.

✔ To maximize a window, tap the middle of the three icons shown in the window's upper-right corner.

✔ To shift your focus from one window to another, tap anywhere on the window that needs your attention.

Managing Files and Folders by Touch with File Explorer

In older versions of Windows, a program named Windows Explorer lets you view your computer's files and storage spaces, shuffling files between them as necessary.

Windows Explorer lives on but with the new name of *File Explorer*. And true to its predecessor, File Explorer also lets you manage your Surface's files, folders, and storage areas. That makes the program particularly handy for moving files on and off your Surface.

To open File Explorer and begin browsing your Surface's files and storage areas, follow these steps:

1. **Open the Desktop app with a tap on its Start screen tile.**

2. **Tap the File Explorer icon (shown in the margin), found on the left end of the desktop's *taskbar* — that strip along the desktop's bottom edge.**

   File Explorer appears, shown in Figure 12-2, letting you manage the files on your Surface.

3. **To see your Surface's storage spaces and the files inside them, tap This PC from File Explorer's left pane, called the *Navigation pane*.**

   There, you see all the storage locations accessible by your Surface: its internal hard drive, removable memory card, network locations, and any storage you've plugged into its USB port (including flash drives, portable hard drives, and even digital cameras).

4. **To see inside a storage area, tap it on the Navigation pane.**

   Tap any storage area you see, and File Explorer lists the files stored inside. For example, tap any of your Surface's main storage areas (your Documents, Music, Pictures, and Videos folders) to see their contents. You can also tap your Surface's memory card, or icons for any flash drives, or portable hard drives. You can even see photos stored on a camera you've attached with its USB cable.

When you want to copy or move files or folders from one place to another, Windows makes you take two steps: First you *select* the items; second, you *copy* or *move* them to their new location.

The next section explains how to select items, be it files on a newly inserted flash drive or folders stored on a network. The section after that explains how to copy or move your selected items to a new destination on your Surface. (It also explains how to rename or delete selected files.)

Although desktop windows contain scroll bars, it's hard to position your fingertip inside those narrow bars. Instead, slide your finger up or down directly inside the Navigation pane; that scrolls the pane's contents up or down. The same applies to the items you see in the File Explorer window's left side.

Storage on OneDrive

Frequently accessed places

Ribbon

Ribbon tabs

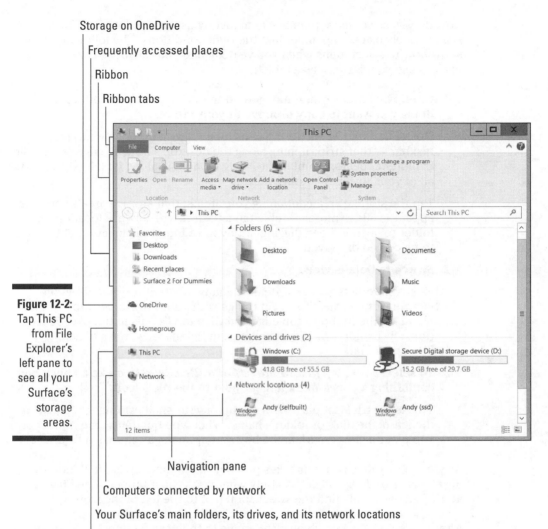

Figure 12-2:
Tap This PC
from File
Explorer's
left pane to
see all your
Surface's
storage
areas.

Navigation pane

Computers connected by network

Your Surface's main folders, its drives, and its network locations

Files stored on libraries of networked computers

Selecting files and folders with a fingertip

To select several items, hold down the Ctrl key on your Surface's keyboard
while clicking items with the trackpad's mouse pointer or a mouse. Simple.

Selecting items or groups of desktop items with your fingers, by contrast, can
be one of a Surface's most maddening chores. It's fairly easy to select one item:
just tap it, and Windows highlights it, showing that it's selected. But when you
tap a second item, Windows selects *that* item instead, deselecting the first.

How do you select more than *one* item just by using your fingers? The key is a precisely placed tap under just the right conditions. The following steps show how to select items when you've detached your keyboard or folded it back to use your Surface as a tablet:

1. **Open File Explorer and navigate to the drive or folder containing the items you want to copy or move to your tablet.**

    Open File Explorer with a tap of its icon (shown in the margin) on the taskbar — that strip running along the desktop's bottom edge. When File Explorer appears, examine the Navigation pane along its left edge: It lists all of your Surface's storage areas.

   Tap the storage area containing your items; that storage area's contents appear in File Explorer. Double-tap a flash drive, network location, or folder to open it. Keep digging until you've found the location of the item to be copied or moved.

2. **Switch to Details view.**

   File Explorer lets you view items in many different ways, and Details view makes it easiest to select things with your fingers. So, tap the View tab along the Ribbon's top edge and then tap Details in the Layout section. File Explorer displays the items in Details view: rows of names of files and folders.

3. **To select a file, tap *just to the left of a file's icon* to make a check box containing a check mark appear next to the file's icon.**

   This is the trickiest part. With the tip of your smallest finger, tap just to the left of the file's or folder's name. When you tap in just the right spot, you place a check mark in the box that appears, as shown in Figure 12-3.

As you quickly discover, this takes practice. If just one tap is off, Windows deselects *everything* and selects only what you've just tapped. Keep trying, and you'll eventually find the sweet spot, just to the left of the icon.

After you select the items you want, move to the next section, "Copying or moving files and folders."

- On the Start screen, a tap opens an item. On the desktop, by contrast, a tap *selects* an item. The desktop requires a *double-tap* — two quick taps in succession — to open an item.

- To select *all* the items in a folder, tap the Select All check mark. (It's next to the word Name atop the Name column shown in Figure 12-3.)

- When selecting many items, it's sometimes easier to tap the Select All check mark and then tap to *deselect* unwanted items.

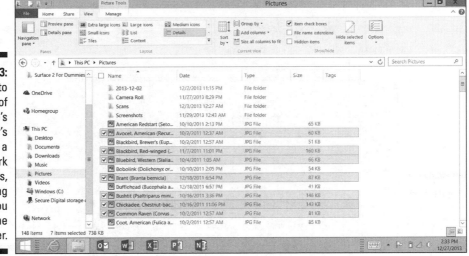

Figure 12-3:
Tap just to
the left of
the file's
or folder's
icon, and a
check mark
appears,
showing
that you
selected the
file or folder.

✔ To delete your selected items, tap the Ribbon's Home tab and then tap the Delete icon (shown in the margin).

✔ If you have a stylus for your Surface, it's often easier to select and deselect items by tapping their check boxes with the tip of the stylus.

✔ You can also *lasso* adjacent items using your finger or stylus: Draw a rectangle around your desired items, and Windows selects them for you.

✔ After fiddling around with your fingers on the desktop for a few minutes, you see why a mouse, trackpad, or stylus can be invaluable for precision desktop operations. In case you didn't buy a Surface Touch or Type Cover keyboard, I describe how to attach mice and keyboards, both wired and Bluetooth, in Chapter 6. (I give tips on buying and using a stylus in Chapter 5.)

Copying or moving files and folders

As you discovered in the previous section, selecting items with your fingers can be time-consuming. But after you've selected the items, it's easy to copy or move them to a new location by following these steps:

1. **From File Explorer, tap the Home tab near the top-left corner.**

   The Ribbon changes to show the icons shown in Figure 12-4.

2. **Tap the Move To or the Copy To icon.**

   A menu drops down from your tapped icon, listing locations where you've previously saved items.

Copy To

Move To Delete

The Home tab Rename

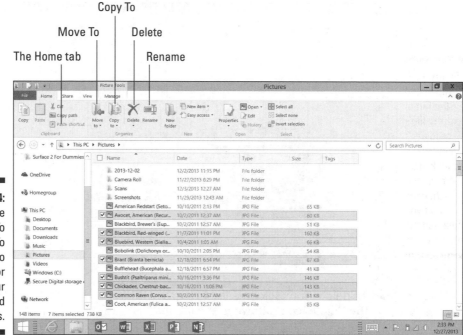

Figure 12-4:
Tap the
Move To
or Copy To
icons to
move or
copy your
selected
files.

3. **If you spot your destination, tap it to complete the process. If you don't see your location, choose the entry at the list's bottom: Choose Location.**

   The Copy Items or Move Items window appears for you to choose the destination for your selected files.

4. **Select the destination from the window and then tap the Copy or Move icon to send your items to their new destination.**

   The Copy Items dialog box, shown in Figure 12-5, works much like a tiny Navigation pane that you see along the left edge of every folder. Tap Libraries to send your items to your Documents, Music, Pictures or Videos libraries, for example.

   Or, to send items to a flash drive, tap your flash drive from the drives listed in the window's Computer section.

   When you've chosen your items' resting place, tap the Copy or Move icon. (The icon's name depends on whether you tapped the Copy To or Move To icons in Step 2.)

TIP

You can enlarge the Copy/Move dialog box by dragging its bottom-right corner outward with your finger. That brings more items into view.

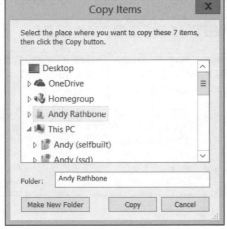

Figure 12-5:
Tap a
location and
then tap
the Copy or
the Move
icon to send
your items
to their final
destination.

Launching Desktop Programs

Although the Desktop app may seem like a self-contained world, it isn't. The Desktop app tosses you back onto the Start screen on several occasions, most noticeably when you want to load a program.

Where did my libraries go?

Introduced in Windows 7, libraries provide a handy way to view the contents of several folders within one window. In Windows 7 and Windows 8, every folder lists *Libraries* in the Navigation pane. A click on the Music library, for example, shows the contents of both your own Music folder and your PC's *Public* Music folder. (Any account holder can access the public folders, making them a convenient way for different account holders to share files.)

Windows 8.1 dropped libraries from the Navigation pane and replaced it with OneDrive, Microsoft's new name for its Internet-based file storage service formerly known as *SkyDrive*. The libraries still exist, though, and they're easy to place back onto

the Navigation pane: Right-click a blank portion of any folder's Navigation pane and choose Show Libraries from the pop-up menu.

To add a folder to a library, right-click the folder and choose Include in Library from the pop-up menu. When a second pop-up menu lists your libraries, choose the library that should receive the folder.

For example, if you store your music in a folder named Tunes on your Surface's memory card, add it to your Music library by right-clicking the Tunes folder, choosing Include in Library, and choosing the Music library from the pop-up menus.

When a program *isn't* a program

Eager to promote its new Start screen system of computing, your Surface refers to its Start screen programs as *apps*. However, your Surface also refers to *desktop programs* as apps. In Windows 8 and 8.1, the word *program* no longer exists.

But because the entire computer industry will take some time to scrub the word *program*

from its menus, software boxes, and websites, this book isn't scrubbing away the history of computing.

In this book, programs that run on the desktop are called *programs.* Programs that run on the Start screen are called *apps.*

The Surface RT and Surface 2 can run only their bundled desktop programs. However, you can easily launch their bundled Office programs by tapping their icons on the taskbar along the desktop's bottom edge.

Follow these steps to load a desktop program:

1. **Return to the Start screen.**

   You can return to the Start screen by tapping the Start icon in the desktop's bottom-left corner. Or, you can press your Surface's Windows button, press a keyboard's Windows key, or swipe in from your Surface's right side and tap the Charms bar's Windows icon.

2. **Tap your desired program's icon from the Start screen.**

   I describe how to load programs from the Start screen in Chapter 4, but here are some quick tips:

   • If your desired program doesn't have a tile on the Start screen, swipe up from the middle of your Surface's screen. The Start screen changes to show icons for *all* of your installed apps and programs.

   • Desktop programs appear along the All Apps screen's farthest right edge.

When you tap the desktop program's icon, Windows returns you to the Desktop app and begins running the program on the desktop.

Snapping an App Alongside Another App

The Windows Start screen and Desktop app live in very separate worlds. The Start screen is "modern," whereas the Desktop app is "traditional." They look and behave nothing alike, and, for the most part, they each work apart from the other.

Adding desktop programs to the taskbar

To skip some trips to the Start screen, add your favorite desktop programs to the desktop's *taskbar* — that strip along the desktop's bottom edge. To stock your taskbar with your favorite programs, follow these steps:

1. **From the Start screen, slide your finger up from the middle to reveal the All Apps screen.**

   The Start screen reveals icons for every app and program installed on your Surface.

2. **Select a favorite desktop program by holding down your finger on its icon until the App bar appears along the screen's bottom edge.**

3. **From the App bar, tap the Pin to Taskbar icon.**

   The next time you visit the desktop, that coveted program's icon is waiting on the taskbar, where you can launch it with a tap. By stocking the taskbar with your favorite programs, you can minimize your trips to the Start screen.

Sometimes, though, it's helpful to mix the two, perhaps placing your Calendar app next to your desktop to show your next appointment.

Windows does that with a feat called *snapping* an app, and the result looks like Figure 12-6.

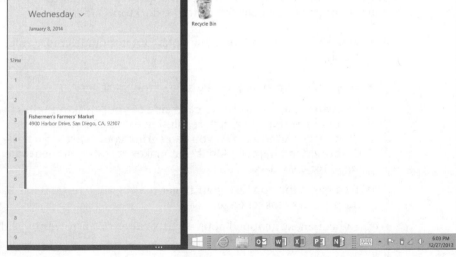

Figure 12-6: Snapping an app places a Start screen app to the side of your desktop or any other app.

Follow these steps to snap any Start screen app to the side of the Desktop app or any other app:

1. **Open the Desktop app and then return to the Start screen and open your desired Start screen app.**

   To reach the Start screen from the desktop, tap the Start button or press the Windows key at the bottom of the screen. Find the app you want to view alongside the desktop and then tap the app to bring it to the screen.

   Although I'm using the Desktop app in this example, these steps work for placing *any* app side-by-side with another app. Just substitute a different app for the Desktop app example I use here.

2. **Switch back to the desktop.**

   Slide your finger inward from the screen's left edge, dragging the desktop back onto the screen.

3. **Snap the app against your desktop.**

   This is the tricky part: *Slowly* drag your finger inward from the screen's left edge; your most recently opened app appears, following along with the motion of your finger. When you see a vertical strip appear onscreen, lift your finger; the app snaps itself to the screen's left edge.

When the app snaps against the desktop's left edge, a small vertical bar separates it from your desktop. The snapped app stays in place even if you head back to the Start screen and run a few apps. When you return to the desktop, your snapped app remains stuck to the desktop's side.

App snapping works well for a few tasks, but it includes more rules than a rebate coupon:

- ✔ You can't snap an app to the side of the Start screen.

- ✔ You can't snap an app onto each side of your desktop unless you connect your Surface to a high-resolution external monitor, described in Chapter 6. (Alternatively, you can shrink your Start screen tile size, described in Chapter 14, but that makes the Start screen's menus too small for easy use.)

- ✔ To unsnap the app, use your finger to drag that vertical bar back toward the screen's closest edge.

- ✔ You can make snapped apps slightly wider or narrower by sliding the vertical bar to the left or right.

- ✔ Not all apps perform well when snapped. Some become so tiny they're nearly unusable.

- ✔ To *unsnap* a snapped app, drag the vertical line back to the screen's closest edge. When that vertical line reaches the edge, the snapped app unsnaps.

Upgrading to Windows Media Center

The Windows Desktop app doesn't offer much to owners of the Surface RT and Surface 2. But on the Surface Pro and Surface Pro 2, the desktop is a fully functioning version of Windows 8.1 Pro. That's right: Those models are powerful desktop PCs that are flattened into a tablet.

Like all versions of Windows 8.1 Pro, you can upgrade your Surface Pro or Surface Pro 2 to Windows Media Center for only $10. Designed to run on a television set screen, Windows Media Center never really took off on desktop PCs. But tablets give this powerful piece of software new life.

If you're already recording TV shows with Windows Media Center on your desktop PC, by all means, upgrade your Surface Pro or Surface Pro 2 to Windows Media Center so you can watch your recorded shows on your Surface. To upgrade to Windows Media Center, follow these steps:

1. **From any screen, fetch the Charms bar by sliding your finger inward from the screen's right edge. Then tap the Search icon.**

2. **Type the words** add features **into the Search box and press Enter.**

3. **Tap the Add Features to Windows 8.1 link when it appears below the Search box.**

   The Add Features to Windows 8.1 window appears.

4. **Tap the words I Want to Buy a Product Key Online.**

   The window lists Windows 8.1 Media Center Pack.

5. **Tap the Choose button, fill out your billing information if necessary, and tap the Next button.**

6. **Follow the steps to purchase and enter a product key.**

When you finish, your Surface Pro or Pro 2 restarts. When it returns to the screen, Windows Media Center appears as a tile on the Start screen's All Apps area. By adding a USB TV Tuner connected to a TV signal, you can even record TV shows for later viewing on the road.

Chapter 13

Working in Microsoft Office 2013

*I*t's no coincidence that the Surface RT and Surface 2 include a free, installed copy of Microsoft's *Office Home and Student 2013 RT.*

That suite of programs — Word, PowerPoint, Excel, and OneNote — are all that many people need. For those who need more, the two tablets also include the Office 2013 RT version of *Outlook,* a powerful e-mail program for the desktop.

Your Surface RT or Surface 2 can read, save, and create Office files stored nearly anywhere: on your Surface, a flash drive, a networked PC, or on *OneDrive,* the online storage place accessible by any brand of PC, tablet, or smartphone.

This chapter helps bring you up to speed on the basics of opening, saving, and printing Office files. (Office programs don't come installed on the Surface Pro or Surface Pro 2, unfortunately, so this chapter doesn't apply to those models unless you buy and install the program.)

Note: The updated versions of Office and Outlook appear on the Surface RT after you update it to Windows 8.1. RT, described in Chapter 1.

Opening, Saving, and Printing in Office 2013 RT

Microsoft's Office Home and Student 2013 RT includes popular programs designed specifically to run on the Surface RT and Surface 2:

- ✔ **Word:** The industry-standard word processor, Word lets you create anything from letters to party flyers to table-filled reports.

- ✔ **PowerPoint:** If you've sat through a corporate presentation shown on a projector or large TV, you've probably seen PowerPoint in action.

- ✔ **Excel:** A staple of accountants, Excel creates large tables for calculating complex formulas, handy for everything from household budgets to stock market projections.

Although the three programs do very different things, they all open, save, and print files in the same way.

The following sections walk you through each step of opening, saving, and printing files. I also explain how to save time by starting work with a free *template* — a preformatted document where you need only fill in the blanks.

OneNote, a note-organizing program, works a little differently, so I give it a separate section near this chapter's end.

Outlook, the full-featured e-mail program, receives its own section at this chapter's end.

Opening a document

Whether you want to create a new document, open an existing one, or start working from a template, follow these steps to open a document in Word, Excel, or PowerPoint:

1. **From the Start screen, tap the tile of the program you want to open: Word, Excel, or PowerPoint.**

   If you don't spot your desired program on the Start screen, you can also launch it directly from the desktop: Tap the Desktop app's tile. When the desktop appears, tap your desired program's icon from the desktop's *taskbar,* that strip along the bottom, and your chosen program fills the screen.

2. **When your chosen program appears, tap the file you'd like to open.**

   Microsoft Word, for example, shown in Figure 13-1, demonstrates how each program offers four ways of starting work:

- **Open a recently accessed document.** The Recent pane along the left edge lists your seven most-recently accessed documents. Tap a document's name, and it returns to the screen, ready for more work.

- **Start a new document.** Tap the Blank Document icon, and the program presents a blank page, ready for you to begin creating a new document from scratch.

- **Open a template.** Office's time-saving templates come preformatted, letting you concentrate on the content rather than the format or design. I give templates their own section later in this chapter.

- **Search for a new template.** Hundreds of free templates await online. For example, type **resume** into the Search box, press the Enter key, and choose among dozens of preformatted resumes.

If you want to open a document not listed here, move to Step 3.

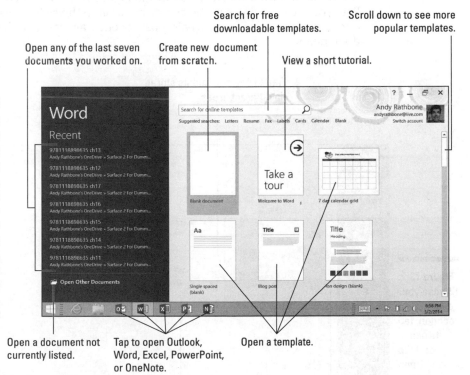

Figure 13-1: You can open an existing document, create a new document, use an existing template, or search for a new template.

Open any of the last seven documents you worked on.

Create new document from scratch.

Search for free downloadable templates.

View a short tutorial.

Scroll down to see more popular templates.

Open a document not currently listed.

Tap to open Outlook, Word, Excel, PowerPoint, or OneNote.

Open a template.

Taking the tour

Mixed in with other documents on the Open screen shown in Figure 13-1 is a tile called Take a Tour. By all means, tap the Take a Tour icon even if you're familiar with the program. It offers a short guide and tips for how to put the program to work.

It's short, and it introduces some new features introduced in Office Home and Student 2013 RT, which Microsoft released in October, 2012. (The programs can still open documents created in older versions of the program.)

---

3. **Tap Open Other Documents, navigate to your existing document, and load it with a tap of the Open button.**

   Tap Open Other Documents from the bottom of the Recent pane, and the Open window appears, as shown in Figure 13-2. The Open window lists your storage areas in the center column; to the right, it lists the currently selected storage area's most recently accessed folders and documents.

Tap to see documents stored in different areas.

Return to previous page.

Recently opened folders in currently viewed area

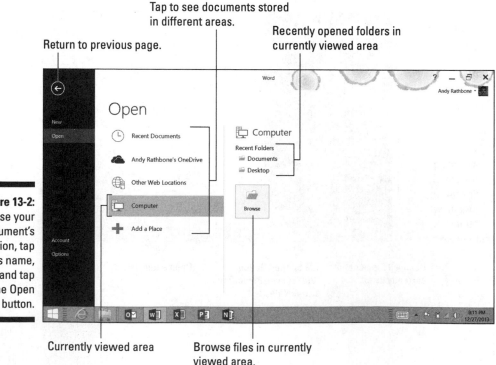

Figure 13-2: Choose your document's location, tap its name, and tap the Open button.

Currently viewed area

Browse files in currently viewed area.

To open a listed document, tap its name. Still don't see it? Then tap one of the Open window's five main storage areas:

- **Recent Documents:** The opening screen shown earlier in Figure 13-1 lists only your past seven recently accessed documents. This area, however, shows the past 24 documents you've opened. If you've opened the document before, chances are good that it's listed here, waiting to be opened with a tap.

- **OneDrive:** Tap here to open files stored on OneDrive, your online storage space covered in Chapter 6. By storing your files on OneDrive, you can work on them either from your Surface or your desktop PC.

- **Other Web Locations:** Most often used by corporations, this option lets you access folders stored on other websites.

- **Computer:** A popular choice, this option shows recently browsed folders. It also offers a Browse button, where you can open files already stored on your Surface or any files stored on an attached flash drive or portable hard drive.

- **Add a Place:** Tap this shortcut to add other online storage places as Microsoft begins supporting them.

Tap the Browse button to navigate to documents inside a storage area. Then open your desired document with a tap on its name.

When you're having trouble finding a document, try any of these tips:

- ✔ When searching for a document you've worked on previously, scan the Recent sections first. Tap likely suspects and take a peek. Guessed wrong? Close them with a tap on the File tab along the top and then a tap on the Close button in the program's left pane. Tap the Open button to start again.

- ✔ Can't find a document *anywhere?* Fetch the Charms bar by sliding your finger inward from the screen's right edge and then tap the Search icon. In the Search box, begin typing a keyword contained in your wayward document. Below the Search box, your Surface lists every file containing the word you typed.

- ✔ To find and edit a file stored on a newly inserted flash drive or portable hard drive, tap Computer in Step 3 and then tap the Browse button. When a miniature File Explorer window appears, tap your flash drive's letter in the This PC section of the Navigation pane along the miniature window's right edge.

- ✔ You can also open documents directly from File Explorer. If you spot your desired document on your recently inserted flash drive, double-tap its name: The program that created the document appears with your document in tow.

The fine print

The version of Office Home and Student 2013 bundled with the Surface with Windows RT is the real thing: It's almost identical to the version of Office Home and Student 2013 sold in the stores for "normal" desktop computers. Microsoft explains the details of the differences at `http://office.com/officeRT`.

In short, the programs may not support some macros, add-ins, or other custom-written programs.

The biggest issue could be that the programs are licensed for *non-commercial* use only. To legally create documents for work, your business needs a licensing contract with Microsoft with commercial-use license coverage. Ask your company's IT person to see whether you qualify and what additional options are available.

Starting from a template

In days of old, people often started from scratch with a sheet of paper. Yet that paper could probably be called a *template*: the preformatted lines across the page gave people something to follow as they wrote.

Today's templates offer much more than simple lines. Microsoft offers thousands of free templates for creating elaborate resumes, reports, invitations, schedules, calendars, or even stock reports that automatically create themselves when you type in a stock symbol.

When you find yourself waiting for inspiration in front of an empty screen, head for the templates. It's much easier to create something when you need only fill in the blanks.

To start working from a template, follow these steps:

1. **From the Start screen, tap the tile of the program you want to open: Word, Excel, or PowerPoint.**

2. **When the program appears, tap the template you want to open and then tap Create to open the template.**

   Figure 13-1, earlier in this chapter, lists just a few of the many free templates available, sorted by current popularity. During the holidays, you see more party invitations in Word, for example; in September, you see more templates for school activities.

To see other popular templates in Excel, scroll down the screen by dragging the scroll bar down the screen. Tap any template's icon for a quick preview, as shown in Figure 13-3. Tap the X button to close a preview if the template isn't the one you want or tap the Create button if it suits your needs.

If the current popular templates don't meet your needs, move to Step 3.

Figure 13-3:
Additional
details
appear
when you
tap a listed
template.

3. **Search for an unlisted template by typing a keyword in the Search for Online Templates bar along the top and pressing Enter. When you see a template you want, tap the Create button to download the template and begin working.**

Microsoft offers thousands of free templates online, searchable by keyword. Type **Expense** into the Search bar (or tap the word Expense beneath the bar), for example, and Excel lists hundreds of expense-related templates, as shown in Figure 13-4.

Narrow down your themes by choosing from the categories, as shown along the left of Figure 13-4. Tap both Monthly and Personal, for example, to show expense-related templates in the categories of both Monthly and Personal.

Tap a template to see a preview, as shown earlier in Figure 13-3; tap the Create button to download and open the template.

Type a keyword.

Return to previous screen.

Tap categories to narrow your search.

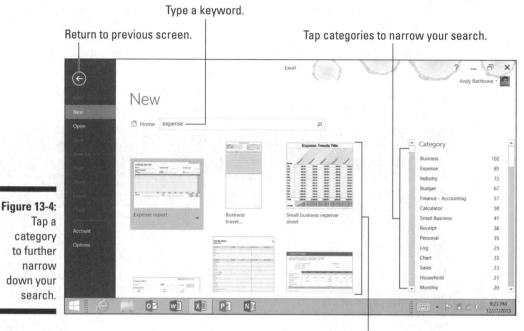

Figure 13-4:
Tap a
category
to further
narrow
down your
search.

Tap to browse customized templates.

Word, Excel, and PowerPoint offer thousands of templates from a wide variety of categories. It's much faster to adapt a template to meet your needs rather than starting from scratch.

✔ To save space, Microsoft didn't bundle Office templates with your Surface. You must be connected to the Internet to download them.

✔ Before beginning a project, spend some time browsing and downloading potential templates. That way you can still work from a template when offline.

✔ To browse Microsoft's templates with Internet Explorer, visit `http://office.microsoft.com/en-us/templates`. Templates you download await you in your Surface's Downloads folder, available in the Navigation pane along the left edge of every folder. (The selections available on Internet Explorer are the same as the selections built into the program, and they can be used in the same way.)

Saving your work

As soon as you begin creating your document, *save it*. By saving it, you've done two things:

✔ You've created something to fall back on just in case you accidentally mess up your current work.

✔ You've created a starting point should you need to rush out the door and return later.

To save your work in Word, Excel, or PowerPoint, follow these steps:

1. **Tap the Save icon in the screen's top-left corner.**

   The Save icon, which resembles a 25-year-old floppy disk, fetches the Save As window, shown in Figure 13-5.

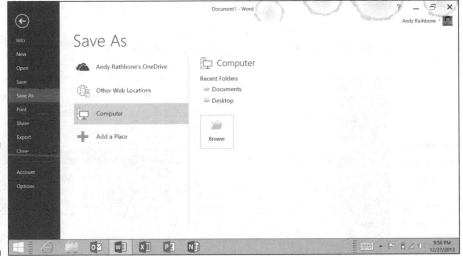

Figure 13-5: Choose a name for your work and a place to save it.

2. **Choose a location for your document.**

   The same locations await you as when you first opened the document earlier in this chapter: OneDrive, Other Web Locations, Computer, or Add a Place.

   Choose OneDrive if you plan on accessing the document from other computers or sharing it online with others.

   To keep it on your Surface or to e-mail it to others, choose Computer and then select My Documents as your final destination. Every program and app on your Surface can easily access files stored inside that folder.

3. **Choose a name for your document and tap the Save button.**

   Your helpful program offers a generic name, such as **Presentation1**, which certainly won't help you locate your work. Change the suggested name to something more descriptive that will help you find the document next week.

Printing your document

After you've finished and saved your document, follow these steps to print your finished work in Word, Excel, or PowerPoint:

1. **Tap the word File from the Ribbon.**

   The Ribbon stretches across each program's top. Tapping different words on the Ribbon — *Format,* for example — shows different commands related to formatting your document.

   Tapping File reveals *file*-related commands, shown in Figure 13-6, including Print.

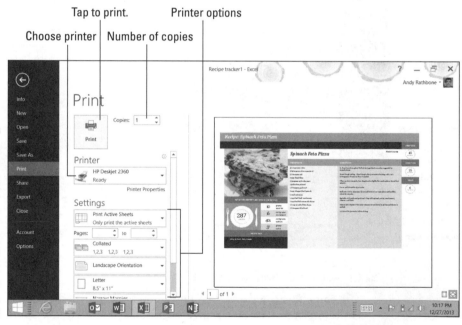

Figure 13-6: Choose Print from the left edge, choose your printing options, and tap the Print button at the top.

2. **Choose your printer, adjust its settings if necessary, and tap Print.**

   If you want only one copy of your document sent to the printer you normally use, just tap the Print button.

   If you need to do a little tweaking, adjust the settings shown in Figure 13-6 before tapping the print button.

I explain how to connect your Surface to a printer in Chapter 6.

✔ Desktop programs include built-in print commands that allow more customized print jobs. Start screen apps, by contrast, require you to open
the Charms bar, choose Devices, and select your printer in order to
print.

✔ Need to give a PowerPoint presentation? I explain how to connect your
Surface to a projector or external display in Chapter 6.

Taking Notes with OneNote

A computerized three-ring tabbed binder, Microsoft's OneNote organizes
your notes. It's not picky, letting you add notes in *any* form: typed by hand,
copied from websites, recorded as audio, captured as a photograph or video,
or even handwritten with a stylus on the Surface's screen.

Many students embrace OneNote because it lets them open a section for a
class, such as a Chemistry section, and then create a new tab for each new
lecture or subject, filling it with freeform notes, including photos of the black-
board or hand-written equations.

OneNote organizes your notes in three main ways:

✔ **Notebooks:** Everything starts with a notebook, which holds all of your
notes. You can create as many notebooks as you want, each designed
around its own theme. OneNote starts with two notebooks: The Personal
notebook contains notes dealing with you and your home; the Work
notebook helps you track your work-related projects.

✔ **Categories:** Each notebook can have several categories to separate your
projects. The Home notebook could have a Remodeling category, for
example, as well as a Shopping List category.

✔ **Pages:** Here's where you break down your categories even further. The
Home notebook's Recipe category could have a page for each recipe.

Follow these steps to create a new Notebook in OneNote, add new categories,
and add pages to the categories:

1. **Open OneNote, tap File from the top menu, and tap New. Then choose
   a location and name for your new notebook.**

   Tap the OneNote icon from the desktop's taskbar along the bottom, or
   tap the OneNote tile on the Start screen.

To create a new notebook, begin by choosing a storage location, usually OneDrive, so it can be accessed from any of your computers. Then type a name for your notebook, for example, *Shopping List*.

2. **Choose whether to share your notebook with others.**

When the Microsoft OneNote window appears, you can tap the Invite People button to give others access to your OneNote file. That's handy when you're creating projects at work, for example, or creating a shopping list that can be on every family member's phone.

To keep it private, tap the Not Now button; you can always share it later.

3. **Type notes into your project, adding Categories and Pages as needed.**

OneNote appears, as shown in Figure 13-7, letting you add Categories and pages to organize your notes. If you want, save time by starting from a template: Tap Insert from the top menu, choose Page Templates from the drop-down menu, and choose from the templates offered on the screen's right edge.

Choose other notebooks.

Current category

Other category

Current notebook — Add new category

Other pages   Current page

Add page

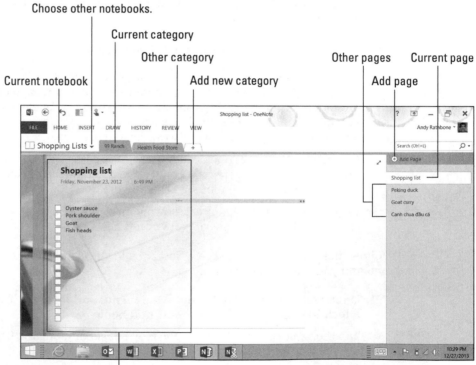

Figure 13-7:
This
Shopping
List
notebook
shows two
categories
and three
pages.

To-Do list template

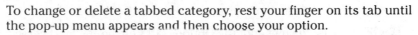

4. **To add a category tab, tap the plus sign to the right of the last tab and then type the category's name.**

   The notebook in Figure 13-7 offers two categories: one for 99 Ranch Supermarket, the other for a local health food store. Each category contains a shopping list for a different store.

   To change or delete a tabbed category, rest your finger on its tab until the pop-up menu appears and then choose your option.

5. **To add a page to the currently viewed category, tap the words Add Page atop the right column and type in a page name.**

   For example, the 99 Ranch category lists some recipes for favorite dishes, making it easy to look over the ingredient list while at the store.

When you're through taking notes, simply stop and close the program with a tap on the X in its upper-right corner. The program automatically saves your work with the name and location you chose in Step 1.

Microsoft offers its OneNote program for desktop PCs, Apple computers, and every smartphone, letting you access your notes from nearly any location. As soon as you make a change in a OneNote document from any device, it's automatically updated for all of your other devices.

One caveat: The RT version of OneNote won't let you record audio directly into the program. But you can record audio with a different app and embed the audio file into the program.

Adding E-Mail Accounts to Outlook

If you think that the Start screen's Mail, People, and Calendar apps don't have enough features, Outlook might be a welcome replacement. Whereas the Start screen's app offers a skeletal approach to basic communication tasks, Outlook is the full beast, writhing with options to handle your mail, calendar, and contacts.

For most people, however, Outlook is overkill on a tablet.

- ✔ Outlook's power adds extra layers of complications to what should be quick and simple tasks.

- ✔ Outlook requires a commitment to the desktop, defeating the purpose of a tablet.

- ✔ Desktop programs don't communicate well with Start screen apps. Unless you log into both your tablet and Outlook with the same Microsoft account, your contacts won't sync between Outlook and the People app.

For simplicity's sake, you should probably choose between either Outlook or the Start screen's Mail, People, and Calendar suite of programs, but not both.

If you still want to give Outlook a try, follow these steps to open Outlook for the first time and add your e-mail account:

1. **From the Start screen, tap the Outlook 2013 tile.**

   If you don't spot the Outlook 2013 tile on the Start screen, look in the All Apps area by sliding your finger up from the middle of the Start screen. When the All Apps area slides into view, scroll to the Microsoft Office 2013 group near the screen's right edge and then tap the Outlook 2013 tile.

2. **When the Welcome to Microsoft Outlook 2013 window appears, tap Next.**

   The program immediately asks whether you want to set up an e-mail account.

   If the program *doesn't* ask whether you want to set up an e-mail account, tap the File tab in its upper-left corner and tap the Account Settings button. Choose Account Settings from the drop-down menu. When the Account Settings window appears, tap the New icon on the E-Mail tab. Then jump to Step 4.

3. **Tap the Yes button and then tap the Next button.**

   The Add Accounts window appears, as shown in Figure 13-8, ready for you to add your e-mail account's information.

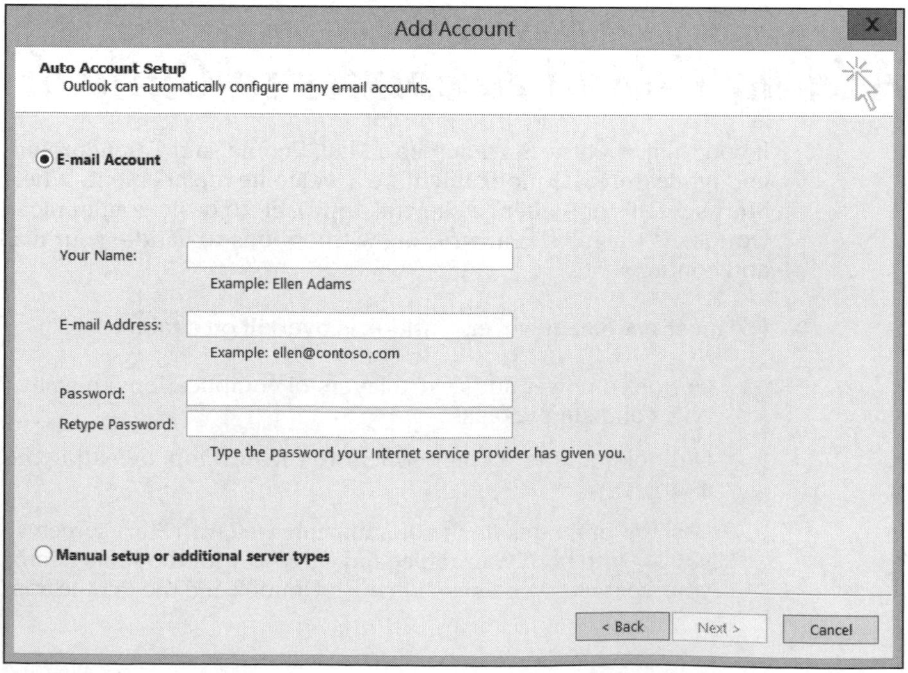

Add Account ☒

Auto Account Setup
Outlook can automatically configure many email accounts.

⦿ **E-mail Account**

Your Name: [   ]
             Example: Ellen Adams

E-mail Address: [   ]
             Example: ellen@contoso.com

Password: [   ]
Retype Password: [   ]
             Type the password your Internet service provider has given you.

○ **Manual setup or additional server types**

[< Back] [Next >] [Cancel]

Figure 13-8:
Enter your name, e-mail address, and password into the Add account boxes.

4. **Enter your name, e-mail address, and password in the Add Accounts window and then tap Next.**

   When you tap Next, Outlook connects with the Internet and tries to discover your ISP's mail settings, sparing you the trouble of entering them yourself. If Outlook succeeds, it tells you so, and you're done. If it doesn't succeed, move to Step 5.

5. **Tap the Manual Setup or Additional Server Types button and click Next.**

   The Add Account window appears, this time ready for you to enter your own e-mail settings.

6. **Enter your mail server settings, tapping the Next button at each prompt.**

   If you don't have your mail server settings, you need to contact your e-mail provider and ask for these tidbits of technical information:

   • **Your e-mail type:** This is usually *IMAP* or *POP3*.

   • **Your incoming mail server name:** This is usually a bit of gibberish like *pop.microsoft.com*.

   • **Your outgoing mail server name:** Just like your incoming mail server name, this is something like *smtp.microsoft.com*.

7. **Tap Finish to complete setting up your account.**

   Or, to set up another e-mail account, tap Add Another Account and return to Step 4.

When you finish, Outlook leaves you at your e-mail Inbox, where you can see the test message left by Outlook.

Chapter 14

Changing Settings

*J*ust about everything comes with settings — ways to change its behavior. Your toaster, for example, lets you choose between light and dark. Some toasters even offer a defrost or bagel mode.

Your Surface offers much more complex settings, of course. But quite often the task of *finding* the right switch consumes more time than deciding which way to flip it.

That's where this chapter comes in. It explains where to locate the settings of your favorite apps, as well as how to find the right switch to make your Surface behave a little better.

This chapter explores every portion of the Start screen's PC Settings area, a formidable array of switches that lets you customize your Surface to your liking.

To jump straight to any setting described in this chapter, fetch the Charms bar, tap Search, and type the setting's name or description in the Search box. Your Surface will place a link to the setting beneath the Search box for quick one-tap access.

Tweaking an App's Settings

Your Surface's apps almost always hide their menus. That's fine when the app behaves correctly. But if you want to change one of your apps, Windows offers several ways to tweak it — if you know where to look.

To find and change the settings of any app, follow these steps:

1. **Open the app that you want to change.**

    Your apps carry their settings with them; you need to open the app before you can access its settings.

2. **Open the Charms bar and tap the Settings icon.**

    The app's Settings pane appears.

That's it; every app includes a hidden Settings pane that lists just about every behavior that can be changed.

Granted, some apps offer more control than others. But when you find yourself dismayed with an app's behavior, head for the Settings pane to see the controls it offers. (To close the Settings pane, tap the screen, away from the Settings pane.)

For a start, these settings may come in handy:

✔ If you add more than one account to the Calendar app, you may find some overlap: Holidays may appear twice, for example. To weed out the duplicates, open the Calendar app's Settings pane and tap Options. There, you can pick and choose which Calendars should display which events, and in which color.

✔ Tired of typing passwords at your favorite websites? From the Start screen's Internet Explorer, open the Settings pane. There, under Options, you can flip the Passwords toggle; that tells the browser to ask whether you'd like to save your password.

✔ When traveling, you may want the Camera app to tag each photo with your *location* (the name of the city where you snapped the photo). To toggle that feature on or off, open the Camera app's Settings pane, tap Options, and tap the Location Info toggle switch.

✔ When shooting photos that you plan to post online, think twice before tagging photos with their location. Some people don't want their locations made publicly available.

✔ Some apps pack so many options on the Settings pane that they scroll off the bottom. To make sure you're seeing all of the options, slide your finger up the pane, dragging the formerly hidden options back into view.

Customizing Your Surface through PC Settings

When tweaking an app doesn't do the trick, call in the big guns. The Start screen's control panel, called the *PC Settings* screen, lets you tweak different parts of your Surface in surprising detail.

Shown in Figure 14-1, the PC Settings screen contains two columns. The pane on the left lists the categories of settings; tap a category, and that category's options spill out toward the right.

Figure 14-1:
The PC Settings screen lets you customize your Surface's behavior.

Follow these steps to open the PC Settings screen and begin tweaking your Surface:

1. **From any screen, slide your finger inward from the right edge to fetch the Charms bar and then tap the Settings icon.**

2. **When the Settings pane appears, tap the words Change PC Settings at the bottom edge.**

   The PC Settings screen, shown earlier in Figure 14-1, opens to show one of two possible views:

   • **Personalize:** Shown in Figure 14-1, this view offers shortcuts to settings that customize three things: the Lock screen that appears when you turn on or wake up your Surface, your account photo, and a picture password.

* **Recent:** This view lists shortcuts to your most recently accessed settings, which is handy when your last switch flip made a situation even worse. (Your most recently changed setting appears atop the list.)

To toggle between the Personalize and Recent opening views, scroll to the opening screen's bottom edge. There, you can find a link to fetch the alternative screen.

The following sections explain each category in the PC Settings area, as well as the settings most likely needing a bit of tweaking. The changes you make, usually by tapping a toggle switch, take place immediately.

✔ When you tap the Charms bar's Settings icon, the Settings pane appears, which lists your six most commonly accessed settings along the bottom: Wi-Fi, Volume, Screen, Notifications, Power, and Keyboard. I describe them all in Chapter 4.

✔ Settings that deal primarily with the Windows desktop can be found in the Desktop app's Control Panel. To visit there, open the PC Settings area and tap the Control Panel link from the bottom left of the PC Settings pane.

✔ The PC Settings area is chock-full of mundane settings, so although I've listed them all, I've called out the most useful ones with a Tip icon.

PCs and Devices

By far the most crowded entry, the PCs and Devices category deals mostly with physical items: your Surface, its display, and connected gadgets like mice or keyboards.

Here's the rundown on the PCs and Devices screen, shown in Figure 14-2:

✔ **Lock screen:** Visit here to choose your favorite photo to display on your Surface's Lock screen. This area also lets you choose which apps can display information on the Lock screen: your number of waiting e-mails, for example, or your next appointment.

✔ **Display:** This lets you adjust your screen's *resolution* — a nerdy term describing the number of pixels on your screen. Rarely needed on the Start screen, this setting is better adjusted through the Desktop app to make it more finger-friendly, as I describe in Chapter 12.

✔ **Bluetooth:** Visit here as well to add Bluetooth accessories, such as mice, keyboards, microphones, and similar cable-less gadgets. (I describe the process in Chapter 6.) This area also lets you remove gadgets you no longer use. If you're running low on batteries, head here to turn off Bluetooth until your next recharge.

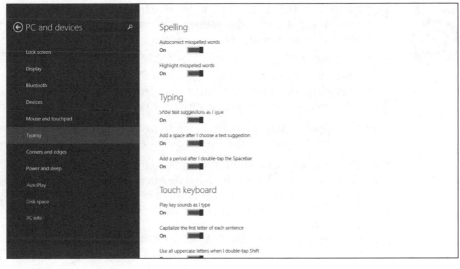

Figure 14-2:
The PC
Settings
screen's PC
and Devices
area
includes
controls
to change
how the
onscreen
keyboard
behaves.

✔ **Devices:** The catch-all for non-Bluetooth gadgets, this area lists nearly every gadget attached to your Surface. In a bit of a letdown, though, it doesn't let you adjust the gadget's settings. You can remove an unused gadget only by tapping its name and then tapping on the subsequent Remove Device button.

✔ **Mouse and Touchpad:** Left-handed Surface owners should visit here to swap the left and right buttons on their mouse and touchpad. The Touchpad area, viewable when you attach a Touch or Type Cover keyboard, lets you adjust the touchpad's sensitivity, which is handy when a shirt sleeve sends your mouse cursor flying.

✔ **Typing:** Drop by here to tweak the onscreen keyboard's sometimes over-zealous AutoCorrect behavior. Be sure to add the last option, *Add the Standard Keyboard Layout as a Touch Keyboard Option,* which adds the full-sized keyboard layout to your Surface's selection of onscreen keyboard. As I describe in Chapter 5, the standard keyboard includes keys missing from the normal keyboard.

✔ **Corners and Edges:** Cherished mostly by mouse-wielding desktop fans, this lets you change what happens when you point in the screen's upper corners. (Most desktop users visit here to prevent the Charms bar and Recent Apps bar from appearing when their mouse touches the screen's top corners.) You can also toggle whether the desktop's taskbar should list Start screen apps.

✔ **Power and Sleep:** When your Surface goes to sleep much too quickly, visit here to increase the two-minute delay to something more convenient. (You can also tell the screen to stay on longer when plugged in than when running on batteries.) Bonus: Visit here to disable the screen brightness control, which annoyingly changes the screen's brightness according to changes in your room's lighting.

✔ **AutoPlay:** This area lets you choose how your Surface behaves when you plug in a particular gadget. For example, you can tell it to show you the contents of a newly inserted flash drive automatically, without having to ask.

When in doubt about a gadget's AutoPlay settings, choose the Ask Me Every Time setting. You can always change the setting to something more specific when you're sure how you want the gadget to behave.

✔ **Disk Space:** Helpful when trying to free up disk space, this lists your apps, main folders, and the amount of space they each consume.

✔ **PC Info:** A gem when you're online with tech support, this area lists all your Surface's details. It also lists Microsoft's tech support phone line for your country, as well as a link to online tech support. (Drop by here to change your Surface's name, as well, if you have trouble recognizing it on networks.)

Accounts

Chances are good that you'll visit the Accounts category for one reason: to take a new selfie and use your smiling mug as a new User Account photo in the upper-right corner of your Start screen.

But if you want to hang around, these three areas await:

✔ **Your Account:** Drop by here to snap your photo for your account or to browse to one already on your Surface.

✔ **Sign-In Options:** This section lets you change your password, switch to a picture password, or even a four-digit number password, as if you were at an ATM. One gem hides here: Normally, you need to reenter your password after the display has been off for 15 minutes. Here, you can change that to Never Require a Password, a boon for people who rarely leave their Surface unattended.

✔ **Other Accounts:** Visit this section to set up standard accounts for other people who may use your Surface or even everybody in your family. If you're adding a child, choose Turn On Family Safety so you can both restrict and monitor little Timmy's behavior. Also, this area lets you change an existing account to either Standard (untrustworthy) or Administrator level (trusted completely).

Newly added users need to follow the walkthrough steps in Chapter 3 to download waiting updates, both from Windows Update and the Windows Store.

Changing your user account

You may want to change the account you use to log in on your Surface. For example, you may want to log in with the same account you use for your Xbox, or you may want to switch to a newly remembered Microsoft account.

The simplest solution is to create a new User Account for your new Microsoft account by following these steps:

1. **Open the Settings charm and then tap Change PC Settings.**

2. **Tap the Accounts category, tap Other Accounts from the Accounts pane, and then tap the plus sign icon next to Add an Account.**

3. **Type the e-mail address associated with your newly remembered Windows Live ID (or the e-mail address associated with your Xbox gamer tag).**

4. **Log back in to your old account and then move all of your data to your new account.**

   You can do this with either OneDrive, a flash drive, or a portable hard drive. Copy the contents of your Documents, Music, Videos, and Pictures folders.

5. **Log into your new account and copy your old files back into your new folders.**

When you're through, you can log out of your old account and log into your new account. After a few days, feel free to delete your old account when you're sure you no longer need it. (Make sure you've elevated your new account to Administrator so you're able to delete the old account.)

Deleting your old account also deletes anything you've purchased with it through the Microsoft Store, including apps, movies, songs, and other items.

OneDrive

OneDrive, Microsoft's cubbyhole in the clouds formerly called SkyDrive, plays a big role in your Surface. It's built into Windows 8.1 and lives in every desktop folder, letting you shuttle files to and from the cloud.

Here's where you control how much of your information automatically flows off your Surface and onto OneDrive.

✔ **File Storage:** This lets you buy more room on OneDrive should you use up your allotted 7GB. (New Surface owners should sign up for their free 200GB, as I describe in Chapter 3.)

A confusing toggle switch here called Save Documents to OneDrive by Default *doesn't* automatically save your files to OneDrive. Turning on that switch merely tells programs to list OneDrive as a *recommended* location. You can still choose a different location to keep your files on your Surface.

- **Camera Roll:** Normally, when you take pictures with your Surface, the Surface places a low-quality copy of every photo you take onto OneDrive. Visit here to stop that practice or to have a full-quality copy sent, instead. (You can even tell your Surface to upload a copy of videos shot, as well.)

- **Sync Settings:** Microsoft kindly remembers the settings of Microsoft account owners. Log into another PC with your Microsoft account, and your settings, passwords, app purchases, favorite websites, and more will ride along, making that other PC behave much like your own. Drop by here to weed out the settings you *don't* want to travel with you.

- **Metered Connections:** Don't bother with this unless you use your Surface with a cellular connection. This area lets you restrict when and why your ever-thirsty Surface can slurp data over those expensive cellular Internet connections.

Search and Apps

The catch-all Search and Apps category for Start screen items lets you control the Charm bar's Search and Share commands, as well as how apps behave on your Surface. Figure 14-3 shows the Notifications area of the Search and Apps category; all of the PC Settings categories look very similar.

Figure 14-3: The PC Settings area lets you control how your Surface alerts you to incoming messages, upcoming appointments, and other announcements.

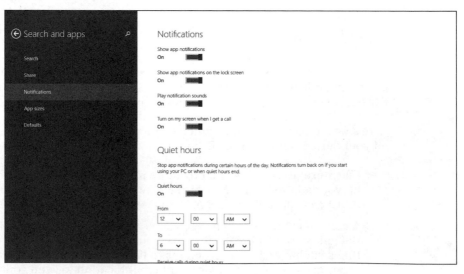

✔ **Search:** Drop by here to delete your past Search History — the words that appear below the Charms bar's Search box when you begin typing.

The Charms bar's Search box routes your searches to the Internet using Bing, Microsoft's search engine, in an effort to grab related information. If you find that to be snooping, toggle off the Use Bing to Search Online button.

✔ **Share:** This rarely used setting lets you choose which apps appear on the Share pane's list of destinations. (To see the Share pane, open the Charms bar and tap Share.)

✔ **Notifications:** When an app gets excited, it often sends you a *notification:* a little box in your screen's top-right corner, accompanied by a beep sound. You may see notifications of a new instant message, for example, or an upcoming appointment. This section, shown earlier in Figure 14-3, lets you turn off all notifications and their announcement sounds. For a less heavy-handed approach, scroll down the screen to the Show Notifications from These Apps section. There, you can choose which specific apps may send notifications, quieting all the rest.

If you value your sleep time, visit the Notifications area's Quite Hours section to set your evening hours when you don't want to be disturbed by notifications from night owls.

✔ **App sizes:** Should your Surface grow short on storage space, tap this to see a list of installed apps, sorted with the largest ones at the top. Delete the biggest hogs to regain some space. (Apps can't be stored on your memory card, unfortunately.)

✔ **Defaults:** When the wrong program keeps opening your files, visit here. It lets you choose which program should handle your e-mail, music, video, photos, calendar, and other common chores.

Privacy

With computers, you must give up some information (your location, for example) to receive other information (localized weather reports and maps). The settings in this area let you choose your comfort level when it comes to how much information you want to give up.

The Privacy category merits an occasional visit to see whether anything has fallen out of your comfort zone.

✔ **General:** Microsoft tries to feed you ads you *want* to see. To do that, it watches the websites you visit and the terms you search for through the Search box. This area lets you adjust what information you want to share with other apps, as well as with Microsoft.

✔ **Location:** When first loaded, some apps — the Map app, for example — ask permission to access your general geographic location. This area lets you change which apps should have that permission.

✔ **Webcam:** Think an app might be spying on you through your Surface's camera? As a first step, visit here to see which apps have permission to use the camera.

✔ **Microphone:** This area shows which apps may listen to you through your microphone.

✔ **Other devices:** If you install another device that may spy on you, it appears here.

Network

Because your Surface moves around with you a lot, it has a chance to connect with a wide variety of networks. The Network category lets you control how your Surface may connect with them.

✔ **Connections:** This lists your currently connected Wi-Fi network. (When troubleshooting, tap the icon to see details like an IP address, security protocol and type, network adapter manufacturer, and driver version.)

If you use your Surface to connect with a corporate network, the big deal is being able to set up a VPN *(virtual private network)* by filling out a short form.

✔ **Airplane Mode:** Enter here to turn on Airplane mode. (You can turn on Airplane mode more quickly from the bottom of the Settings pane, as I describe in Chapter 4.)

Visiting the Airplane mode setting here offers two perks: You can stay in Airplane mode but turn back on your Bluetooth and Wi-Fi. That way you can take advantage of the plane's Wi-Fi service, if available, and keep using your Bluetooth mouse.

✔ **Proxy:** Used mostly by techies, this lets you set up an alternative server, usually to handle your web requests.

✔ **Homegroup:** If you've set up a homegroup — a special type of network — on your home or office computers, visit here to join or leave it. There's one caveat: The Surface RT and Surface 2 can't *start* a homegroup, but they can join an existing one. The Surface Pro and Pro 2, by contrast, can both start and join an existing homegroup.

✔ **Workplace:** If you work at a "Bring Your Own Device" company, here's where you type the user ID that your company handed to you.

Time and Language

Frequented mostly by bilinguals, translators, and globe trotters, the Time and Language category lets you change your Surface's time and language to mesh with your currently visited country.

- ✔ **Date and Time:** If your Surface doesn't automatically keep time correctly — even during Daylight Saving Time — visit here to turn on the Set Time Automatically toggle.

    While here, you can also change the date and time formats to match your current region, as well as change your time zone.

- ✔ **Region and Language:** Bilingual Surface owners tap this to add keyboard layouts used in other countries. (That lets them type foreign symbols not found on the usual keyboard.)

Ease of Access

These switches in the Ease of Access category help adapt the Surface to people with physical challenges. The High Contrast switch, for example, helps the vision-impaired by reducing all distraction. And the Narrator, a Windows chestnut for years, reads menus and text with its robotic tone.

Update and Recovery

Tossed in at the bottom of the PC Settings section is the Update and Recovery category. These three sections found there make or break your Surface:

- ✔ **Windows Update:** Microsoft regularly issues updates for your Surface to fix problems and smooth out rough spots. Tap the Check Updates link here to find, download, and install the latest updates. For more information about Windows Update, flip back to Chapter 3.

- ✔ **File History:** Drop by here to turn on Microsoft's backup program. File History can backup files to a portable hard drive or a network location, as I describe in Chapter 15. (It also backs up to a memory card in your Surface's memory card slot, but if you lose your Surface, you've also lost your backup.)

- ✔ **Recovery:** I cover this section's last three options, Refresh, Remove Everything, and Advanced Startup, in Chapter 15. They're powerful tools to cure ailing Surfaces.

Chapter 15

Troubleshooting and Repair

*E*ven the best-treated Surface occasionally falls ill. This chapter covers general-purpose cures, as well as a few tweaks to solve specific problems.

The Surface doesn't contain any user-serviceable parts, so don't bother reaching for a screwdriver (or even finding any screws on the darn thing).

Instead, this chapter offers different ways to cure your Surface's software problems: how to turn it on when it refuses and how to turn it off when it stops listening to you.

I explain how to refresh your Surface when it's *really* misbehaving. And I show how to reset your Surface to factory condition when you're ready to start over from scratch.

In case nothing seems to fix it, the last section explains how to contact Microsoft for repairing or replacing your Surface.

Checking for New or Missed Updates

Your Surface is a comparatively new product for Microsoft, so Microsoft constantly releases a stream of patches to fix nagging problems and hopefully prevent new ones from occurring.

The Surface RT and Surface 2 automatically install every new update; the Windows Update service can't be turned off. However, your Surface often waits a day or two before installing new patches so the updates won't interfere with your work.

If you're planning a trip or you'll be away from the Internet, you can force your Surface to install new updates by following these steps:

1. **Fetch the Charms bar by sliding your finger inward from the screen's right edge. Then tap the Settings icon.**

2. **Tap Change PC Settings at the bottom of the Settings pane, tap the Update and Recovery category, and then tap Windows Update.**

3. **Tap the Check Now button.**

   Shown in Figure 15-1, the Check Now button tells your Surface to connect to the Internet and look for any recently released updates from Microsoft.

4. **If updates are available, tap or click the View Details link.**

5. **Tap to select the updates you want to install and then tap the Install button.**

   Your Surface immediately installs the waiting updates.

- Depending on the update, you may need to restart your Surface after Windows Update finishes installing the patches.

- If you spot a waiting update labelled Firmware, plug your Surface into its power charger *before* installing it. Firmware patches are more extensive than other patches. They take longer to install, and you don't want your Surface to run out of power before they're completely installed.

- To view your history of installed updates, which is handy when trouble-shooting, tap the View Your Update History in Step 3. Windows displays a list of downloaded updates, and the word *Installed* or *Failed* appears next to each one. Your Surface automatically tries to reinstall failed updates the next time it connects with Windows Update.

- Your Surface RT and Surface Pro must have all updates installed *before* the Upgrade to Windows 8.1 link appears in the Windows Store. If you can't upgrade to Windows 8.1, keep vising Windows Update until you've installed all the waiting updates.

- Windows Update is always turned on and set to automatic on the Surface RT and Surface 2. On the Surface Pro and Surface Pro 2, make sure it's set the same way by tapping the Choose How Updates Get Installed link in Step 3. Then choose Install Updates Automatically (Recommended) from the Important Updates drop-down menu, and tap the Apply button.

Figure 15-1:
Tap the
Check Now
button to
look for new
updates.

It Won't Turn On!

When your Surface won't even turn on, it's not always an End-of-Tablet-Life situation. No, it usually means the battery needs charging. Grab your Surface's battery charger and begin running down these steps:

1. **Unplug everything from your Surface: USB gadgets, memory cards, keyboards, docking stations, and anything else connected to your Surface.**

   You want to isolate your Surface completely and rule out any third-party culprits that may be interfering.

   Like most chargers, your Surface's charger may not work when the temperature drops below freezing.

2. **Plug the charger into the wall outlet and plug its other end into your Surface's power connector.**

   I show how to plug in the charger in Chapter 2. When your Surface is charging correctly, you'll spot a glowing dot of light either at the charger's tip (shown earlier in Chapter 2) or near the tip's end.

   If you spot the light, press and release your Surface's power switch. If it turns on, you're through. Let your Surface charge for a few hours and try to remember to plug it in more often.

If you *don't* spot the glowing charger light, plug the charger into a different wall outlet.

If the charger light glows, your first wall outlet is bad. Leave your Surface plugged in to slurp up electricity.

Still no glowing charger light? Move to Step 3.

3. **Clean the connectors.**

The power supply's connector tip can't connect with the Surface's charging port if one of them is dirty or covered with oil. Unplug the power cord from the wall outlet. Then put some rubbing alcohol on a rag and wipe off the magnets on both the charger's connector and the Surface's charging port. When it's dry, plug in the charger and try to charge your Surface one last time.

If the charging light still won't turn on when connected between the wall outlet and your Surface, it probably needs replacing. Contact the Surface Online Service Center (http://myservice.surface.com) for help. I describe the process at this chapter's end.

   ✔ If your Surface has a tiny amount of charge left, only the Battery Is Critically Low icon appears. That's a sure sign you need to charge your Surface as soon as possible.

   ✔ If your Surface is too hot to turn on, perhaps from being left on a car's dashboard, the Surface Is Too Hot icon may appear. Remove your Surface from the heat and let it cool off completely before trying to turn it on.

Turning on a stubborn Surface Pro or Pro 2

If your Surface Pro or Pro 2 receives power from the charger but still won't turn on, it might be stuck in a rare limbo state where it's neither completely on nor off. Before giving up, try this resuscitative effort to ensure that the Surface turns off *completely*:

Note: This trick doesn't work on the Surface RT or Surface 2.

1. **Hold down the Volume Up switch and simultaneously hold down the power button for at least 15 seconds.**

The Surface may flash a Surface logo, but keep holding down the buttons, counting slowly to 15. You want to make sure your Surface turns off completely.

2. **Let go of both buttons and wait ten seconds.**

3. **Press and release the power button.**

Your Surface Pro or Pro 2 should turn back on and behave normally. If it still doesn't turn on, it's time to head for this chapter's last section, "Servicing Your Surface through Microsoft."

It Won't Turn Off!

When your Surface seems too deep in thought to listen to any of your frantic commands, try this trick:

Hold down the Surface's power button for ten slow seconds. (Count them.) After ten seconds, the Surface stops what it's doing and turns off.

Give it a moment to rest. Then press and release the power button. Your Surface should wake up, display the welcoming word *Surface* on the screen, and drop you off at your Sign In screen, once again eager for your attention.

Fixing Problem Apps

Sometimes apps don't work correctly. They crash when you press a button, for example. Or they freeze on the screen. When an app doesn't seem to be working correctly anymore, this trick usually works: Uninstall it and then reinstall it from the Windows Store.

This trick works for both free and paid apps; the Windows Store remembers your purchase and lets you download the app again without paying twice.

1. **From the Start screen, select your problem app's tile or icon.**

   To select an app, hold your finger down on it. After a second or two, a check mark appears by the app, and the App bar appears along the screen's bottom edge.

2. **Tap the Uninstall icon on the App bar.**

   Your Surface uninstalls the app.

3. **Visit the Windows Store and reinstall the app.**

   From the Windows Store, slide your down finger slightly from the screen's top and then tap the words Your Apps that appear at the top.

   When the list of all of your apps appears, slide your finger down slightly on the icon of your formerly misbehaving app. When the App bar appears along the screen's bottom edge, tap the Install icon.

Your app reinstalls itself onto your Start screen's All Apps area. With any luck, your app has enjoyed its vacation and returned in a better mood.

> ✔ To pin your app back to the Start screen, slide your finger upward from the middle of the Start screen. When the All Apps area comes into view, tap and hold your newly reinstalled app; when the App bar appears along the screen's bottom, tap the Pin to Start icon.

✔ You can also uninstall and reinstall apps that came bundled with your Surface, such as the News, Finance, and Weather apps. The Mail, Calendar, and People apps are actually one app. Uninstalling one removes all three. To reinstall them, install the Store's app called "Mail, Calendar, and People."

✔ If an app still acts up, contact the app's publisher: Drop by the app's entry in the Windows Store and scroll to the Details section of the app's description page. There, under the Learn More category, tap the support link. That takes you to the publisher's website or opens an e-mail for you to use to contact the app's publisher.

Backing Up Your Surface

Your Surface does a remarkable job of backing itself up. For example, your Microsoft account remembers how you personalize your Surface, as well as the settings you change. It also remembers your e-mail accounts, calendar information, contacts, favorite websites, and even many of your passwords.

Aided by your Microsoft account, the Windows Store remembers the apps you've installed and purchased, making it easy to download them again. Any files you store on OneDrive are backed up there.

So, what's left to back up? Well, it's the files stored in your Windows main folders: Documents, Music, Pictures, and Videos. Your Surface's built-in File History program can back those up, but there's a catch: Microsoft didn't turn on File History by default.

To turn on the File History backup program, you need to choose a backup location and tap the program's On switch by following these steps:

1. **Insert your memory card into your Surface's memory card slot, or plug a portable hard drive into your Surface's USB port.**

   I describe how to do both in Chapter 6.

   If you prefer to back up your Surface to a wireless network location (perhaps a shared folder on another PC), you can do that in Step 3.

2. **Visit the PC Settings' File History category.**

   Fetch the Charms bar by sliding your finger inward from the screen's right edge and then tapping the Search pane's Settings icon.

   Type **File History** into the Search box and then tap the File History Settings link.

   The File History settings page appears, as shown in Figure 15-2. File History quickly looks for any available drives and lists the most promising candidate (the largest available drive). If you haven't plugged any drives into your Surface's USB port, File History recommends your memory card as a backup location.

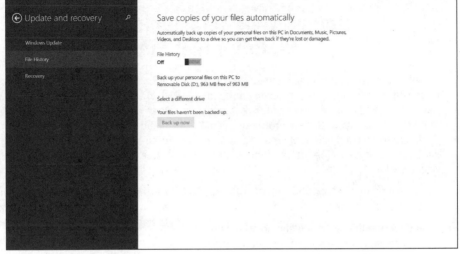

Figure 15-2:
You can choose your backup drive from the File History settings page.

3. **Choose your backup drive and tap the Turn On toggle switch.**

   If you're backing up to your memory card — and that's the only available backup spot available — tap the Turn On toggle switch, and you're through. Your Surface starts backing up your files on the memory card. File History refers to the memory card as "Removable Disk (D:)."

   But if you want to back up to a different drive, tap the Select a Different Drive link. A pop-up menu appears, listing all the drives available to your Surface. Choose your drive's name from the pop-up menu, tap File History's On/Off toggle switch to On, and you're done.

   If you want to back up to a network location, tap the Select a Different Drive link. When the pop-up menu appears, choose Show All Network Locations at the bottom of the pop-up menu. When your list of network locations appears, tap the one you want and tap the program's On/Off toggle switch to On. Whew!

After you've chosen the backup location and turned on File History, your Surface backs up your files every hour.

- ✔ If you're using a portable drive, store it in a safe, yet convenient, place. You must remember to reconnect it often so your Surface can create another, more-recent backup.

- ✔ To view your backups, open the Desktop app, tap the Charms bar's Settings icon, and tap Control Panel from the top of the Settings pane. When the Control Panel appears, open the System and Security section and tap File History.

Bringing your data back to a new or factory-reset Surface

Whether you've bought a replacement Surface or done a factory reset on your existing Surface, here's how to bring all of your files, settings, and apps back to your Surface. Your Surface is designed to be used with a Microsoft account, so if you don't have one, some of these steps won't work.

1. **Turn on your Surface and sign in with your Microsoft account.**

   I describe the steps you should take when first turning on a new Surface in Chapter 3. For example, be sure to visit Windows Update and install all of the waiting updates.

2. **Tell your PC to sync your settings.**

   Fetch the Charms bar, tap Settings, and tap OneDrive on the PC Settings screen. From the OneDrive pane, tap Sync Settings and then tap Sync Your Settings on This PC.

   When given a choice of which PC to grab the settings from, choose your old Surface from the list.

3. **Visit the Windows Store and reinstall your apps.**

From the Windows Store, slide your finger down slightly from the screen's top and then tap the Your Apps button that appears along the screen's top edge. From the first drop-down menu, choose your old Surface's name. Then tap the Select All icon from the App bar and tap the adjacent Install icon.

Or, if you spot icons for your uninstalled apps on the Start screen, tap their icons to begin downloading them anew. (On the Start screen, icons for uninstalled apps have a little downward-pointing arrow in their lower-right corner.)

4. **Restore your files from File History.**

If necessary, plug in the drive containing your File History backup or insert the memory card. Then fetch the Charms bar, tap Search, and in the Search box type **Restore File**. From the Search pane, tap the Restore Your Files With File History link to fetch the File History program. When the program window appears, tap the green button in the window's bottom center to copy your files back in place.

Refreshing Your Surface

When your Surface isn't working correctly, you can tell it to reinstall its operating system but leave your files on your tablet. Refreshing your Surface is a quick fix because you can easily reinstall your apps from the Windows Store. But it poses a problem for owners of the Surface Pro and Pro 2.

On the Surface Pro and Pro 2 models, the Refresh feature also removes all of the *programs* you've installed on your Desktop app. Before using the Refresh feature, make sure you have your program's original installation files handy because you need to reinstall them all.

To refresh your Surface, follow these steps:

1. **Swipe in from the right edge of the screen, tap Settings, and then tap Change PC settings.**

2. **Tap the General section.**

3. **In the Refresh Your PC Without Affecting Your Files section, tap the Get Started button.**

   Your Surface will restart.

4. **When your Surface wakes up, you're left with a few tasks:**

   • Visit the PC Settings screen's Windows Update section and download any waiting updates.

   • Open the Windows Store app and reinstall your apps.

   • On the Surface Pro or Pro 2, open the Windows desktop. There, you find a waiting list of your uninstalled desktop programs, along with links to where you can download and reinstall them. If you don't find links to missing programs, you need to reinstall the programs from their original discs.

Refreshing your Surface RT or Surface 2 takes less time than refreshing a Surface Pro or Surface 2 Pro because you needn't worry about reinstalling desktop programs. (The Office programs will still be there, although you need to update them again with Windows Update.)

On a well-used Surface Pro or Surface Pro 2, by contrast, tracking down and reinstalling all those desktop programs can be a nightmare.

Resetting Your Surface

This last-resort option wipes your Surface completely clean, removing *everything*. When it wakes back up, your Surface behaves like it was just removed from its shiny new box. Although it's a drastic measure, this last-ditch effort can often salvage a Surface that seems beyond repair.

Resetting your Surface is also a good way to restore your Surface to factory conditions before giving it away, either to friends or charity.

Resetting your Surface deletes *all* of your personal files, apps, desktop programs, and settings.

I can't even sign in!

If your Surface seems beyond repair, you're not without hope. You can troubleshoot, refresh, or reset your Surface to factory conditions by following these steps:

1. **With your Surface turned off, attach any type of keyboard.**

   A desktop keyboard plugged into your USB port will do if you don't have a Touch or Type Cover keyboard cover.

2. **Turn on your Surface by pressing its power button.**

3. **At the Sign In screen, press and hold the left Shift key.**

4. **Tap the Power icon in the screen's bottom-right corner and then choose Restart from the pop-up menu.**

A light-blue screen appears on your Surface, offering several options, including Troubleshoot.

5. **Tap Troubleshoot.**

   The Troubleshoot screen lets you refresh or reset your Surface, options described in their own sections in this chapter. But before trying those, tap Advanced Options and then tap Automatic Repair.

If your Surface can't repair itself, follow these steps again but choose Refresh or Repair in Step 5.

In Step 5, owners of the Surface RT and Surface 2 find a way to boot from their USB Recovery Drive, which I describe how to make in Chapter 3. Surface Pro or Surface Pro 2 owners see an option to load a System Image backup.

To reset your Surface to factory conditions, follow these steps:

1. **Swipe in from the right edge of the screen, tap Settings, and then tap Change PC settings.**

2. **Tap the General category.**

3. **In the section called Remove Everything and Reinstall Windows, tap Get Started, tap Next, and follow the instructions.**

If you're giving away your Surface, choose the Fully Clean My Drive option. That option takes much longer, but it scrubs your drive clean of any identifying information.

When your Surface returns to life, flip back to Chapter 3. Your Surface behaves just as it did when you first turned it on, and you need to choose a language and begin installing updates.

Servicing Your Surface through Microsoft

If your Surface includes problems you can't fix alone, drop by Microsoft's website at this address:

```
https://myservice.surface.com
```

After you enter your Microsoft account, the website walks you through registering your Surface, reporting problems, checking the status of service orders, checking your warranty status, replacing accessories, and, if desired, buying a service plan.

To find your Surface's serial number, flip open its kickstand; the serial number is printed below the word *Surface*. The serial number for your Touch or Type Cover keyboards is printed in extraordinarily tiny letters on the right side of the keyboard's spine. (You need to detach the keyboard from your Surface to see it.)

When your new or refurbished Surface returns from the repair shop, fill it back up with your files and settings by following the steps in this chapter's sidebar, "Bringing your data back to a new or factory-reset Surface."

Part V
The Part of Tens

For a list of ten popular apps that work well on your Surface, visit www.dummies.com/extras/surface.

In this part . . .

- ✔ Get essential tips and tricks to make the most of your Surface

- ✔ Find out which accessories work best for your particular model.

Chapter 16

Ten Essential Tips 'n' Tricks

A *For Dummies* book wouldn't be the same without a Part of Tens section: ten tidbits of information that didn't quite fit anywhere else in the book.

With the Surface, the hard part is limiting this chapter to only *ten* tips. After paring down the list from 20, here are 10 essential tips 'n' tricks to wring the most out of your Surface.

When Lost, Swipe in from the Screen's Left Edge

Whenever you tap a link or open another program on your Surface, the new item fills the screen, pulling you in deeply. When you finally close the app, the Start screen jumps in to fill the void.

But what were you working on *before* you went off track by tapping the link?

To find out, slide in your finger from the screen's left side. Your finger pulls your original app back onto the screen, bringing you full circle to where you were before the distraction.

Search for Items by Typing Directly on the Start Screen

If you've attached any type of keyboard to your Surface, you have a special perk: To search for something, begin typing its name directly onto the Start screen. Windows automatically fetches the Charms bar, enters your search into the Search box, and begins listing matches.

For example, type **camera** directly into the Start screen.

As you type the first letter, the Start screen switches to Search mode; as the letter *c* enters the Search box, the Search pane lists every app, setting, or file containing the letter *c*. The list narrows as you keep typing, eventually showing only camera-related apps and settings, followed by popular camera-related listings on the Internet, as shown in Figure 16-1.

Figure 16-1:
Typing
the word
camera
directly into
the Start
screen
fetches
the Search
box and
lists match-
ing apps,
settings,
files, and
websites.

Don't have a keyboard attached to your Surface? You can do the same thing by tapping the Search icon in the Start screen's upper-right corner. When the Search pane's Search box appears, tap inside the Search box to call up the onscreen keyboard. Then start typing your search term. That takes a few more keystrokes but works the same way.

Select Onscreen Items within Apps

Some items seem difficult to select, which is a precursor to deleting, moving, renaming, copying, or any other host of tasks. For example, a tap on an e-mail in the Mail app *opens* rather than *selects* the e-mail. Holding down a finger on the e-mail won't select it, and perplexed finger jabs just scroll the item back and forth.

The trick to selecting difficult items is to slide your finger across them in the *opposite* direction that they scroll.

Mail normally lets you scroll through e-mail by sliding your finger up or down the list. So, select a single piece of e-mail by sliding your finger left or right across it. This "slide in the opposite direction" trick works when selecting many other seemingly difficult-to-select items.

Take Screenshots

To take a snapshot of what you're seeing on the screen, hold down the Windows key below your Surface's screen and press the Volume Down button. The screen dims, and a screenshot appears in your Pictures library's Screenshots folder.

Taking screenshots comes in particularly handy when an error message pops up. You can e-mail the screenshot to a techie who can tell you how to deal with the error.

Stop the Screen from Rotating

Most of the time, you want the screen to rotate as you hold your Surface. That way, the screen is always right side up. Occasionally, though, you don't want it to rotate — perhaps you're reading a book or browsing websites.

To keep the screen from rotating, open the Charms bar and tap on Settings. When the Settings pane appears, tap on the Screen icon near the bottom right (shown in the margin).

When the brightness bar appears, look at the Rotation Lock icon atop the bar; tap that icon to toggle autorotation on and off.

Note: The rotation lock automatically turns on when your Touch or Type Cover keyboard is attached and folded out for use. The lock turns off when you fold back the keyboard (or detach it) to use your Surface as a tablet.

Tweak Your App's Settings

 Every app offers a way to fine-tune its behavior through the Charms bar's Settings area. When something about an app irks you, see whether you can change it: Fetch the Charms bar by sliding your finger in from the screen's right edge and tapping the Settings icon. If an app can be changed, the Settings pane offers a way.

Make a Recovery Drive

I tossed this in as a sidebar in Chapter 3, but creating a Recovery Drive isn't very difficult. If you have a flash drive, dedicate it as a Recovery Drive for your Surface. If your Surface won't start someday, that Recovery Drive just might be the only thing to bring it back to life.

The Surface RT and Surface 2 need a USB drive of at least 4GB; the Surface Pro and Pro 2 models need a USB drive of at least 8GB.

Find a Lost Start Screen App

Can't find an app on your Start screen? Then check the All Apps area; from the Start screen, slide your screen upward until the All Apps area appears. Look for your app in the alphabetical list. When you spot it, launch it with a tap.

 Or, if you want it on the Start screen, where it's easier to launch, hold your finger down on its icon. When the App bar appears along the bottom, choose Pin to Start.

 Don't see Pin to Start? Then tap the App bar's Find on Start icon instead. The Start screen returns with the formerly missing app's tile highlighted with a white border.

If you still can't find the app, head to the Windows Store. You may need to reinstall it.

Increase Your Surface's Storage Space

The biggest challenge when moving from a desktop PC to a Surface is the amount of storage space. Most Surfaces offer from 32GB to 128GB of storage; the Surface Pro 2 offers up to 512GB. Yet, most desktop PCs still offer much more storage than that.

Also, Windows consumes quite a bit of that space. On a 32GB Surface 2, you're left with only 18GB of space to store your own files.

The easiest, fastest, and best way to maximize storage on your Surface is to insert a microSDXC memory card into its memory slot. You can buy cards with up to 64GB of space and store your files there. Turn to Chapter 6 if you're not sure how to insert or access your memory card.

Don't have a memory card? Then follow these steps to delete any unneeded files, leaving more room for storage on your Surface:

1. **Run the desktop's Disk Cleanup program.**

   Type **free up disk space** into the Charms bar's Search box. Then tap the similarly named link that appears beneath the box. The Disk Cleanup program appears, as shown in Figure 16-2.

Figure 16-2:
Tap the check boxes next to the categories you want to delete and then tap the OK button to delete them.

2. **Tap the Clean Up System Files button near the window's bottom.**

   That tells the program to also list files created by Windows itself rather than you. You can safely delete most of them.

3. **Select the boxes next to the items you want to delete.**

   If you've refreshed your Surface, you may spot a category named Temporary Windows Installation Files. Select that one, and you free up several gigabytes of space.

4. **Tap the OK button to delete the files.**

   When you delete the files, they're gone for good. Unlike most desktop files, you can't retrieve them. If you're in doubt about deleting an item, don't select its check box.

If you still need more disk space, consider carrying around a portable hard drive, which can store 3TB or more.

Add Your Contact Information to Your Surface

If you lose your Surface, your information usually remains safe. If you've chosen a secure password for your Microsoft account, nobody can move past the Lock screen.

But if a Good Samaritan finds your Surface, how will the finder know how to return it to you? You can solve that problem in either of two different ways.

For a quick-and-easy solution, grab a permanent magic marker and write your name and phone number on the back of your Surface. Use large letters on the back or write with a fine-point marker along the top of your Surface. (To keep your personal information less visible, write it beneath the kickstand.) That not only ensures that the finder will see your contact information, but it will raise suspicions at the pawn shop.

If you want to preserve your Surface's resale value, though, there's another way:

Use the desktop's Paint program or another graphics editor to write your name and phone number onto the wallpaper you use for your Lock screen. That makes it easy to update if your phone number changes.

Then whoever finds your Surface will see your contact information every time your Surface turns on.

Chapter 17

Ten Handy Accessories

"**M**y Surface would be perfect if *only* . . . " Have you ever thought that to yourself?

This chapter tackles accessories that smooth out the spots that keep your Surface from being your favorite computer.

Whether you never leave the desk or you travel the globe, these accessories turn your Surface into a faithful digital assistant.

Power Adapter

Your Surface came with a power adapter, so it isn't really an accessory. But if you're traveling with your Surface, it's essential that you tote this along.

Just like an iPad, your Surface can't be charged through its USB port.

The adapter that came bundled with your Surface works the best. However, any Surface charger works with any Surface. Just remember that chargers for the Surface RT and Surface 2 take much longer to charge than a Surface Pro or Surface Pro 2.

Touch or Type Cover Keyboard

Your Surface's onscreen keyboard works fine for typing snippets of text on the Start screen and its gang of apps. But when you're creating some serious work on the desktop, the onscreen keyboard falls short.

First, it covers half of your screen space, leaving little room for your desktop or app. Second, the onscreen keyboard isn't designed for speedy touch-typing.

Your Surface generously offers you several options, but the most versatile replacement is either a Touch or Type Cover keyboard. Custom-made for the Surface, the keyboard snaps into place, as shown in Figure 17-1, and folds down for typing. When you're done typing, the keyboard folds up to double as a screen protector.

Figure 17-1:
The Touch or Type Cover keyboards work best for extended typing on your Surface.

Photo image provided by Microsoft

Lightweight and durable, either keyboard is a natural fit for your Surface. I prefer the Touch Cover for casual use and the Type Cover when typing for longer periods of time.

The newer Touch Cover 2 and Type Cover 2 keyboards work better than the original models, but all of the Touch and Type Cover keyboards still work on all Surfaces.

Any Bluetooth keyboard also works with your Surface, including the Microsoft Wedge Mobile Keyboard. Portable Bluetooth keyboards are rarely bigger or better than the Touch or Type Cover keyboards, however.

Don't forget: If you're holing up in the desert to write the Great American Novel, take your full-size desktop keyboard with you. Plug it into your Surface's desktop-sized USB port, and your portable Surface will feel as comfortable as your staid desktop PC.

Memory Card

If you own a large music or video collection, a memory card is essential. A 64GB microSDXC memory card, costing less than $50, can store thousands of songs or photos, and dozens of movies.

If your Surface leaves you cramped for space, by all means, buy a memory card and slip it into your Surface's memory card slot. Your Surface should recognize it immediately. It's one of the cheapest and easiest updates.

I describe how to buy and insert a memory card into your Surface in Chapter 6.

Portable Mouse

The trackpads built into the Touch and Type Cover keyboards work fine for small jobs. For example, a few nudges of the trackpad let you maneuver the cursor to the right spot to start, pause, or stop music and movies. And on the desktop, a trackpad works *much* better than your fingertip.

But I've always found trackpads to be cumbersome compared with a real mouse. When I'm ready for serious computing work, I want a *real* mouse. Thankfully, the Surface offers several options.

If space isn't a concern, just toss your favorite desktop mouse into your bag. Plug the mouse into your Surface's USB port, and you're set.

If space rules supreme in your gadget bag, though, look for something more portable. I've tried both Microsoft's Arc Touch mouse and Wedge Touch mouse, and both work very well.

Being a minimalist at heart, I prefer the Wedge Touch mouse, shown in Figure 17-2. Granted, it's miniscule, but it's convenient and responsive. It's easily detected by your Surface; if you have more than one Surface, it's not hard to switch it from one to another.

Figure 17-2:
Microsoft's minimal-ist Wedge Touch mouse fits in any bag but works better than any trackpad.

Photo image provided by Microsoft

Powered by a single (and easily replaced) AA battery, the mouse turns on and off automatically, making its battery last for up to four months.

Microsoft released Surface-branded versions of the Wedge and Arc mice. The new Surface Wedge Touch mouse simply has black sides rather than chrome, so there's little gain there.

The Surface Arc Touch mouse, though, brings an improvement: It works directly with Bluetooth, and you no longer need to tote around the Arc Touch mouse's little Bluetooth nub that consumed the USB port.

Portable USB Hub

Your Surface's built-in, full-size USB port gives it a burst of utility unmatched by all other tablets, including those from Apple and Android.

The only problem is that there's only one. If you plug in a mouse, for example, there's no room to plug in the flash drive, keyboard, mouse, cell phone, fax modem adapter, or any other USB accessories.

The solution is a *portable USB hub*. Small and inexpensive, the hub is a tiny box that plugs into your lone USB port. In exchange, the box contains four or more USB ports for plugging in other gadgets.

If you're using a Surface RT or you're not particularly concerned with transfer-ring files at high speeds, pick up an inexpensive USB 2.0 hub. If you'll be trans-ferring large files through the hub, buy a slightly more expensive USB 3.0 hub.

You don't need a *powered* hub — a hub that needs to plug into a power outlet — unless you plan to run on plugging in particularly power-hungry accessories, such as portable DVD players, cell phones that need charging, or more than one portable hard drive.

Case

If you're fine with your Surface and its click-on keyboard, you don't need a case. Being both lightweight and flat, your Surface and keyboard combo fits easily into a suitcase.

But if you plan on taking a few accessories, perhaps a mouse, USB hub, portable hard drive, and a few cables, you probably want a case.

It's not hard to find a case that fits your Surface, though, because it fits into nearly any case sold for laptops. Your Surface is thinner than nearly all laptops, so don't worry about the thickness as much as the other dimensions.

When shopping for a case, make sure its dimensions are at least 11 inches by 7 inches. A case that size will fit any Surface model. Choose your case's thickness and amount of pockets to match the amount of accessories you plan to carry around.

Flash Drive

Many people find it difficult to live with the Surface's small storage space; others have no problem: It's simply a tablet to use on the road for e-mail and web access.

But if you need just a little bit more storage, a flash drive fits the bill. A flash drive, like the one shown in Figure 17-3, is like a miniature hard drive that plugs into your Surface's USB port. Because it's detachable, it's an easy way to transfer files between your Surface and other computers.

Figure 17-3:
A flash drive plugs into your Surface's USB port to provide extra storage.

Photo image provided by SanDisk

A 32GB portable flash drive should handle most needs, but they're available in sizes up to 256GB.

Portable HDMI Cable

Compared with the screen of a smartphone, your Surface's 10-inch screen looks gigantic. Still, it doesn't present the cinematic experience of a large high-definition TV set.

To watch your Surface's movies on your HDTV, pick up a portable HDMI cable, shown in Figure 17-4. By connecting the cable between your Surface and your TV, everything you see on your Surface can fill the room with HDTV glory.

Figure 17-4:
An HDMI cable lets you plug your Surface into an HDMI TV set, monitor, or some digital projectors.

Photo image provided by Amazon

Even if the concept seems silly at home, toting around a small cable can be cheaper than dishing out $15 for a hotel room's pay-per-view movie. Just unplug the HDMI cable from the TV's HDMI port. Then connect your own HDMI cable between the TV's HDMI port and your Surface and watch a movie from your Surface. You send the movie from the Surface's Video app, Netflix, or something streamed through Internet Explorer.

When shopping for an HDMI cable for a Surface RT or Surface 2, buy a micro-HDMI-to-HDMI cable. (The cable's male micro-HDMI side fits into your Surface; the male plug on the HDMI cable's other side plugs into the TV set.)

For a Surface Pro or Surface Pro 2, buy a Mini DisplayPort-to-HDMI cable. (The cable's male Mini DisplayPort plugs into your Surface; the male HDMI port plugs into the TV set.)

Even if you never plan to connect your Surface to a TV, these cables also work for connecting your Surface to an external monitor or some digital projectors.

USB-to-Ethernet Adapter

An Internet connection ranks high on the essentials list for every Surface owner. Many people work fine with their Surface's built-in wireless Internet connection.

However, *wired* Internet access — piped in through an *Ethernet* cable — comes in handy for several reasons.

- ✔ **Security:** Some businesses don't offer wireless Internet access for security reasons, leaving only wired access.
- ✔ **Hotels without Wi-Fi:** Some hotels still don't offer Wi-Fi. But nearly every hotel has an Ethernet jack that offers wired Internet access.
- ✔ **Reliability:** Although Wi-Fi strength constantly changes, wired Internet access remains constant and fast, an important fact for people who watch streaming Internet videos.

If you can relate to any of these categories, just about any USB-to-Ethernet adapter works on the Surface Pro or Surface Pro 2. Some adapters also work on the Surface RT and Surface 2 if you're willing to jump through an ever-changing number of hoops to make it work.

Portable Hard Drive

People who need this usually know who they are. They want to carry *everything* with them: all of their movies, photos, books, and songs.

If you want all of your materials around you for access any time, you need a portable hard drive.

People who shoot high-definition video and need to backup or process their footage on a Surface Pro or Pro 2 *definitely* want one of these.

Look for a USB 3.0 drive to take advantage of the USB 3.0 speeds of your Surface Pro and Surface Pro 2. That extra speed makes all the difference when moving large files.

Portable Car Charger

When traveling with a Surface, a portable car charger brings some extra peace of mind. Slipped into the glove box, it's there in case you ever forget to pack your Surface's plug-in charger.

The car charger is essential if you're using your Surface on the road for work and can't deal with any down time. Microsoft's portable car charger, shown in Figure 17-5, can charge your Surface while you're stuck in traffic, so you're ready for work whenever you arrive.

Figure 17-5:
Microsoft's portable car charger lets you charge both your Surface and your phone in your car.

Photo image provided by Microsoft

As a bonus, the charger includes a USB charging port on the back, so you can simultaneously charge your phone.

Index

• S •

About the Author

Andy Rathbone started geeking around with computers in 1985 when he bought a 26-pound portable CP/M Kaypro 2X. Like other nerds of the day, he soon began playing with null-modem adapters, dialing computer bulletin boards, and working at Radio Shack.

He wrote for various techie publications before moving to computer books in 1992. He's written the *Windows For Dummies* series, *Upgrading and Fixing PCs For Dummies, Windows 8 For Tablets For Dummies*, and many other computer books.

Today, he has more than 15 million copies of his books in print, and they've been translated into more than 30 languages. You can reach Andy at his website, www.andyrathbone.com, where he answers a reader's question online each week.

Publisher's Acknowledgments

Sr. Acquisitions Editor: Katie Mohr

Project Editor: Rebecca Senninger

Copy Editor: Virginia Sanders

Technical Editor: Frank Garcia

Editorial Assistant: Anne Sullivan

Sr. Editorial Assistant: Cherie Case

Project Coordinator: Sheree Montgomery

Cover Image: Photo by Andy Rathbone

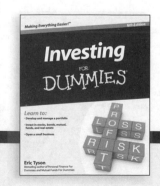
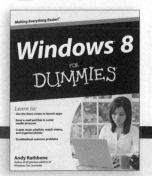

Math & Science

Algebra I For Dummies,
2nd Edition
978-0-470-55964-2

Anatomy and Physiology
For Dummies,
2nd Edition
978-0-470-92326-9

Astronomy For Dummies,
3rd Edition
978-1-118-37697-3

Biology For Dummies,
2nd Edition
978-0-470-59875-7

Chemistry For Dummies,
2nd Edition
978-1-1180-0730-3

Pre-Algebra Essentials
For Dummies
978-0-470-61838-7

Microsoft Office

Excel 2013 For Dummies
978-1-118-51012-4

Office 2013 All-in-One
For Dummies
978-1-118-51636-2

PowerPoint 2013
For Dummies
978-1-118-50253-2

Word 2013 For Dummies
978-1-118-49123-2

Music

Blues Harmonica
For Dummies
978-1-118-25269-7

Guitar For Dummies,
3rd Edition
978-1-118-11554-1

iPod & iTunes
For Dummies,
10th Edition
978-1-118-50864-0

Programming

Android Application
Development For
Dummies, 2nd Edition
978-1-118-38710-8

iOS 6 Application
Development For Dummies
978-1-118-50880-0

Java For Dummies,
5th Edition
978-0-470-37173-2

Religion & Inspiration

The Bible For Dummies
978-0-7645-5296-0

Buddhism For Dummies,
2nd Edition
978-1-118-02379-2

Catholicism For Dummies,
2nd Edition
978-1-118-07778-8

Self-Help & Relationships

Bipolar Disorder
For Dummies,
2nd Edition
978 1 118 33882-7

Meditation For Dummies,
3rd Edition
978-1-118-29144-3

Seniors

Computers For Seniors
For Dummies,
3rd Edition
978-1-118-11553-4

iPad For Seniors
For Dummies,
5th Edition
978-1-118-49708-1

Social Security
For Dummies
978-1-118-20573-0

Smartphones & Tablets

Android Phones
For Dummies
978-1-118-16952-0

Kindle Fire HD
For Dummies
978-1-118-42223-6

NOOK HD For Dummies,
Portable Edition
978-1-118-39498-4

Surface For Dummies
978-1-118-49634-3

Test Prep

ACT For Dummies,
5th Edition
978-1-118-01259-8

ASVAB For Dummies,
3rd Edition
978-0-470-63760-9

GRE For Dummies,
7th Edition
978-0-470-88921-3

Officer Candidate Tests,
For Dummies
978-0-470-59876-4

Physician's Assistant Exa
For Dummies
978-1-118-11556-5

Series 7 Exam
For Dummies
978-0-470-09932-2

Windows 8

Windows 8 For Dummies
978-1-118-13461-0

Windows 8 For Dummies
Book + DVD Bundle
978-1-118-27167-4

Windows 8 All-in-One
For Dummies
978-1-118-11920-4

Available in print and e-book formats.

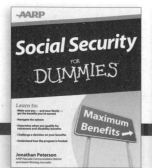

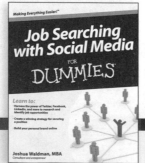

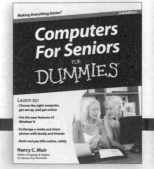

Take Dummies with you everywhere you go!

Whether you're excited about e-books, want more from the web, must have your mobile apps, or swept up in social media, Dummies makes everything easier.

Dummies products make life easier

- DIY
- Consumer Electronics
- Crafts
- Software
- Cookware
- Hobbies
- Videos
- Music
- Games
- and More!

For more information, go to **Dummies.com®** and search the store by category.

A Wiley Bran